Guide #16

Getting Started with Cloud Computing

A LITA Guide

Edward M. Corrado
Heather Lea Moulaison
Editors

with a Foreword by Roy Tennant

facet publishing

Published by
Facet Publishing
7 Ridgmount Street
London WC1E 7AE
www.facetpublishing.co.uk

Facet Publishing is wholly owned by CILIP: the Chartered Institute of Library and Information Professionals.

First published in the USA by Neal-Schuman Publishers, Inc., 2011.
This simultaneous UK edition 2011.

British Library Cataloguing in Publication Data
A catalogue record for this book is available from the British Library.

ISBN 978-1-85604-807-1

Printed and bound in the United States of America.

Contents

iii

PART II: TECHNOLOGIES

v

List of Illustrations

FIGURES

ix

TABLES

x

Foreword

From one perspective, the history of computing can be viewed as a cyclical gyration of centralization versus decentralization of computing power. The first machines were too expensive for any organizations or individuals except government agencies and eventually very large businesses. Centralization was broken by the advent of the personal computer, which put computing power in the hands of individuals for the first time. The era of the minicomputer consolidated decentralization, as each individual organization installed "dumb" terminals lashed to a minicomputer, including the library where I worked in 1983.

Then came the Internet, which provided a way to interconnect all of these nodes. This enabled another wave of centralization, as we increasingly accessed servers so far away and anonymous that we never knew where they actually sat. To some degree, cloud computing represents taking centralization to its logical conclusion. With cloud computing, the very idea of "clients" and "servers" fades into the background. You have a phone, or a pad device, or a laptop, or a desktop, and it is able to do many wondrous things because it is seamlessly integrated over the network with farms of servers that operate transparently and that automatically grow with demand.

It is indeed a brave new world we live in, and this book demonstrates that librarians are not only aware of these changes but are already using them to more effectively and efficiently fulfill their needs and the needs of their users. In that way this book is both a lesson and an inspiration. It is an inspiration as it demonstrates the resiliency of librarians in acquiring new skills and applying new technologies to serve the needs of their users ever better. It is a lesson because in these pages are both foundationally instructive pieces as well as case studies of exactly how to bring these new technologies to bear in your own organizations.

This is no different from the era in which I became a librarian, when the Internet was beginning to transform our world. Both instructional explication and case studies were needed, to illustrate both what could be accomplished with this new tool as well as exactly how librarians were using it. Therefore, you now have in your hands the chapter and verse on what cloud computing is and how to use it effectively in your library.

For me the most powerful aspect of cloud computing is that it enables libraries to stop dealing with technical issues that have nothing to do with their day-to-day mission and services. Cloud computing offers the ability to simply requisition technological resources that can expand as required to meet expanding needs while requiring little or nothing from the library providing the service. Additionally, using cloud computing services it is possible to get a full-featured website going in minutes—I've done this multiple times myself using Amazon's EC2 service and I'm still astonished. It quite literally has never been easier to get a website going than it is today.

So within these pages rests the future of libraries. We must get out of the business of buying, configuring, installing, and maintaining servers unless we absolutely must do so. Otherwise, we should be simply and easily requisitioning services from the cloud, and immediately and effectively putting them into service. After all, this is exactly what everyone else is doing.

Roy Tennant
Senior Program Officer
OCLC Research

Preface

Getting Started with Cloud Computing: A LITA Guide is designed as a start-up guide to cloud computing in libraries. Although librarians have been interested in cloud computing for a while and many libraries have used it, until now no book has tackled the intricacies of cloud-based computing and services from an information professional's point of view.

Library data is different, and library ethics and budgets require that librarians think differently about the information they have and the services they offer. If you are a librarian, a library administrator, or someone interested in how libraries can implement and make the most of the myriad cloud computing options, you need a book that will address your unique perspective on a very complex topic.

Getting Started with Cloud Computing is meant to help readers understand more about cloud computing in general in easy-to-understand terms; it also is designed to explain cloud computing as it pertains to the library community. Cloud computing can be defined in a number of ways, but this book takes the broadest possible approach, considering any use of remote computing power accessed through the Internet as a kind of cloud computing that will be of interest to librarians. This guide has two additional parts to help readers learn about some of the cloud-based tools that are available and that show some real-world examples of how libraries are using the cloud to offer superior service to their users while meeting their own computing needs in the process. This book aims to convey the current state of affairs in library uses of cloud computing, give ample ideas of projects that libraries and cultural institutions can undertake, and share expertise from a variety of information professionals who use cloud computing in their jobs. After learning more about cloud computing and seeing how it pertains to libraries, readers will understand the requirements for trying various cloud computing projects at their own institutions.

This book is composed of 20 chapters written by leaders in library technology. The chapters are designed so that both a computer professional working in libraries and a librarian or library administrator who is merely interested in new technology will gain solid knowledge of cloud computing in the library environment. It may also be of interest to library and information science educators who are in need of a collected volume of essays on cloud computing.

Organization and Content

Getting Started with Cloud Computing is divided into three parts: General Concerns, Technologies, and Case Studies. Part I: General Concerns (Chapters 1–6) describes cloud computing in general but focuses conceptually on approaches that will be relevant and of interest to those in libraries or other cultural heritage institutions. In Chapter 1, the editors, Heather Lea Moulaison and Edward M. Corrado, introduce the general topic of cloud computing in libraries, highlighting some of the benefits and issues particular to libraries with a special emphasis on what the reader might keep in mind while continuing through the rest of the book. In Chapter 2, Rosalyn Metz describes the components of cloud computing working from the NISO guidelines; Metz gives clear and precise examples at each step of the way and, in the process, provides an ideal introduction to cloud computing for the librarian reader. H. Frank Cervone follows in Chapter 3 by further describing features of cloud computing in libraries; he also enumerates pros and cons of moving to the cloud. In Chapter 4, Erik Mitchell describes trends in cloud computing, including practical aspects that pertain to libraries. He also builds on Metz's discussion but takes the topic a step further as he looks to the future. In Chapter 5, Carl Grant of Ex Libris describes cloud computing from the point of view of a library vendor. Finally, in Chapter 6, Christinger R. Tomer and Susan W. Alman describe implications for cloud computing in libraries via efforts in library and information science (LIS) education at present.

In Part II: Technologies (Chapters 7–12), the discussion of issues gives way to a pointed look at a variety of cloud computing technologies that can be used in libraries today. The part begins in Chapter 7 with a discussion by well-known and well-respected Marshall Breeding on the use of discovery layers in the cloud. In Chapter 8, Christopher R. Nighswonger and Nicole C. Engard, using Koha as an example, next describe what is needed to host a library's open source integrated library system (ILS) in the cloud. In Chapter 9, Karen A. Coombs of OCLC describes a host of free and innovative web services that are cloud based and that can be integrated into any library's web presence. In Chapter 10, John Davison of OhioLink describes setting up a DSpace repository in the cloud; it was announced in December 2010 that the project's implementation, the Digital Resource Commons (DRC), won the ALA Cutting-Edge Technology Practices award. The final two chapters of the Technologies section describe cloud-based tools that can be used by practically any library or cultural heritage institution. In Chapter 11, Heidi M. Nickisch Duggan and Michelle Frisque, a LITA past president, describe tools and considerations for file sharing in the cloud, and in Chapter 12 Jennifer Diffin and Dennis Nangle give tips and tricks to consider in the creation of an institutional intranet using Microsoft SharePoint that is hosted in the cloud.

Lastly, Part III: Case Studies (Chapters 13–20) gives insights into projects that libraries throughout the United States have undertaken. Each chapter features subsections giving a background to the library and to the problem. Chapter sections describe the cloud-based tools considered, how the selected solution was implemented, and an evaluation of the end product. In Chapter 13, Edward Iglesias begins by describing how his library saves archival quality images in the cloud. In Chapter 14, Karen A. Reiman-Sendi, Kenneth J. Varnum, and Albert A. Bertram describe their experience integrating the cloud-based LibGuides with their locally hosted website by taking advantage of Springshare's XML output feature. In the following case study in Chapter 15, Caitlin A. Bagley details the use of Dropbox for file sharing between and among librarians and for the remote access of library instruction documents by embedded librarians at her institution. In Chapters 16 and 17, respectively, Anne Leonard and Robin Elizabeth Miller both describe experiences using free software from Google: Leonard describes benefits and uses of Google Calendar, and Miller describes innovative uses of Google Forms for instruction. In Chapter 18, Leland R. Deeds, Cindy Kissel-Ito, and Ann Knox describe their experience using Ning both in the library and for distance education at their college. In Chapter 19, Ann Whitney Gleason describes using DimDim for web conferencing. Although the DimDim software is no longer on the market, Gleason's experiences with a cloud-based web conferencing tool can still inform librarians' thought processes as they consider other web conferencing tools for library services. Lastly, in Chapter 20, Jennifer Ditkoff and Kara Young describe their uses of VoiceThread for instruction.

xv

Although the chapters in this book are written in such a manner that they can stand on their own individually, *Getting Started with Cloud Computing* is designed to be a complete volume that is possible to read from cover to cover. The chapters and indeed the parts of the book build on each other; readers are encouraged to start from the beginning and read their way sequentially through the book's chapters. However, if readers are trying to implement a cloud-based solution similar to one of the case studies, they should feel free to jump in at the point that makes the most sense, as readers would do with any technical handbook covering new technologies.

The editors hope this book paves the way for easier implementation of cloud computing and helps readers think about cloud computing in libraries as they never have before.

Acknowledgments

The editors would like to acknowledge the University of Ottawa's School of Information Studies for the use of facilities during the preliminary phase of editing.

xvii

Part I

GENERAL CONCERNS

Chapter 1

Perspectives on Cloud Computing in Libraries

Heather Lea Moulaison and Edward M. Corrado

Introduction

During the first decade of the current millennium, the term "cloud computing" has become almost ubiquitous in certain circles. Gmail is in the cloud. Facebook is in the cloud. Remotely hosted integrated library systems (ILSs) are also in the cloud. The term "cloud" is on everyone's lips, yet, depending on the community, the term may well mean different things both in theory and in practice. While businesses may look to the cloud for low-cost solutions to data storage and computing power problems, libraries may be interested in targeted solutions for sharing data with other libraries and providing low-cost services to users. Many types of computing problems can benefit from the use of cloud computing solutions, but those solutions may involve a different set of considerations for libraries due in part to the nature of their mission and activities.

Different models for deploying the cloud have made cloud computing an interesting proposition for businesses as well as for nonprofits, and those involved with libraries and cultural heritage institutions are right to explore their options. This book is designed to help librarians and administrators think about cloud computing as a powerful technology, to consider some tools that are available for use in libraries, and to learn about the experiences of libraries already using these technologies.

The Promise of Cloud Computing

Because authors in the following chapters of this guide will give very complex definitions of cloud computing, this introduction will remain general so as to focus on the promises and the issues as they pertain to libraries. A variety of technical definitions of cloud computing exist. Simply put, cloud computing offers access to computing power over the Internet. In moving machines offsite, organizations like libraries have to rethink their computing strategies and the services they provide, both for internal communications and for services to patrons.

Cloud computing is designed to give users flexibility for dealing with their computing needs. Because of the inherent elasticity that is part of the cloud computing model, cloud computing is especially useful in industries where there is a sharp rise and decline in activity. Holiday shopping activities are classic examples of a smart way that online merchants make use of cloud computing. Companies offering online purchasing may not have enough computing power locally to support web sales in December, but it does not make economic sense for them to purchase additional servers and hire additional staff year-round for the single month per year that the computing power is necessary. Instead, these companies are better served to host some aspect of their operations in the cloud and to let their providers bill them for the use incurred on a monthly basis. If they were so inclined, librarians could certainly arrange for a similar computing power to be available to them to support their diverse computing needs.

Cloud computing can also be beneficial when expertise is lacking or when future computing needs are unsure. A large percentage (43.3 percent) of respondents from the Zenoss open source systems management community indicated that flexibility is the main reason they choose to use virtualization software (Zenoss, 2010: 6). Librarians, especially at smaller libraries, may see the same advantages in cloud computing. Ambitious librarians wanting to start new services may also appreciate using resources in the cloud, because, with cloud computing, there is "[t]he elimination of an up-front commitment by cloud users, thereby allowing companies to start small and increase hardware resources only when there is an increase in their needs" (Armbrust et al., 2010: 51).

Some librarians are excited about cloud computing because it offers an avenue for better cooperation. Using a data as a service (DaaS) model, for example, it would be possible for libraries to better cooperate to maintain bibliographic and authority records. As Karen A. Coombs describes in Chapter 9, one way this can be done is by taking advantage of application programming interfaces (APIs).

The cloud also allows libraries to cooperate with other libraries and library software vendors to secure rights to article metadata from publishers and database providers. With a few possible exceptions for large or well-funded libraries, negotiating access to locally store this metadata and then make it available to end users in a meaningful manner would likely be cost prohibitive. However, as Marshall Breeding elaborates on in Chapter 7, some library software vendors are now able to provide discovery services, utilizing metadata provided by many different content providers, to libraries that offer a more complete, single search experience for library patrons.

On-demand computing power is not the only reason to consider turning to the cloud. Other reasons to use cloud computing include hardware savings (33.3 percent), administrative ease of use (8.7 percent), and labor cost savings (6.0 percent) (Zenoss, 2010: 6). If librarians can save on buying and maintaining servers, for example, they can save their parent institutions money. Depending on the service, they can also rely on the software provider to carry out all updates, thereby allowing their own employees to take care of other obligations in lieu of monitoring version changes and upgrades. Furthermore, quite a few of the cloud-based software platforms are available for free, meaning that librarians can make use of services without incurring any cost for their libraries. The promise of saving money and easing the administrative workload is enticing in the for-profit sector, but is especially interesting for libraries and cultural heritage institutions that may be increasingly forced to find ways to decrease the bottom line while continuing to offer the same or even better services.

The Reality: Cloud Computing Is Not a Silver Bullet

While it might be tempting to focus on the promises of cloud computing, it is nonetheless important to keep one's feet on the ground. Libraries are not like businesses that see a spike in sales in the month of December. Public libraries and academic libraries may see predictable patterns of use throughout the year, but it is not obvious the extent to which these sorts of patterns require scalable computing solutions. The services that libraries can acquire through the use of cloud computing platforms may indeed be valuable, but the cost of Internet access, even if bandwidth is not currently at a premium, can become a considerable hurdle to effective provision of services. Imagine a library relying solely on Google Docs for word-processing needs. If every librarian and every user had to connect to Google to do the smallest word-processing task, the strains on the bandwidth would become pronounced. Also, questions of security and privacy need to be posed. At what point is it ethical to give over all word-processing functions (for example) to a for-profit third-party provider? With the new questions in the blogosphere about cloud computing service providers raised by the December 2010 United States diplomatic cables leak by WikiLeaks (see Anderson, 2010), librarians may find renewed cause for concern over the reliability of the storekeepers of data in the cloud.

In addition to security, there are also questions of privacy. Librarians are acutely aware of the sensitivity of the kinds of data they maintain but often are operating as relatively small organizations when compared to big businesses with thousands of employees worldwide. Libraries may feel behind the black ball because of their small size when negotiating service level agreements (SLAs) with cloud vendors.

> Another potential challenge with using the cloud surrounds how significant an influence—if any—an organization can have with respect to modifying the way the cloud operates, imposing and/or strengthening the liability terms of the contracts, requesting and receiving the assurances required from the vendor, and having a firm grasp on the enforcement of the solid legal agreement once it is put in place. (Chaput and Ringwood, 2010: 242)

5

Working in organizations that may not have recourse to legal counsel and in ones that will not have the kind of large accounts that American Express has, librarians may find themselves on their own for thinking through some of the issues of cloud computing. This can be somewhat daunting given that both costs and obligations need to be understood and considered (Chaput and Ringwood, 2010: 241). Indeed, this book is intended to get librarians and administrators thinking about using cloud computing services, but it is understood that each library will need to assess the cloud landscape for itself before making decisions to rely in any way on cloud computing.

Some library administrators may be interested in cloud computing because of the perceived cost savings in staff. It is true that with many, if not most, cloud computing solutions there is no need to purchase or maintain servers, and there are associated cost savings in that area. However, the added fees paid to the provider may or may not outweigh the costs of a non-cloud-based solution. Also, while you may not need someone to administer a server, there is most likely still a need for someone to administer the software application itself. Migrating to a cloud-based application may turn out to be cost neutral but at the same time still have the benefit of allowing staff to concentrate more on library-specific issues.

At present, many libraries in the United States have free or low-cost accounts for software that is hosted in the cloud or pay to host data that is not sensitive. For example, several chapters in the Technologies section and the Case Studies section address free and low-cost options for software in the cloud. Chapters in the General Concerns section and the Technologies section describe the use of hosted solutions either through a library vendor or through a standard account available to any user. This volume does not feature chapters describing instances where libraries are hosting sensitive data in the cloud quite simply because none have come to the attention of the editors.

Privacy in Libraries' Clouds

Because of the nature of the web, there are inherent privacy concerns in putting library data into any cloud environment. Libraries have a professional and legal obligation to keep certain data, such as circulation records and patron information, private and secure. Librarians need to be aware how national laws such as Canada's Personal Information Protection and Electronic Documents Act (PIPEDA) and the United States' Health Insurance Portability and Accountability Act (HIPAA) and Family Educational Rights and Privacy Act (FERPA) might affect what they do in the cloud. Besides issues about what data can be placed where, organizations placing personal data in the cloud need to understand the risks and liabilities and must know if the cloud provider will provide indemnification if there is a breach of privacy or security that is the provider's fault. Librarians should also make sure that any contracts with cloud providers specify how quickly and in what manner the provider must notify the library if such a breach occurs.

As Thomas J. Trappler (2010) points out, if it is in the cloud, get it on paper. If a library does not have the ability or resources to negotiate changes in the contract, librarians should at least make sure they are aware of the terms in the standard agreement.

Legal Aspects of Sensitive Library Data

Libraries must also be alert to legal implications of allowing sensitive data to be placed in the cloud. While libraries in the United States were acutely aware of the implications of the Uniting and Strengthening America by Providing Appropriate Tools Required to Intercept and Obstruct Terrorism (USA PATRIOT) Act passed in 2001, the legislation also affected Canadian data housed in the United States. Canadian businesses as a result have hesitated to trust sensitive data to providers in the United States, and libraries have likewise been hesitant to store their sensitive circulation data outside of the confines of the library's walls. However, it should be noted, although perhaps lesser known, the Canada Anti-Terrorism Act (ATA) has many provisions and goals similar to those of the USA PATRIOT Act (Kavur, 2010; PrivacySense.net, 2010; Wispinski, 2006). Librarians may want to make sure there are clauses in contracts with cloud providers that identify what obligations the vendor has to notify the library should a legal request be made to access its data.

Various countries, states, and other legal jurisdictions have laws about where data can be located that need to be considered while implementing a cloud-based solution. For example, in Australia, organizations "may not transfer information to somebody in a foreign country unless the recipient of the information is subject to a law or binding scheme similar to the National Privacy Principles that apply in Australia, or another exception such as consent applies" (Dawson and Hilton, 2010).

Encryption of Library Data

Encrypting sensitive data as it travels to and from the cloud is one option for protecting the data as it is en route. It is also advisable to leave data encrypted while stored in the cloud. In this way, privacy can be more strongly ensured if the data cannot be interpreted as it is. Again, because such uses of cloud computing have not come to our attention, it is difficult to provide any kind of best practices scenarios to readers of this introductory guide.

Security in Libraries' Clouds

Closely linked to the idea of privacy, the concept of security is a major concern in libraries and in any organization that trusts sensitive or necessary information to an offsite group. In a recent survey, 39.4 percent of respondents from the Zenoss open source systems management community indicated that security is their primary concern with cloud computing (Zenoss, 2010: 10). In talking about portability and interoperability, Chaput and Ringwood (2010: 252) remind us, "Planning for contingency is paramount for outsourcing arrangements and cloud arrangements are no different. It is important to identify who owns the data and ensure that both parties agree." For further thoughts on this question, see Carl Grant's chapter (Chapter 5) for the point of view of a vendor/librarian.

Trust Must Be Earned

Trust in the individuals, enterprise, and resources maintaining data must be earned. While some critics of the cloud point out that it might be unwise to trust your data in the cloud, there are also risks with running your own servers in-house with your own employees. As Quing Hu, a professor and chair of logistics, operations, and management information systems at Iowa State University points out, his studies and others suggest "that internal computer fraud is a more significant issue than external hacking" even if external hacking grabs the headlines (Iowa State University, 2009). It is possible and may be likely that cloud providers will be in a better position to employ more and better trained computer security staff than an individual library could afford to hire. They may have better plans and procedures for security and backups than a smaller business or library. As the blogging website JournalSpace.com found, one disgruntled employee could wipe out and shut down an entire business (Humphries, 2009). Similarly, improper backup procedures wiped out the social bookmarking website Ma.gnolia (Halff, 2009). These two examples show that who to trust is not always a simple question. Ma.gnolia and JournalSpace.com trusted their employees, and their users trusted them, yet there was a failure. When evaluating cloud providers, things such as past experiences, reputation, track record, staffing, and other factors should be used in determining the level of trust.

Trust but Verify: The SLA

As Barack Obama (2010) said, "To borrow an old phrase, we will trust, but we will verify." Although Obama was referring to the April 2010 BP oil spill and Ronald Reagan typically used his signature phrase "trust but verify" in relation to the Soviet Union, this phrase also applies to dealing with cloud computing providers. Most, if not all, contracts with cloud providers will have details about SLAs. SLAs typically cover things such as uptime, performance, and security. However, these SLAs and any other contract clauses are not worth much if they cannot be monitored or verified. Librarians should ask for the right to review and verify any third-party audits and certifications. This is especially true if sensitive or mission-critical data or applications are cloud based.

Risk

There is a certain amount of risk any time sensitive data is recorded and entrusted to any party for any reason. While it may be easier to trust those who are known, it may not be possible to ensure that data is truly any more secure within the metaphorical walls of the library than beyond them. Using cloud services "is neither inherently insecure nor secure" (Chaput and Ringwood, 2010: 241). As with the Ma.gnolia and JournalSpace.com examples earlier, there is a risk both to housing library data in the cloud (the risk the users of the websites took) and to using internal staffing (the risk the owners of the websites took).

There are other risks with cloud computing besides employee sabotage or error. Librarians will want to consider the possibility of the cloud computing provider's going out of business. Is that provider the only place the library's data is housed? If so, will the library be able to get the data back, and, in the case that it can, will it be in a timely manner? Librarians contemplating moving to a cloud-based service will need to determine what level of risk they are willing to take and what those risks are compared to hosting the application in-house. The answers will differ depending on the organization and on the cloud provider.

Data Ownership

Data in the cloud brings many concerns such as the aforementioned privacy and security implications. Another concern libraries need to be aware of is data ownership. Questions regarding data ownership need to be addressed before embarking on a cloud computing project—especially one that places data and applications critical to day-to-day library operations such as an integrated library system (ILS) into the cloud. Who owns the data placed in the cloud, and what rights do the library and provider have to the data? After the contract expires, how and in what format will the data be returned to the library, or how will the library retrieve the data? Libraries should make sure that any contract they sign with a cloud provider includes information about access to the data on an ongoing basis and at the end of the contract. The process and time frame for receiving data in an agreed-upon format should be delineated (Trappler, 2010).

Evaluation

While this book does not address the concept of evaluation of cloud services directly, it acknowledges that evaluation is an essential component of any new service's implementation in libraries. The editors of this guide recommend that evaluation of cloud computing be carried out the way any other evaluation is carried out at a reader's library. Although the evaluation component offered in the Case Studies section tends to be informal, it is a first step toward getting libraries to quantify their cloud computing experiences and to share that information outside the walls of their institution.

Conclusion

Cloud computing has generated a great deal of buzz in technology circles in general and within the library community in particular for good reason. The advantages of cloud computing include flexibility, ease of use, cost savings on hardware, and possible time savings for staff that would allow technology staff to concentrate on tasks more closely related to the library mission than the maintenance of servers.

Cloud computing, however, is not a panacea that will cure all library technology ills. While libraries have ebbs and flows in computing needs, they are not at the same scale as an Internet retailer during the holiday season. There are various concerns that librarians need to consider when moving services, especially mission-critical services, to the cloud. If the network connection goes down or is unbearably slow, staff and patrons may not be able to access necessary applications, data, or other content entrusted to the cloud computing service. There are various data security and privacy concerns that are specific to libraries and that need to be addressed by library institutions on an individual basis. Also, librarians need to consider when first implementing a cloud-based solution how they will get their data out of the cloud should they need or want to change providers. Libraries are entrusted with content that must be safeguarded and protected, and they must provide services to help users access that content. When content and services are outsourced to third-party cloud computing providers, librarians may feel that they have lost a degree of control that would be maintained had they hosted their content and services themselves.

Questions of control are mitigated when there is a sense of trust in the professionalism of the cloud computing provider. While there are certainly privacy and security risks with cloud computing, it is not necessarily any more risky than running one's own servers. In fact the cloud may be more secure, depending on the availability and skill level of local technology staff. Hackers can compromise a local server just as easily as a cloud-based one if the proper security steps have not been taken. Librarians need to take a critical look at cloud providers to see how much trust they should be afforded and should act accordingly.

For better or for worse, the cloud allows librarians to experiment with technology like never before and with little or no up-front costs. For example, instead of having to purchase servers to house a DSpace repository, libraries can outsource their computing needs to Amazon as John Davison describes in Chapter 10. Economies of scale can be exploited, partner libraries can be brought on board, and projects can be expanded, scaled back, and changed with little to no inconvenience to an institution's librarians.

Librarians and library administrators, especially those interested in library technology, have reason to be excited about cloud computing and the possibilities it offers. As with any other service or product, however, librarians need to evaluate cloud-based solutions to see if they offer a good return on investment and if they further the library's mission. The chapters that follow are designed to guide the reader in that quest for understanding and for finding inspiration.

References

Anderson, Kent. 2010. "Is the Cloud Too Weak to Support What Paper Can?" *The Scholarly Kitchen* (blog), December 8. http://scholarlykitchen.sspnet.org/2010/12/08/ is-the-cloud-too-weak-to-support-what-paper-can/.

Armbrust, Michael, Armando Fox, Rean Griffith, Anthony D. Joseph, Randy Katz, Andy Konwinski, et al. 2010. "A View of Cloud Computing." *Communications of the ACM 53*, no. 4: 50–58. doi:10.1145/1721654.1721672.

Chaput, Shawn R., and Katarina Ringwood. 2010. "Cloud Compliance: A Framework for Using Cloud Computing in a Regulated World." In *Cloud Computing: Principles, Systems and Applications,* edited by N. Antonopoulos and L. Gillam, 241–255. London: Springer-Verlag London Limited. doi:10.1007/978-1-84996-241-4_14.

Dawson, Sophie, and Andrew Hilton. 2010. "Privacy Changes Could Affect Cloud Projects." *CIO,* December 20. http://www.cio.com.au/article/370772/privacy_changes _could_affect_cloud_projects/.

Halff, Larry. 2009. "Whither Ma.gnolia?" *Citizen Garden* 11. Video. 25:04, uploaded February 13. http://vimeo.com/3205188.

Humphries, Matthew. 2009. "Disgruntled Employee Kills JournalSpace with Data Wipe." *Geek.com* (blog), January 5. http://www.geek.com/articles/news/disgruntled-employee-kills-journalspace-with-data-wipe-2009015/.

Iowa State University. 2009. "Iowa State Researcher Says Internal Security Breaches Pose a Bigger Threat than Hackers." *Iowa State University News Releases,* July 31. http:// www.news.iastate.edu/news/2009/jul/security.

Kavur, Jennifer. 2010. "Don't Use the PATRIOT Act as an Excuse." *IT World Canada,* July 5. http://www.itworldcanada.com/news/dont-use-the-patriot-act-as-an-excuse/ 141033.

Obama, Barack. 2010. "Remarks by the President on the Ongoing Oil Spill Response." Transcript, and MP4 Video, 7:20, uploaded May 14, The White House. http://www.whitehouse.gov/blog/2010/05/14/relentless-efforts-stop-leak-and-contain-damage.

PrivacySense.net. 2010. "The Canadian Equivalent to the PATRIOT Act." Privacy-Sense.net. Accessed December 23. http://www.privacysense.net/canadian-equivalent-patriot-act/.

Trappler, Thomas J. 2010. "If It's in the Cloud, Get It on Paper: Cloud Computing Contract Issues." *EDUCAUSE Quarterly Magazine 33*, no. 2. http:// www.edu-cause.edu/EDUCAUSE+Quarterly/EDUCAUSEQuarterlyMagazineVolum/ IfItsintheCloudGetItonPaperClo/206532.

Wispinski, Jennifer. 2006. "The USA PATRIOT Act and Canada's Anti-Terrorism Act: Key Differences in Legislative Approach." Parliamentary Information and Research Service (PIRS) of the Library of Parliament, March 31. http://www2.parl.gc.ca/ Content/LOP/ResearchPublications/prb0583-e.pdf.

Zenoss. 2010. *2010 Virtualization and Cloud Computing Survey.* Annapolis, MD: Zenoss.

Chapter 2

Understanding the Cloud: An Introduction to the Cloud

Rosalyn Metz

Introduction

Cloud computing is the new "it" thing in the information technology community. Everyone from Microsoft to Google to Amazon purport to have some type of cloud offering. Microsoft recently released a series of advertisements in which people, faced with difficult tasks, go "to the cloud" to accomplish what they need. In one advertisement a couple stuck in an airport uses a laptop to remotely watch TV shows from their home computer. In another, a mother uses Windows to merge multiple family portraits into one, creating a more idyllic, singular portrait.

Google has quietly offered a number of cloud-based solutions to users for quite some time. These include Google Docs and its even more popular YouTube service. But, Google's offerings do not stop there. Its popular Google App Engine allows developers to create and host applications on Google's data centers, minimizing development costs and allowing a company to get their application out the door more quickly. Their latest offering, Google Storage for Developers, provides "a RESTful [Representational State Transfer] service for storing and accessing your data on Google's infrastructure" (Google, 2010), minimizing the costs associated with storing large quantities of data and creating redundancies to prevent data loss.

The cloud provider that often eclipses them all is Amazon. With its myriad services, Amazon has one of the most robust offerings of any of the vendors out there. Using Amazon's Simple Storage Solution (S3), subscribers can store as much data as they need. They can also provision a server in just a few clicks using Amazon's Elastic Compute Cloud (EC2). Or hook into a MySQL database using its Relational Database Service (RDS).

Defining the Cloud

While all of these services and actions sound exciting, they still leave many people wondering: What does "the cloud" mean? In October 2009, the National Institute

13

of Standards and Technology (NIST) released their definition of cloud comput-ing. In a note at the beginning of the definition, the authors state: "Cloud com-puting is still an evolving paradigm. Its definitions, use cases, underlying technologies, issues, risks, and benefits will be refined in a spirited debate by the public and private sectors. These definitions, attributes, and characteristics will evolve and change over time" (Mell and Grance, 2010).

A quick review of books on cloud computing reinforces this idea. While on the surface there may seem to be different definitions of what the cloud is, most cover the same generally accepted principles outlined in the NIST definition, which is intended to capture all of these major concepts (Mell and Grance, 2010) and is generally considered to be a well-balanced definition (Hoff, 2009). This chapter will take an in-depth look at the five characteristics, three service models, and four deployment models outlined in the NIST definition of cloud comput-ing. Additionally, it will discuss scenarios and cloud-based services that illustrate each of the major points outlined in the definition.

Five Characteristics of the Cloud

To understand the different types of cloud-based services, we must first under-stand what qualifies something as "cloud-like." The NIST defines the cloud as containing the following five characteristics:

1. On-demand self-service
2. Broad network access
3. Metered service
4. Elasticity
5. Resource pooling

Other definitions of the cloud seem to echo this sentiment. In her book, *Cloud Computing for Dummies,* Judith Hurwitz (2010) defines the cloud as having elas-ticity, self-service provisioning, application programming interfaces (APIs), and metering of services. In *Cloud Security and Privacy,* the authors use the technolo-gies that brought the cloud together to help define its characteristics. These tech-nologies are thin devices, high-speed access, data centers and server farms, cheap storage, virtualization, and APIs (Mather, Kumaraswamy, and Latif, 2009). While a cursory review of these definitions shows some differences, upon further inspec-tion each of these definitions can easily be encompassed by the NIST's definition. The following sections will take a closer look at the five characteristics outlined in the NIST definition as well as how these generally accepted principles are illus-trated in currently available cloud-based services.

On-Demand Self-Service

When an institution makes a decision to implement a system, it generally works with a vendor to make the system operational. For example, a library might decide to purchase an integrated library system (ILS); one of the first likely steps would be to purchase a server for the ILS. After consulting with the ILS vendor to determine the requirements for the server, the library will call on a number of hardware vendors, provide them with the server specifications, and get price quotes. Once the vendor and price have been determined, the vendor's sales representative will place an order for the server and the server will be shipped to the library. When it's received, the library will need to rack the server, connect it to its network, and install the operating and supporting software.

When implementing the same system in the cloud, the process for purchasing a server is radically different. Although the institution would still need to determine the server requirements from the ILS vendor, the rest of the process would change. For cloud-based server providers, rates are usually posted on their websites, thereby eliminating the need to work with a sales representative to get a price quote. In the case of some providers, like Amazon Web Services, there is even an online calculator to help the client project its monthly bill (Amazon, 2010c).

Ordering a server would no longer be an obstacle either. Instead, cloud providers allow their clients to create an account, attach it to a credit card, and begin purchasing services immediately. Rackspace, which allows clients the ability to provision servers on demand, provides a simple to use form that walks clients through the process of creating an account. Once it is created, access to its cloud-based servers is available instantly. Users simply need to find the server in the list of available templates, provision it, and then log into the server to begin using it. Contrast this to the hours it can take to set up a locally hosted system that requires network drops, racking a server, and installing the server's base operating system. This new process can save both network and system administrators a considerable amount of time.

Broad Network Access

Many network administrators, systems administrators, and other IT professionals have used a picture of a cloud to symbolize a network in system diagrams. In fact, a quick search for "network diagram" using Google Image Search reveals a number of diagrams using a cloud to represent some aspect of a network or system. While many believe that broad network access is the defining characteristic of cloud-based services, it is important to remember that it is just one of the five characteristics used to define the cloud.

In *Cloud Security and Privacy,* the authors attribute the rise of cloud computing to, among other things, thin devices, high-speed Internet access, and APIs (Mather, Kumaraswamy, and Latif, 2009). They argue that these things have changed how we use the Internet. Reports from the Pew Internet & American Life Reports on Internet evolution confirm this, showing some of the trends that have and still permeate our lives. One such trend is mobile Internet access. In an early report, an opening statistic reads, "17% of Internet users have logged on using a wireless device" (Rainie, 2004). Whereas six years later a similar report indicates, "59% of American adults now go online wirelessly using either a laptop or cell phone" (Smith, 2010). In the earlier report there is only one mention of using mobile phones for access to the Internet, but in the later there are 164. The way we use thin devices and the way we access the Internet has radically changed and led to the evolution of cloud computing.

So what does it mean that cloud-based services are available through broad network access? The NIST asserts that "capabilities are available over the network and accessed through standard mechanisms that promote use by heterogeneous thin or thick client platforms" (Mell and Grance, 2010). This means that users can use cloud-based services through any type of Internet-ready device, unlike in the past when users were required to download an application in order to work with the computing service they had purchased.

Being able to access computing resources over the Internet is just the tip of the iceberg. In the past, methods for accessing computing services were usually offered only through the service provider. For instance, to upload a picture to a particular provider's website, one was required to download and install an application created and distributed by the provider itself. Today, APIs have made it possible for third parties to create their own applications for use with the providers' services. The Android Market illustrates this brilliantly; the market contains dozens of web applications available for Flickr users, none of which was created by Flickr. Most, if not all, cloud services provide some type of API so that users can access the service through whatever means they want.

The most prominent example of a service available through broad network access is Google Docs. In 2007, Google launched Google Docs, which allowed users to create and edit documents via the web. Traditional word processors and spreadsheet editors required users to install software locally. Google Docs, on the other hand, linked users to existing Google accounts, creating a space for them to produce and collect documents using the web-based software, eliminating the need to install it locally. Over the years, Google Docs has become more full featured, adding new upgrades like charts for spreadsheets and collaboration tools for documents. Because the software itself is available through any web browser, Google can make upgrades transparently and seamlessly for its users. In 2010, Microsoft released its Office Web Apps, a recent competitor to Google Docs. This trend indicates that the future of word processing may very well occur over the network.

Metered Service

There are countless books, blog posts, and articles out there comparing cloud computing to electricity. The most prominent is Nicholas Carr's (2008) book *The Big Switch*. In it he discusses the rise of electricity as we know and use it today. He discusses, in fascinating detail, how Edison originally saw electricity as something that would be created and used strictly on-site in a business or home. It was his clerk,

Samuel Insull, who saw the bigger picture. He created a system of generators and a delivery network, thus making electricity a public utility. Carr goes on to argue that the same thing is happening with computing. Instead of services being located on-site, we are farming computing out to a select few providers (Carr, 2008). While many argue that the analogy has been taken too far (Urquhart, 2009), one place where the comparison becomes readily apparent is in the metering of services.

Outsourcing is not a new concept for technology. People have been using virtual private servers and hosting providers for years. The pricing structures for these services are either by the month or year or through some other contract the institution sets with the hosting provider. Generally, the users of these services are limited in the amount of computing resources they can consume. For example, a customer may be allowed to use only 350 GB of bandwidth each month and 100 GB of storage. If they go over these limits the hosting provider may deny users access to the website or turn the service off altogether. These old pricing structures are similar to Edison's view of electricity: you use only what you have, and you can't have any more without a significant investment.

The cloud model is different, though; you pay according to your use. This means that if users use 3 TB of storage the first month but only 1 TB in the second month, the bill will be adjusted accordingly. In previous payment models, users would be charged for 3 TB of space regardless of whether or not they were using that space.

Figure 2.1 provides an example of a bill from Amazon Web Services. In it, users are charged for hours a device is running, I/O (input/output) requests to the device, storage on the device, storing an image of the device, and any GETs made to the device. Similar to a public utility, subscribers are charged based on which resources are used and how much they are being used. While the metered payment model is not a new one to the business world, it is new to the computing industry and is changing the way institutions provide computing services.

17

Figure 2.1. Amazon Web Services Bill

		Totals
Amazon Elastic Compute Cloud View/Edit Service		
US East (Northern Virginia) Region		
Amazon EC2 running Linux/UNIX		
$0.085 per Small Instance (m1.small) instance-hour (or partial hour)	96 Hrs	8.16
$0.17 per High-CPU Medium Instance (c1.medium) instance-hour (or partial hour)	4 Hrs	0.68
Amazon EC2 EBS		
$0.10 per GB-month of provisioned storage	7.458 GB-Mo	0.75
$0.10 per 1 million I/O requests	3,550,311 IOs	0.36
$0.01 per 10,000 gets (when loading a snapshot)	87,707 Requests	0.09
$0.01 per 1,000 puts (when saving a snapshot)	4,946 Requests	0.05
Elastic IP Addresses		
$0.00 per Elastic IP address remap - first 100 remaps / month	1 Count	0.00
	Download Usage Report »	**10.09**
Amazon CloudFront		

Elasticity

Setting up a new system can often be a guessing game. Common questions we might ask vendors or the institution are:

- How much storage is needed?
- How much RAM is needed?
- What kind of redundancy should be implemented?
- Will the system grow?
- How process intensive is the system?

The purpose of asking these questions is to better understand the type of infrastructure needed to implement a system.

Let's say that a large library system plans on implementing a new search tool. They hope to first release it to particular graduate school libraries; if the project is a success, they will release it to the entire campus. The user base at the beginning of the system's implementation may be dramatically different when compared to the end of its implementation; the infrastructure developed must take this into account. At the beginning of the project, the team is faced with one of two decisions:

1. Create a system that will work with the pilot project. Perhaps the team can reuse an existing server. Later, if the project is a success the team will need to determine how to expand the infrastructure while maintaining any changes or keeping data they may have added to the system.
2. Create a system that will work for the eventual population. This may include purchasing new servers, backup tools, or anything else the infrastructure might need. Essentially the team is planning on the success of the project and spending money accordingly.

Neither of these options is ideal. Many institutions now deploy virtual servers that allow for expansion and contraction, but sometimes institutions are still faced with purchasing expensive hardware to ensure that a system can be expanded when needed.

The cloud, however, offers the ability to expand without the worry of purchasing hardware or other components to improve the system's infrastructure. This means that an institution can quickly expand from a system that works for a thousand users to a system that works for tens of thousands.

An example of a cloud-based service that allows for quick and easy expansion is Amazon Web Services' Relational Data Service (RDS). With RDS, a user can create a MySQL database and later choose to expand its space. Figure 2.2 shows the modify database instance screen available through the Amazon Web Services Management Console. Here are a number of options available to users. One allows users to change the database from a small instance, which according to Amazon's website is "1.7 GB memory, 1 ECU (1 virtual core with 1 ECU), 64-bit platform, Moderate I/O Capacity," to a four times large instance that has "68 GB of memory,

Figure 2.2. Amazon Web Services' Modify Database Instance Screen

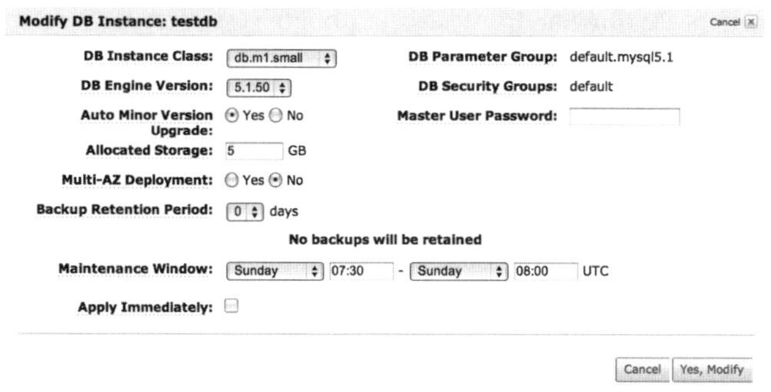

26 ECUs (8 virtual cores with 3.25 ECUs each), 64-bit platform, High I/O Capacity" (Amazon, 2010a). Still another option allows users to specify the amount of storage needed for the data. This can be as small as 5 GB or as large as 1 TB. These features and others make Amazon's RDS easily scalable simply by clicking a few buttons or making a few API calls.

Resource Pooling

Traditionally when an institution purchases infrastructure for a system, it must purchase according to the system's needs during peak loads. Consider a library purchasing a new discovery interface. Administrators know that during midterms and finals the system will be under an intense load, so they purchase a server based on the load they expect during those four time periods. During the rest of the year, they will only utilize a quarter of the server's capacity. In the end, the institution is wasting money by not taking advantage of the infrastructure's true potential.

If the same institution's administrators choose to use the cloud, they could provision a server based on their normal use case. They could then utilize APIs or other services to scale the system up or down based on the load to the server. The rest of the time the computing power they are not using is released back into the general pool to be used by other institutions.

Perhaps another institution's administrators use the cloud to provision a number of high-capacity servers to process large quantities of data. This work is something that they need to do once a year, and purchasing servers just for this work would be a fiscal waste. By using the cloud, the institution provisions the servers, processes the data, and releases the servers back into the general pool of resources.

The idea of sharing computing resources with the larger pool is often referred to as *multitenancy:* "a single instance of software [that] runs on a server, serving multiple client organizations (tenants)" (Wikipedia, 2010). The best example of

19

multitenancy is Salesforce.com. Salesforce hosts their customers' software; so instead of companies purchasing and maintaining their own hardware and software, customers are drawing from a larger pool of resources for software, including Salesforce's app exchange, which allows companies to share applications with other Salesforce customers. It is important to remember that multitenancy can expand beyond software though. As Lori MacVittie (2010) writes in a blog post, infrastructure multitenancy "is primarily achieved through server virtualization and configuration." This allows companies like Amazon to pool together infrastructure in order to provision servers based on their users' needs rather than on the physical makeup of servers. The idea of resource pooling as a primary characteristic of the cloud is an important one and it will become a point of controversy as we begin to discuss the different deployment models for the cloud.

Three Service Models

The NIST definition of the cloud outlines three ways to serve up the cloud to users:

- Software as a service (SaaS)
- Platform as a service (PaaS)
- Infrastructure as a service (IaaS)

It is important to remember these three service models are just that: service models. Many computing resources are delivered via one of these three models, but that does not necessarily mean they are a cloud-based service.

Before discussing these three types of systems, it is important to understand what we mean when we talk about software, platform, and infrastructure. Figure 2.3 shows a hypothetical systems architecture an institution might use for Ex Libris' link resolver SFX. The hardware for the system would be composed of, at a basic level, a server and a network connection. Once the data center puts this in place, the next step would be to install the supporting software or platform that

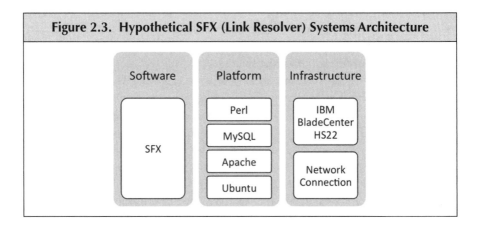

Figure 2.3. Hypothetical SFX (Link Resolver) Systems Architecture

will run the end-user software. In the case of SFX this consists of the programming language Perl, the Apache web server, the open source database MySQL, and the operating system Ubuntu. Once these pieces are in place and functioning, the software itself can be installed on top of the platform and infrastructure.

Software as a Service (SaaS)

Software as a service, or SaaS as it is commonly referred to, is defined as software that a user purchases without needing to also purchase the underlying infrastructure or platform in order to run that software. To better understand the difference between traditional software and cloud-based software, let us compare Microsoft Word and its cloud-based SaaS counterpart Microsoft Office Live's Word Web App.

In the case of Microsoft Word, the infrastructure would simply be any laptop or personal computer, while the platform might be Microsoft's Windows Operating System or Apple's OS X. Once users have acquired the infrastructure and platform, they can then install the software. As new releases, bug fixes, and versions are released, users will be required to update the system. This is usually prompted by automated checks run by the software. With Word Web App, though, users are not required to purchase infrastructure or a platform. Instead, Microsoft's data center provides the infrastructure for the software and JavaScript as its primary platform (Anderson, 2010). Users acquire the software by registering for an account on Office Live's website and logging in. Updates, bug fixes, and new releases are pushed out and applied by Microsoft rather than prompting users to update the software manually.

Software as a service is by no means a new idea. There are many software applications that are hosted in software vendors' data centers, but this does not mean they are cloud based. In the library community, just about any application can be hosted. Innovative hosts Millennium, Ex Libris hosts MetaLib, Serials Solutions hosts 360 Link, and so on. Just because these applications are hosted does not mean they are cloud-based software; they still need to be available on demand, elastic, metered, available via broad network access, and part of a larger pool of computing resources.

Platform as a Service (PaaS)

Platform as a service, or PaaS, is often the hardest concept for people new to the cloud to understand. Essentially, PaaS allows a software provider to develop and deploy his or her own software without having to worry about the underlying infrastructure. PaaS users would decide which platform (usually based on the programming language), corresponding web server, and database engine they would like to use. For example, a number of platform providers offer their users Ruby on Rails, Thin, and SQLite; Java, TomCat, and Google Datastore; or Python, Apache, and MySQL. Once users have decided which platform to use, they deploy their application based on the way the provider has configured the platform.

This idea of platform as a service is not new. Traditional web-hosting providers have been hosting platforms for users for quite some time but without the advantages the cloud provides. A good example of a traditional web-hosting provider is Go Daddy. Go Daddy provides users of its service access to a number of different programming languages, including Ruby on Rails, PHP, Perl, and Python; each of these programming languages is usually coupled with the Apache web server. But, hosting providers like Go Daddy usually limit users to a certain number of databases, storage space, and/or bandwidth. Additionally, setting up services provided by these types of hosting providers is often cumbersome; there are usually quite a few hoops to jump through in order to make the new web space work in the way users require.

Conversely, cloud-based platform providers offer users the flexibility that traditional providers do not offer; one such provider is Heroku. Heroku itself runs on Amazon Web Service's infrastructure and utilizes a platform consisting in part of Ruby on Rails, Thin, Rack, PostgreSQL, and a variety of other platform service options (Heroku, 2010). Users of Heroku can use as little or as much space as they want, create as many applications as they want, and even connect their service to other cloud providers. Setting up space within Heroku is as simple as creating an account and executing a few commands. The user's web space is instantly available for whatever Ruby on Rails application they need to host.

PaaS is slowly growing. Aside from Heroku, other major providers of cloud platforms include Google App Engine, and its ability to program in both Java and Python and Microsoft Azure, with its ability to program in ASP.net. The services these providers offer are some of the most innovative services available in the cloud.

Infrastructure as a Service (IaaS)

When most people think of the cloud, they usually think of the giant in the room, Amazon Web Services, with its infrastructure services like the Elastic Compute Cloud (EC2) or Simple Storage Service (S3). In the past, if institutions did not want to host their own servers, they usually contracted with a data center to do the work for them. Servers were still purchased, installed, and usually dedicated to one particular customer. If the server crashed, the hard drive failed, or power was lost in that particular area, the user was usually out of luck until the problem could be fixed.

Cloud-based IaaS, however, offers a number of advantages that users did not previously have available to them. For example, utilizing Amazon Web Services customers can create replications of their servers in multiple data centers throughout the United States and Europe. Backups can easily be provisioned and launched with the click of a few buttons, opening up a whole new world of possibilities for disaster recovery efforts, load balancing, and a host of other issues the modern data center faces.

IaaS doesn't just stop with servers though. Amazon and other providers also offer a number of storage and network solutions. For example, Google recently announced its Google Storage for Developers, combining "the performance and scalability of Google's cloud with advanced security and sharing capabilities" (Google, 2010), and Rackspace, a major competitor to Amazon, provides users with on-demand IP addresses that can easily be associated or disassociated with any of the "servers" customers provision. These infrastructure services are dramatically changing the way users are creating and implementing technology.

A Note

It is important to remember that many do not believe that these three service models are the only possible service models. In his book *Cloud Computing with Windows Azure Platform,* Roger Jennings (2009) outlines other service models, including files as a service, data as a service, communication as a service, and monitoring as a service. While it may be possible to provide any type of computing resource as a service, it is also possible to broaden these ideas and fit them into one of the three NIST-defined service models.

Four Deployment Models

Much of the controversy that comes into play in the cloud computing community is what is and is not the cloud. Nowhere does this occur more than in the debate about the different deployment models for the cloud. The NIST definition outlines four different deployment models for the cloud:

- Public cloud
- Community cloud
- Private cloud
- Hybrid cloud

The following section will move through each of the deployment models, providing examples and discussing issues and controversies associated with the different models as well as how one might deploy a system within that model.

Public Cloud

A public cloud is a cloud service that is available for use by the general public. Users of this type of cloud need to simply sign up for an account and the service is made available to them instantly. Users would make payments to the cloud provider based on their usage of the different services. Some examples of public cloud providers are Google, Amazon, Microsoft, and Rackspace.

If an institution was interested in setting up a system in Amazon's cloud it might first search through the available Amazon Machine Images, or AMIs, to see if an image of that system already exists. If it does, the institution can easily launch the system with a few simple clicks. If it does not, the institution can choose an

AMI that contains the proper supporting platform or it can choose to build that platform itself. Once it has that platform in place, it can install the software and deploy its new system.

There are, of course, a number of concerns that institutions have with deploying systems into a public cloud; chief among these is security. What information can we trust cloud providers with? Legally, what information are we allowed to trust cloud providers with? It is important for any institution that is looking to move to the cloud, or even to outsource a system, to properly assess the risk involved in giving up some portion of control over that system.

There are a number of services that different cloud providers offer their users in order to help make their systems more secure. Amazon offers a Virtual Private Cloud that allows users "to connect their existing infrastructure to a set of isolated AWS compute [sic] resources via a Virtual Private Network (VPN) connection, and to extend their existing management capabilities such as security services, firewalls, and intrusion detection systems to include their AWS resources" (Amazon, 2010b).

In its *Cloud Computing Risk Assessment* report, the European Network and Information Security Agency (ENISA, 2009) outlines a number of security benefits for the cloud:

- Security and the benefits of scale
- Security as a market differentiator
- Standardized interfaces for managed security services
- Rapid, smart scaling of services
- Audit and evidence gathering
- More timely, effective, and efficient updates and defaults
- Benefits of resource concentration

Deploying applications to a public cloud may bring up many questions and concerns for an institution. It is important that, before implementing a system in the cloud, institutions thoroughly evaluate it, the cloud provider, and the data they plan on storing in that system.

Community Cloud

Community cloud is cloud infrastructure that "is shared by several organizations and supports a specific community that has shared concerns (e.g., mission, security requirements, policy, and compliance considerations). It may be managed by the organizations or a third party and may exist on premise or off premise" (Mell and Grance, 2010). The most commonplace community clouds are governmental clouds; the U.S. government, the European Union, and a number of other governmental bodies around the world use the cloud in order to share resources among their different agencies (Di Maio, 2010). In higher education, community clouds are already beginning to appear. OSHEAN, the Rhode Island Research and Education Network, is in the process of building and expanding its Cumulus Cloud Computing (C3), which allows OSHEAN members to "annually subscribe to a dedicated Resource Pool" (OSHEAN, 2010).

Community clouds offer many advantages over public clouds. The payment structure for a community cloud might differ greatly from that of the public cloud. Institutions may pay an annual fee based on FTE or may pay based on their annual usage; all of this would depend on how the community chooses to set up payment structures. Additionally, security concerns might be reduced when using a community cloud based on prior relationships the institution may have with the community offering the cloud service. And, within a community cloud, institutions may feel they have a greater voice in how the cloud itself is operated and secured.

Educational institutions and libraries, in particular, are perfectly poised to provide community clouds. These institutions have been working together, creating vast networks of cooperation among one another. The idea of sharing computing resources is not a new one either, and creating a community cloud is simply the next step in sharing with one another.

Private Cloud

Private cloud is by far the most controversial of all the deployment models. Private cloud is defined as an individual institution operating its own cloud. The cloud can be operated either by the institution or by a third party, and it can be hosted at the institution or off-site (Mell and Grance, 2010).

Many argue that a private cloud is not the cloud. In the blog post, "When Is a Cloud Not a Cloud?" Phil Wainewright (2009) points out that cloud computing comes from the notion of the Internet and the countless diagrams using clouds to represent the Internet. When a private cloud is launched at an institution, it is essentially captive or cordoned off from the rest of the Internet. Wainewright (2009) argues that this is the primary reason that it is not the cloud. It doesn't need the Internet to run; just its local network will suffice.

Conversely, private cloud allows institutions to reap the benefits of the cloud (metering, scalability, on-demand self-service, etc.) but without the risks (security, lack of control, and so on). Established computing vendors like Oracle, IBM, EMC2, and VMWare all offer some type of private cloud-based service in conjunction with their traditional computing offerings, helping to legitimize the private cloud as a true cloud deployment model.

Hybrid Cloud

Hybrid cloud allows institutions to deploy an application or system using more than one type of deployment model. Figure 2.4 is an example of how an institution might deploy Redmine, an issue/software management system, in the cloud. Perhaps in this case the institution is interested in keeping control of the data maintained in the MySQL database but isn't as interested in hosting the files associated

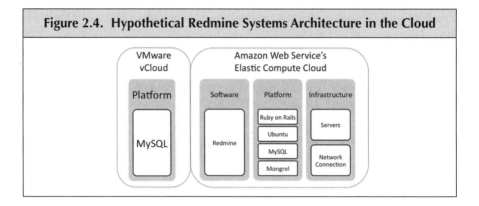

Figure 2.4. Hypothetical Redmine Systems Architecture in the Cloud

with the application. The institution decides to use VMWare's vCloud service to host the database and Amazon EC2 for the remainder of the system's architecture.

Hybrid cloud, though, can go beyond the normal decoupling IT shops are used to implementing. "Eucalyptus is an open-source software platform that implements IaaS-style cloud computing using the existing Linux-based infrastructure found in the modern data center" (Eucalyptus, 2010). When users implement Eucalyptus in their data center they receive an experience similar to that of an Amazon Web Services user. Eucalyptus also integrates with EC2, allowing users to employ cloud bursting, which is

> the practice of "bursting" into a cloud when capacity has been reached in the corporate cloud/data center. The business case for cloud bursting primarily revolves around seasonal or event-based peaks of traffic that push infrastructure over its capacity but are not consistent enough to justify the cost of investing in additional hardware that would otherwise sit idle. (MacVittie, 2009)

When Amazon released its Virtual Private Cloud, or VPC, data centers everywhere stood up and cheered. This new offering provided data center operators with the ability to place greater control on Amazon's cloud offerings, essentially moving the public cloud under the umbrella of the institution's data center.

Hybrid cloud allows users of the cloud to integrate the different deployment models, public, community, and private, into one seamless cloud. Users are then able to benefit from all of the things each of these deployment models has to offer.

Conclusion

The NIST definition of cloud computing offers a sound foundation of understanding for anyone interested in learning more about the cloud. The five characteristics of the cloud help users recognize what attributes cloud services possess. The four deployment models provide users with an understanding of where they can set up their systems. Finally, the three service models supply a framework of how providers deliver these services to their users.

The cloud is an ever evolving and changing computing paradigm. As more and more vendors enter the space, the definitions and concepts surrounding the cloud will change. New services will be offered and new concepts brought to light. One thing is for certain, though, cloud computing is here to stay and will change the way IT departments provide systems to their users.

References

Amazon. 2010a. "Amazon Relational Database Service (Amazon RDS)." Amazon Web Services. Accessed November 7. http://aws.amazon.com/rds/.

———. 2010b. "Amazon Virtual Private Cloud." Amazon Web Services. Accessed November 7. http://aws.amazon.com/vpc/.

———. 2010c. "Simple Monthly Calculator." 2010. Amazon Web Services. Accessed November 7. http://calculator.s3.amazonaws.com/calc5.html.

Anderson, Tim. 2010. "Microsoft's Office Web Apps—Google Killing Not Included." *The Register* (London, UK), April 27. http://www.theregister.co.uk/2010/04/27/office _2010_web_apps_review/.

Carr, Nicholas G. 2008. *The Big Switch: Rewiring the World, from Edison to Google.* New York: W.W. Norton & Co.

Di Maio, Andrea. 2010. "Community Clouds from Governments to Banks Will Challenge Vendors." *Gartner Blog Network* (blog), April 27. http://blogs.gartner.com/ andrea_dimaio/2010/04/27/community-clouds-from-governments-to-banks/.

ENISA (European Network and Information Security Agency). 2009. "Cloud Computing Risk Assessment." ENISA. November 20. http://www.enisa.europa.eu/act/ rm/files/deliverables/cloud-computing-risk-assessment.

Eucalyptus. 2010. "Products Overview." Eucalyptus. Accessed November 7. http://www.eucalyptus.com/products/overview.

Google. 2010. "Google Storage for Developers—Google Code." Google Code. Accessed November 7. http://code.google.com/apis/storage/.

Heroku. 2010. "How It Works." Heroku. Accessed November 7. http://heroku.com/ how/architecture.

Hoff, Chris. 2009. "On the Draft NIST Working Definition of Cloud Computing. . . ." *Rational Survivability* (blog), May 8. http://www.rationalsurvivability.com/blog/ ?p=870.

Hurwitz, Judith. 2010. *Cloud Computing for Dummies.* Hoboken, NJ: Wiley.

Jennings, Roger. 2009. *Cloud Computing with the Windows Azure Platform.* Indianapolis, IN: Wiley.

MacVittie, Lori. 2009. "Cloud Balancing, Cloud Bursting, and Intercloud." *F5 DevCentral* (blog), July 9. http://devcentral.f5.com/weblogs/macvittie/archive/2009/07/09/cloud-balancing-cloud-bursting-and-intercloud.aspx.

———. 2010. "Architectural Multi-tenancy." *F5 DevCentral* (blog), May 18. http:// devcentral.f5.com/weblogs/macvittie/archive/2010/05/18/architectural-multi-tenancy.aspx.

Mather, Tim, Subra Kumaraswamy, and Shahed Latif. 2009. *Cloud Security and Privacy.* Beijing: O'Reilly.

27

Mell, Peter, and Tim Grance. 2010. "Cloud Computing." National Institute of Standards and Technology. Last updated August 27. http://csrc.nist.gov/groups/SNS/cloud-computing/.

OSHEAN. 2010. "Cumulus Cloud Computing (C3) Service, by OSHEAN." OSHEAN. Accessed November 7. http://cumulus.oshean.org/.

Rainie, Lee. 2004. "The Rise of Wireless Connectivity and Our Latest Findings." Pew Research Center's Internet & American Life Project. April 13. http://www.pewtrusts .org/our_work_report_detail.aspx?id=22660&category=54.

Smith, Aaron. 2010. "Mobile Access 2010." Pew Research Center's Internet & American Life Project. July 7. http://pewinternet.org/Reports/2010/Mobile-Access-2010.aspx.

Urquhart, James. 2009. "In Cloud Computing, Data Is Not Electricity." The Wisdom of Clouds. CNET News. August 1. http://news.cnet.com/8301-19413_3-10296370-240.html.

Wainewright, Phil. 2009. "When Is a Cloud Not a Cloud?" ZDNet. August 28. http://www.zdnet.com/blog/saas/when-is-a-cloud-not-a-cloud/846.

Wikipedia. 2010."Multitenancy." Wikipedia. Revised October 13. http://en.wikipedia.org/ wiki/Multitenancy.

Chapter 3

Cloud Computing: Pros and Cons

H. Frank Cervone

Introduction

Cloud-based computing is a hot topic right now because many people believe that it will dramatically transform the way we use and provide access to technology. Others, however, are not so sure (Farber, 2008). Nonetheless, while perhaps not as transformational as the Internet itself, cloud computing will provide an evolutionary step in the provision of network-based services by changing the way people access applications and other services. This emphasis on services is important as it is the main attraction of moving to cloud computing. While the underlying technology is interesting to technologists, it is ease of access and provisioning of services that is the real benefit to organizations.

As is often the case with newer technologies, as many people and organizations begin to adopt the new technology, there is a lot of confusing information swirling around, and much of it is based on subjective opinion rather than objective reasoning or facts. Cloud computing is no exception. Today, much of the information related to cloud computing approaches the topic from either one of two perspectives. The first approach takes the position that it is the savior of all the ills in the information technology world. The other perspective is that cloud computing is a bad idea and will lead to the inevitable failure of an organization if adopted. While these depictions may be a bit exaggerated, they demonstrate the two polar opposite approaches to cloud computing being sold today. However, neither of these perspectives is completely correct.

The research firm IDC predicts that cloud computing will move from a technology used by "early adopters" to one that is part of everyday information technology operations by 2012 (Gens, 2008). Therefore, the goal of this chapter is to present a balanced view of both the pros and cons of using cloud computing so that librarians and employees in other information organizations can make informed decisions on how and when to proceed. Not surprisingly, as is the case with most technologies, the usefulness of cloud computing will depend greatly on

29

the particular context in which it is used. There is no definitive answer as to whether cloud computing is appropriate in a given context. Nevertheless, by considering all of the facts, understanding the environment, and evaluating the options, librarians can make an informed decision whether cloud computing is right or not for their situation.

What Cloud Computing Is Not

Today, the definition of cloud computing is somewhat vague given the marketing hype that has sprung up around the technology. Most people, however, would agree that the most obvious aspect of cloud computing is that the user relies on the Internet, which is where the "cloud" is located, for the majority of their computing needs. As one moves from this basic definition, the specifics of cloud computing become a bit more concrete. For most technologists, as Rosalyn Metz discusses in Chapter 2, "cloud computing" is a term used for a particular type of information technology architecture that is based on resources that are provided from a variety of sources, most of which are not necessarily located within the physical premises of the organization. Technologists may have very specific ideas about what constitutes and what does not constitute cloud computing and may have very strict interpretations of cloud computing's relationship to outsourcing, software as a service (SaaS), and virtualization.

Technologists specify that outsourcing differs from cloud computing primarily because cloud computing is about providing standardized technology stacks. That is, in a cloud environment, the operating environment (operating systems, programming language, database back ends) tend to be standardized so that services can be moved from one physical implementation to another with ease. In most data centers today, most organizations run a variety of computing platforms to support the various technology needs of their users. In a mixed environment such as this, the economies of scale would not allow one to simply move everything to a cloud because of the diversity in the environment. However, the operation could be outsourced if the outsourcing provider can supply all of the platforms that would be needed.

Similarly, technologists also specify that cloud computing is not necessarily the same thing as SaaS. SaaS is remotely hosted software that is accessed directly. While there may be economies of scale in using SaaS, this is not the primary motivation for using it. For example, WorldCat Local may not strictly be considered cloud computing; it is SaaS. One of the major reasons one can make this claim is because it is clear the services and resources provided through WorldCat Local are coming directly from an OCLC data center. In a true cloud computing environment, it would not necessarily be clear where the data center was actually located, and there would be clear economies of scale to the end user. That is, it would be clearly less expensive to run your catalog on WorldCat Local than it would be to run it using locally installed software.

Finally, while cloud computing generally makes extensive use of virtualization technologies, virtualization is not inherently cloud computing. Virtualization technologies use software, in the form of a hypervisor, to simulate hardware. This enables an organization to run multiple operating environments concurrently on the same physical hardware regardless of whether the physical server is located in-house or in the cloud.

Pros of Cloud Computing

There are a number of perceived benefits of cloud computing. The most commonly reported benefit of cloud computing (Wittman, 2010) is that it is easier and faster to deploy than traditional technology solutions. This is because vendors typically use economies of scale in setting up the provided service, thereby allowing implementation to proceed faster. For the most part, this is possible because the vendor has preimplemented systems with all the basic configuration information for the new system predefined. All the vendor need do is to clone the preconfigured system onto a new host and, voila, your organization now has a system available for local customization. As an example of how quickly new applications can be implemented using this model, Westmont College (Sheard, 2010) has completed six significant cloud application deployments in 12 months with no additional staff or budget.

An additional benefit of cloud computing is that the organization can pay only for the resources that it uses, as the services are typically provided on some type of metered basis. During busy periods, charges may be higher as more computer processor or disk storage may be used. This could be offset by other periods where demand is less. This model is very similar to the heating and cooling bills most librarians are familiar with.

In cloud computing, because the hardware and most of the software infrastructure is maintained outside the organization, fewer in-house staff members are required to maintain hardware and software. This can lower cost overall and allows the existing staff within the organization to do other work that truly is localized or unique to the organization. Ideally, this would allow staff to focus on research and development of new innovative services.

These benefits are in addition to some of the characteristics of cloud computing previously mentioned:

- **Immediate availability.** Because of the commoditized nature of cloud services, additional resources can be added or removed on demand.
- **Scalability.** As the need for greater or lesser capacity changes over time, it is simpler in a cloud-based environment to make those adjustments.
- **Round-the-clock availability.** As cloud-based resources are typically housed in massive data centers, personnel are on duty 24 hours a day, 7 days a week, 365 days a year to respond to any issues.
- **Resiliency.** Cloud computing provides sustainability for disaster recovery and business continuity.

Cons of Cloud Computing

Cloud-based computing, however, is not without its drawbacks. Security can be a major concern (Kim, 2009), and there are several aspects of security that can be problematic. One example is authentication to cloud-based systems. An organization will have to work with the vendor to provide a common authentication framework that is both secure and reliable. With the work of groups such as InCommon and technological infrastructures such as Shibboleth, this is becoming less of a concern. Larger concerns include ensuring the transmission of data across the network is always secured, most typically through encryption, as well as ensuring that the cloud-based infrastructure upon which the system is based is secure as well. As Brenner (2010) has noted, confidence in the ability to secure computing assets in the cloud is low primarily because of uncertainty about the ability to enforce security policy in the cloud. Additionally, many cloud providers are not particularly forthcoming in revealing the details of their security infrastructure, including how their systems are audited and what types of ongoing security training they provide their employees.

Performance of cloud-based services can also be a concern as services are delivered over the network; therefore, a major issue is ensuring that there is sufficient bandwidth to cover all applications. Additionally, protocols for adding hardware-based resources, such as computing power or storage space, need to be defined so that these resources can be added quickly and efficiently during periods of heavy usage.

Availability of services can also be a concern. Most organizations have SLAs (service level agreements) with their in-house IT departments that define the services that will be provided as well as the operational parameters within which those services will be provided. For example, SLAs will often include information about the percentage of the time services will be available, the number of users who can be served simultaneously, as well as benchmarks with which performance will be compared. When relying on free or low-cost solutions, many of these items will not be specifically addressed, as the service is provided on an "as is" basis. For enterprise level applications, an organization must ensure that appropriate SLA standards are in place.

For some, the inability to customize applications may be a major drawback. For most applications, there are fewer options for local customization of a system, as most of the benefit of cloud-based services comes for commoditization. While this may have some drawbacks, it also has benefits. Given that the customizations outside of those typically provided are usually rather expensive to implement, it forces an organization to critically evaluate the worth of such local customizations.

Finally, cloud-based services can be difficult to integrate with in-house information technology operations. Often this is related to the limited options for local customization that cloud-based services provide. Because of these limited options, it may be difficult to integrate local systems with cloud-based systems, particularly if the local systems use idiosyncratic or nonstandard interfaces.

Things to Consider When Evaluating Cloud Services

Perhaps one of the most important considerations in evaluating cloud computing is separating the fact from the hype. There is a lot of hype surrounding cloud computing, much of which revolves around some common themes (Ryan, 2008). The first of these themes is that all computing will move to the cloud. This is unlikely, as the majority of services that are being moved to the cloud are commodity services, such as e-mail, where there is no real intrinsic benefit to hosting the service in-house. The major exception to this is for services that cannot be provided in-house. An example of this is Ex Libris' bX recommender system, which analyzes search and use patterns across a wide range of institutions to recommend articles to individuals as they browse through the results of their searches.

Second, cloud computing may not make economic sense in all cases. In large environments where there is a robust IT infrastructure in place, it may actually cost more to move services to the cloud. Similarly, it is unlikely that cloud computing will eliminate IT expenditures on hardware as, for the foreseeable future, some types of services simply will not translate well to the cloud environment.

Finally, the hype that cloud computing will eliminate the need for professional IT staff in-house is rather shortsighted. While the skill sets of internal IT staff will need to be different in a cloud-based environment, organizations will still need to have IT administrators and developers to monitor the cloud applications as well as address the needs that cannot be fulfilled through the cloud.

This being said, organizations considering cloud computing should carefully evaluate the following:

1. **Pricing** for cloud computing varies greatly. Some services are provided for free, others at low cost, and others at considerable cost, and there is no standard for reliability based purely on cost.
2. **Performance assurances** are critical and must be defined through an SLA. Many free services do not provide an SLA or provide an SLA that is very rudimentary. For mission-critical applications, most organizations would find this unacceptable, so it is important to understand what expectations are reasonable and what can be expected based on the pricing model chosen.
3. **The provider must have an understanding of the unique circumstances of the organization.** The needs of libraries differ from those of the commercial sector. Consequently, it is important for the cloud provider to understand the unique characteristics of library and educational applications. Choosing a provider that specializes in this area is likely to generate a better long-term partnership.

4. **The organization must retain the ability to move cloud offerings back in-house or to another provider.** This is particularly critical for enterprise applications where considerable intellectual effort has been spent on creating the application environment.

In addition to these points, Heiser and Nicolett (2008) of the Gartner Group suggest the following security points be considered:

1. **External audit and security certification of the cloud-based provider.** Ultimately, an organization is responsible for the security and integrity of its data, regardless of where it is held. Service providers must undergo external audits and security certifications for the good of the library.
2. **Storing and processing data in specific jurisdictions.** A library may be subject to laws and regulations that govern where data can (and, more importantly, cannot) be stored. Librarians will need to work with their provider to both understand and ensure that their data is being stored in legal locations.
3. **Investigative support.** This is critical in certain circumstances. The cloud provider must be able to ensure that if the data is subpoenaed or requested for other investigation, it will be able to produce it within a reasonable time frame.
4. **Provider long-term viability.** If the cloud services provider being used goes bankrupt or is acquired, librarians must ensure that their data will be accessible after such an event.

Conclusion

While still new, adoption of cloud computing is gaining steam because most organizations see that the advantages of controlling all aspects of information technology implementations are outweighed by the benefits of outsourced models that can provide a greater range and diversity of services than could be provided in-house. In addition to reducing the startup costs for new services, cloud computing can be more cost effective in the long term as services are usually based on a pay-as-you-go model, similar to utilities. By reducing costs, cloud computing allows organizations to use their resources to focus on the truly unique aspects of service they need to provide to their community.

This is not to say that there are not concerns associated with cloud computing. Issues related to security, pricing, and availability need to be addressed before any large-scale deployment of cloud-based services. Vendors need to be carefully evaluated to ensure they have the capability and resources to deliver the services promised. Additionally, organizations need to consider the long-term viability of their cloud services providers.

Many libraries will find that introduction of cloud-based services will come on a piecemeal basis as their traditional vendors experiment with this new model. By introducing cloud-based services one at a time, libraries can assess the appropriateness and value of such services. Proceeding in this manner also helps address concerns related to vendor lock-in. If librarians dislike the service, it is likely that it can be swapped out with a competing service that is more in tune with the local context.

Perhaps the most compelling argument for cloud-based computing is that moving to the cloud computing model will help libraries become more agile and better able to compete in an uncertain environment by eliminating the overhead of technology support and allow for a greater focus on service provision and innovation.

References

Brenner, Bill. 2010. "Reset." *CIO Magazine* 24, no. 2: 30–36. http://www.cio-digital .com/ciodigital/20101015.

Farber, Dan. 2008. "Oracle's Ellison Nails Cloud Computing." CNET News. September 26. http://news.cnet.com/8301-13953_3-10052188-80.html.

Gens, Frank. 2008. "IT Cloud Services User Survey, Pt. 1: Crossing the Chasm." *IDC Exchange* (blog), September 29. http://blogs.idc.com/ie/?p=205.

Heiser, Jay, and Mark Nicolett. 2008. "Assessing the Security Risks of Cloud Computing." *Gartner Research.* June 3. http://www.gartner.com/DisplayDocument?id=685308.

Kim, Won. 2009. "Cloud Computing: Status and Prognosis." *Journal of Object Technology* 8, no. 1: 65–72. http://www.jot.fm/issues/issue_2009_01/column4/.

Ryan, Vincent. 2008. "A Place in the Cloud." *CFO Magazine.* September 1. http://www.cfo.com/article.cfm/11954936.

Sheard, Reed. 2010. "Cloud Computing in Education: A Practitioner's View." *Campus Technology.* Accessed December 28. http://campustechnology.com/Articles/ 2010/09/22/Cloud-Computing-in-Education-A-Practitioners-View.aspx?p=1.

Wittman, Art. 2010. "Practical Analysis: Our Maturing View of Cloud Computing." *Information Week.* Accessed December 28. http://www.informationweek.com/story/ showArticle.jhtml?articleID=224701815.

Chapter 4

What Cloud Computing Means for Libraries

Erik Mitchell

Introduction

This chapter examines the role that cloud computing has played in transforming libraries and information technology organizations. It begins with a history of technology adoption in libraries and concludes with an exploration of current trends in cloud computing and how these trends are beginning to transform libraries.

Our Information Technology Environment

The information technology (IT) landscape of libraries has changed dramatically over the past 20 years. In the 20 years since the advent of the web, libraries have almost ubiquitously adopted Internet access and have become key players in the provision of Internet services to their communities (Kinney, 2010). During this time libraries have redirected services both to support in-house Internet use and to serve the needs of users via digital means (Blowers, 2010). This shift in focus is found in the United States as a whole. For example, it took only 24 years for *Time* magazine to transition from naming the computer as "Machine of the Year" (*Time*, 1983) to naming "You" as the person of the year (Grossman, 2006). During this time Internet adoption in the home grew to 79 percent of the U.S. population (A. Smith, 2010). As the computer and the Internet became mainstays in U.S. culture, our vision of them transitioned from a machine-centric view to a social and network-centric view. This included the development of highly successful social web services and the emergence of complex network-based user services. The adoption of network-based services has been so widespread that in 2008 the Pew Internet Trust found that 69 percent of Internet users use some form of cloud computing service (Horrigan, 2008). A more recent EDUCAUSE survey found that undergraduate student use of these types of technologies was nearly ubiquitous (Smith and Caruso, 2010).

Over this time, substantial changes have occurred in IT hardware, information structures, and technology cost that have driven the pace and scope of IT change. In the early 1980s, the personal computer (PC) market was driven by word processing and other localized productivity applications. Over the past 24 years mobility and network connectivity have played key roles in transforming the most popular applications to cloud-based versions of traditional productivity applications. A key example of this shift can be seen in the use of Google Docs as opposed to traditional productivity application formats. Research (Low, 2010) on users who have both Google Docs and traditional productivity suites installed on their machine show that they are more frequently using the Google products but that time spent in an application may depend on the type of application (e.g., Microsoft Excel outweighed Google Spreadsheets in time spent).

During this time information formats also changed. For example, the most commonly accessed information services on smartphones are communication based, not publication based (A. Smith, 2010). These formats include text messaging, e-mail, Facebook, and Twitter. While there are many publication formats accessed via mobile environments, they often include point-of-need information such as weather, transit availability, or location information. Likewise information structures changed from primarily narrative-based text to a mix of multimedia, structured metadata, and text-based information. This shift extends from client-based computing to larger scale data analytics. Geoffrey Moore (2010) asserts that use analysis now requires a cloud computing orientation: "The IT stack is changing from being data centric to cloud centric—you cannot do metadata analytics at scale in a data centric environment." The shift in computing platform and in information structure is joined with a shift in appliance use. Cloud-based service providers such as Skype (http://skype.com) represent an abstracted means of accessing voice and video communication services, and file synchronization sites such as Dropbox (http://dropbox.com) and Jungle Disk (http://jungledisk.com) provide cloud-based disk services that both abstract the service from the hardware and provide a suite of advanced services that are not easily deployed in a client-hardware environment (e.g., version control, continuous data protection, automatic replication).

Finally, the cost of technology has driven innovation and change. Not only has technology continued to follow the pace of advancement suggested by Moore, who said that circuits on a chip double every 24 months (Intel, 2010), the cost of computing resources has dropped considerably—$200/MB for storage in 1980 compared with $.08/GB for storage in 2010 (I. Smith, 2010). As this drop in price has occurred, service subscription models have been created that do not rely wholly on hardware cost to provide computing services. For example, the Amazon AWS service platform (http://aws.amazon.com) provides computing resources, disk space, notification services, and monitoring services at by-the-hour pricing models. As of November 2010, the cost per month for 1 GB of disk space was $.14 per month. While considerably more expensive than comparable costs for local hard-drive space, Amazon is providing advanced services such as automatic redundancy, version history, and guaranteed uptime. The same trend is occurring throughout the IT industry as resource providers offer computing resources combined with service level agreements (SLAs), enterprise level redundancy services, and value-added support models. Organizations are increasingly turning to these models as opposed to locally purchased and managed hardware for a number of reasons, including lower initial cost, lower total cost of ownership (TCO), improved service, and improved functionality.

These factors—client platform needs, information resource needs, and infrastructure costs—are three of the primary driving factors for users considering their computing environments. Research by the Pew Internet Trust and EDUCAUSE has shown that our patrons' computing environments are increasingly diverse, online, and socially focused (Smith and Caruso, 2010; A. Smith, 2010). Based on this perspective, Nicholas Carr observes that "for consumers, the cloud revolution has already happened" (Anderson and Rainie, 2010). Likewise, the EDU-CAUSE Center for Applied Research (ECAR) report of 2010 observes that one of the outcomes of this computing environment is a shift in how enterprise IT is managed. "The enterprise-driven model of controlling learning technology is likely facing a relative decline. Students will set the direction, choose the tools and determine the behaviors" (Smith and Caruso, 2010: 24). The following section examines how libraries have deployed services to address this shift in patron focus and discusses how libraries can weigh these factors to make decisions for future cloud computing adoption.

How Cloud Computing Responds to Current IT Needs

It is perhaps enough to state that the idea of cloud computing is taking over a number of previous concepts, including grid computing, data centers, and web services. While each of these types of computing maintains distinct definitions and service approaches, cloud computing providers are beginning to demonstrate how a cloud-centric approach differentiates itself from traditional approaches. In relation to these ideas are two related concepts that are often used together in cloud computing. The first of these concepts is "web services." Web services are defined as "a software system designed to support interoperable machine-to-machine interaction over a network" (Haas and Brown, 2004). The second concept is the application programming interface (API). An API can be thought of as a set of standardized methods that enables access to a software program or system. These two types of IT services are typically important facets of cloud computing provider platforms. For example, Amazon offers its cloud services via both a browser-based console and a suite of command-line API tools. These tools are capable of both real-time human-computer interaction and automated computer-to-computer interaction (web service). While cloud services do not necessarily need to make use of web services or APIs, these tools tend to be important in enabling scalability and on-demand service as discussed in the definitions given earlier.

Although cloud computing definitions can be a complex concept, the model has already become an everyday experience for most Internet users. While the platform cited most frequently by the Pew Internet Trust research showed that users most often used e-mail, other services include productivity suites involving word processing, spreadsheets, and calendaring software. In addition to this everyday use, both library patrons and professionals are making use of point-of-need cloud services for advanced projects. For example, Anali Perry (2010) is using YouTube as a storage platform for her Library Minute videos. Likewise, the Z. Smith Reynolds (ZSR) Library uses Vimeo as a storage platform combined with harvested and locally stored metadata to create a video-based tutorial toolkit (ZSR Library, 2010). Vimeo (http://vimeo.com) offers video hosting, conversion, and sharing services in a software as a service (SaaS) environment. Vimeo offers automation services including desktop clients, API methods, and advanced authentication services for content control. This shift in seeking cloud-based services to integrate locally or to replace wholly traditional service platforms has enabled libraries to provide complex services without a large amount of IT overhead.

While libraries commonly use "everyday" cloud applications to serve informal needs, it is becoming more common to use cloud computing to solve formal and more complex needs. The IT service industry in libraries has begun to focus on cloud-based services. Nearly every type of library system (e.g., OpenURL resolver, Digital Asset Management System, Integrated Library System, Research Guides, digital publishing system) is available in an SaaS, PaaS (platform as a service), or IaaS (infrastructure as a service) environment. The solution selected depends on a number of factors, including desired level of control over the system, level of in-house expertise, cost, desired service level, and comfort level. Table 4.1 indicates major issues that should be considered when selecting and implementing cloud-based services for key library IT resources.

In an EDUCAUSE Live presentation, Theresa Rowe of Oakland University discussed three primary factors in considering whether to migrate a system to the cloud—cost, service agility, and resource availability (Rowe, 2010). First, Rowe indicated that cost savings can be a major factor and is particularly evident in commodity-based services such as e-mail and storage space. Rowe pointed out that these types of services are both very important to the university and require considerable resources to manage internally. There currently exist a number of external cost-effective options in the cloud marketplace, including Google Apps for Education (http://google.com/a/edu) and Microsoft's Live@edu service (http://microsoft.com/liveatedu). Second, Rowe cited service agility as a factor, indicating that there are important but highly localized services that either are not relevant outside of the department's need (e.g., human resource hiring service) or need to move more quickly than local IT can. Finally, Rowe discussed the impact that cloud computing can have on local resource availability. By selecting resources

Table 4.1. Factors and Issues with Cloud Platforms

Service Type	Influential Factors	Important Issues
SaaS	• Low in-house expertise at content or IT level • Seeking minimal involvement • Willing to pay additional cost for management services	• Service agreement must define availability, IT and data management responsibilities, support responsibilities, and security. • Outsourced expertise limits may curb innovative potential. • Turnkey solution may offer least flexibility.
PaaS	• Balanced IT expertise, high level of local service involvement • Appropriate in cases where library needs a level of flexibility or customization • Often includes the ability to add limited services	• Platform tools must be available and useable by local staff. • SLA issues are similar to SaaS issues but need to include additional support definitions. • Clear roles for library staff and service provider need to be defined.
IaaS	• Maximum control over environment desired • Seeking minimal external support • Scalability and on-demand access are key requirements	• IT and library staff must be prepared for high level of involvement. • SLA is important, but locally defined SLA must include service definitions. • Traditional IT management procedures must be put in place to ensure sustainability.

to outsource that do not contribute to the differentiating factors of the university, organizations can make better resource allocation decisions to enable IT staff to focus on important applications.

While cloud-based solutions for library IT needs are still emerging, it is worth noting that the shift is in line with the changes in subscription models for periodicals. In each case, libraries select a different approach (SaaS, IaaS, PaaS) based on factors such as cost, internal expertise, and desired service level. Libraries are positioned to capitalize on cloud-based solutions for a number of reasons. First, libraries often rely on a mix of internal and external IT expertise for system management. By looking toward cloud solutions libraries can create partnerships that allow them to leverage their local resources without replicating expensive IT skill

Table 4.2. Example Distribution of Services on Cloud Platforms

	APPROACH	SYSTEMS
SERVICE CATALOG	SaaS	OpenURL resolver, statistics management, research guides, online reference, digital library system
	PaaS	Integrated library system, interlibrary loan, copyright compliance systems
	IaaS	Discovery platform, digital repository, archives management, website storage, institutional repository

sets. Second, libraries often lack the large-scale infrastructure that would enable them to deploy new services without considerable capital investment. By selecting PaaS and IaaS solutions libraries can gain access to these resources on a subscription basis without capital investment. Finally, libraries have to find a balance between services with very rapid life cycles (e.g., video tutorial sites) and services with very stable life cycles (e.g., integrated library systems). While it can be difficult to find a single IT service management (ITSM) approach that equally supports these services, ITSM approaches that leverage cloud-based solutions with appropriate SLAs and management policies are good matches with how libraries approach IT. Table 4.2 shows an example of how a library might approach the distribution of its services based on these factors.

How Will Cloud Computing Change Libraries and IT Organizations?

The introduction of the Internet to libraries was part of a significant shift from print/in-house-focused service to online/externally provided service. While libraries have historically turned to large capital investment for their IT resources, they have adopted online and subscription-based models for a number of other services, including resource management, patron-driven acquisition, and resource aggregation services. Given the success of these services, libraries are positioned to view the subscription focus of cloud-based IT in a positive light. By itself, subscription models are not entirely representative of the cloud computing service platform, but the concepts of capital-based purchases and just-in-case resource/staffing models that libraries rejected when they began utilizing subscription-based services are in line with cloud computing goals.

In fact, cloud computing is one facet of a changing landscape of information that is leading to new forms of information creation and use. Moore (2010) observes that this shift is leading to new location-based services, transparent pricing, consumer-specific discounts, immediate gratification, mobile push, branded apps, and social reward applications. The impact of this transition is that not only is our approach to accessing computer resources changing, but the ways in which these resources are used to create, share, and leverage information are also changing. While predicting the evolution of the cloud computing movement so early in its life cycle is ultimately not particularly productive, it is worth thinking about some large-scale changes that cloud computing may introduce into information-centric organizations. Three areas in particular stand out as being potentially affected by cloud computing changes. These areas are personal empowerment, IT issue redefinition, and reallocation of organizational resources.

Personal Empowerment

One of the key outcomes of cloud computing is the ability to lower barriers to use and ultimately empower individuals through access to enterprise-scale technology. By both lowering the cost and moving to a subscription model from a capital investment model, cloud providers are enabling everyday users to enter the IT market. Amazon EC2, for example, offers microserver instances for only two cents per hour of CPU time as well as high memory and CPU instances. When combined with auto-scaling services, the EC2 model enables IT departments to allocate computing resources as necessary and without a large capital investment. There are also PaaS and SaaS style services such as Omeka.net (http://omeka.net) that offer on-demand digital publishing services. While these services are not free, they enable small libraries to leverage the expertise and IT support of much larger organizations at relatively low cost.

43

Redefine IT Issues

Second, cloud computing has the ability to redefine key IT issues. For example, security, stability, and data integrity are important aspects of any IT service approach. By addressing these issues, and by further allowing organizations to purchase these services, cloud computing enables organizations to deploy services with the same or better SLA levels that would have been made available in local computing environments. Furthermore, cloud computing offers the ability to fundamentally change how IT providers approach technology issues such as stability and data integrity. By using virtualization and redundancy-focused technologies, cloud service providers can provide advanced versions of these services that would be cost prohibitive for end users to implement on their own. Likewise traditional issues with capital allocation and the challenges of responding to rapidly changing user needs are fundamentally redefined in a cloud environment. By removing the need for large capital investment and by allowing IT departments to publish IT resources as services rather than commodities, cloud computing providers facilitate the introduction of new IT services outside of formal capital request cycles. As a result, IT organizations can begin approaching the provision of IT service from a user-centric perspective.

Reallocation of Local Resources

Third, cloud computing offers both large and small IT organizations the opportunity to realign their staff and IT resources. While new skills are required (such as the skill to launch, monitor, manage, and kill cloud services), cloud computing changes the balance of work required to guide a service through the service life cycle. Server management, resource allocation, and end-user support all fundamentally change when implemented on cloud platforms. While the impacts on staffing levels and focus will be different for each organization, cloud computing approaches do allow organizations to further distribute IT responsibilities and bring in staff who would otherwise not be part of the ITSM approach of the organization. This should lead to the accomplishment of new goals and the establishment of new priorities that would otherwise not be possible.

Conclusion

This chapter has taken a very positive view of the role and potential impact of cloud computing in libraries and other information organizations. To be sure, potential pitfalls such as security, privacy, information ownership, resource access, and IT sustainability are significant issues facing cloud adopters. Rather than considering any one of these issues to be insurmountable, organizations should consider the decision-making and resource allocation models discussed here to help guide decisions surrounding cloud computing. As cloud platforms mature, providers are becoming more accustomed to providing traditional ITSM services, including the definition of SLAs and implementation of ITSM procedures, to ensure that security and service levels meet the needs of the subscribing organization. In each of these cases it is important to balance the risk against the service need and to select appropriate providers and service agreements based on criteria relevant to the subscriber.

References

Anderson, Janna, and Lee Rainie. 2010. "The Future of Cloud Computing." Pew Research Center's Internet & American Life Project. June 11. http://www.pewinternet.org/Reports/2010/The-future-of-cloud-computing.aspx.

Blowers, H. 2010. "From Realities to Values: A Strategy Framework for Digital Natives." *Computers in Libraries* 30, no. 4 (May): 6–10.

Grossman, Lev. 2006. "*Time*'s Person of the Year: You." *Time,* December 13. http://www.time.com/time/magazine/article/0,9171,1569514,00.html.

Haas, Hugo, and Allen Brown. 2004. "Web Services Glossary." World Wide Web Consortium. http://www.w3.org/TR/ws-gloss/.

Horrigan, John. 2008. "Use of Cloud Computing Applications and Services." Pew Research Center's Internet & American Life Project. http://www.pewinternet.org/Reports/2008/Use-of-Cloud-Computing-Applications-and-Services.aspx.

Intel. 2010. "Moore's Law and Intel Innovation." Intel. Accessed November 20. http://www.intel.com/about/companyinfo/museum/exhibits/moore.htm.

Kinney, Bo. 2010. "The Internet, Public Libraries, and the Digital Divide." *Public Library Quarterly* 29, no. 2 (April): 104–161.

Low, Montana. 2010. "Google Is Eating Microsoft's Lunch, One Tasty Bite at a Time." *Rescuetime* (blog), June 17. http://blog.rescuetime.com/2010/06/17/google-is-eating-microsofts-lunch-one-tasty-bite-at-a-time/.

Moore, Geoffrey. 2010. "Atmosphere: Core, Content and the Cloud." YouTube video, 42:33, posted by EVENTS@Google, April 12. http://www.youtube.com/eventsatgoogle#p/u/8/0swJCYLH2Ck.

Perry, Anali. 2010. *The Library Channel.* Accessed September 10. http://lib.asu.edu/librarychannel.

Rowe, Theresa. 2010. "Spotlight on Cloud Computing: Impact! *EDUCAUSE Live!*" (presentation). EDUCAUSE. September 17. http://net.educause.edu/LIVE1026.

Smith, Aaron. 2010. "Mobile Access 2010. Pew Internet & American Life Project." Pew Internet. July 7. http://www.pewinternet.org/Reports/2010/Mobile-Access-2010/Summary-of-Findings.aspx.

Smith, Ivan. 2010. *Cost of Hard Drive Space.* Updated December 3. http://ns1758.ca/winch/winchest.html.

Smith, Shannon D., and Judith B. Caruso. 2010. *ECAR Study of Undergraduate Students and Information Technology, 2010.* ECAR Study of Undergraduate Students and Technology. October 22. http://www.educause.edu/Resources/ECARStudyofUndergraduateStuden/217333.

Time. 1983. "MACHINE OF THE YEAR 1982: The Computer Moves In." October 5. http://www.time.com/time/magazine/article/0,9171,952176,00.html.

ZSR Library (Z. Smith Reynolds Library). 2010. Toolkit. June 2. http://zsr.wfu.edu/toolkit/.

Chapter 5

Head in the Clouds?
A Librarian/Vendor Perspective
on Cloud Computing

Carl Grant

Introduction

Overview and Benefits of Cloud Computing

According to The Quotations Page website (http://www.quotationspage.com), it was Arthur C. Clarke who said, "Any sufficiently advanced technology is indistinguishable from magic." To listen to all the current claims being made about cloud computing it might easily qualify as magic under Clarke's definition. The claims have gotten so overblown that the Gartner group noted on October 7, 2010, that cloud computing, along with many other new technologies, has moved into the "Peak of Inflated Expectations" (Gartner, 2010). In this chapter, the goal is to provide you with an understanding of the realities of cloud computing from the point of view of someone who is both a librarian and a vendor.

So let's start with a reality. Cloud computing is really not new, and it is not magic. It is at best an evolutionary step in a long line of computing products and services that can be utilized by libraries. Let's put that evolution in perspective. Mainframe computer technology in the 1960s was a clear early ancestor of cloud computing, as it was based on a centralized server with remote users. This technology was later used to support travel reservation booking systems, point-of-sale systems, and numerous other examples that started in the 1970s and exist yet today. There have also been e-mail hosted systems for a long time. Remember AOL™ and Compuserve™? These too were hosted wide-area network-based applications. Even for libraries, library automation vendors and cooperatives have long offered hosted systems. OCLC originated in 1967 when 54 Ohio college and university libraries formed the Ohio College Library Center to develop a cooperative, computerized regional library network. OCLC's bibliographic database, the Online Union Catalog, began its operation in 1971. So the basic concepts of cloud computing are really not new.

At a practical and entirely logical level, cloud computing also offers both the vendor and library some distinct advantages over the existing environments. These include:

1. **Platform neutrality.** The history of hardware vendors is nearly as convoluted as the surface of the human brain. They come, they go, they acquire and divest. As it happens, so do operating systems. For the software vendors, delivering application software products into this environment is equally complex. It increases the number of quality assurance tests that must be run, the number of staff needed to program and support applications, and overall time needed to get a new or updated application to library customers. The use of a cloud computing–based approach allows the vendor instead to consolidate, over time, the number of platforms to be supported and thus will allow them to be as focused as the customers on being efficient and effective.

2. **Reducing overall costs.** This is a benefit that most librarians and vendors understand the cloud computing environment is intended to achieve. For libraries this occurs because the cost of provisioning hardware and the staff to run it can be redirected to the vendor, who through having a larger base over which to spread those costs can do it in a more efficient manner and at a lower cost to the library. In addition, because libraries need purchase only computing services to meet their needs and can quickly scale those services, cost efficiencies are realized there as well. For the vendors, it means gaining the maximum use out of the investment they make in hardware through optimal use of talented staff, thus gaining the greatest efficiency.

3. **Ability to refocus library and/or IT staff and redirect cost of services to more important value-added services.** "Cloud computing offers an economic advantage by allowing institutions to focus more resources on differentiating value" (Oblinger, 2010: 4). In discussions with librarians about cloud computing, they'll frequently mention that they do not see that they are adding substantial value to the running of computing infrastructure. In times of economic crisis, this becomes a far more important factor, and thus library directors seek to redeploy staff in order to create substantial value-add for the end user and the library.

4. **Better support.** It is natural for libraries to be concerned that moving support to their vendor may introduce room for new unknown variables over what they have today. In doing so, however, consider that the vendors will, just like the libraries, be able to take existing staff and better focus and train them as a result of the consolidation of platforms to be supported.

Many librarians also note that, in the current model, institutional IT support is not necessarily the same as library IT support. When that is the case, it can result in the institutional IT being a barrier in terms of making needed changes. They may require education on the reasons for the changes, and even once that is done, there may still be conflicts, problems, and security issues. That leaves the library having to justify and argue with institutional IT support in order to do its job. When librarians compare that support to what they can obtain from their system vendor, and if costs are comparable, they should find support will likely be better in the cloud computing model.

5. **Data as a Service (DaaS).** Depending on the architecture of the cloud computing solution, if data is part of the hosted offering and it's enabled for sharing, one of the most important advantages is that of moving to a model where data becomes a service rather than a function replicated library by library. Cloud computing allows data to be built once and used over and over by many institutions. When this is mentioned what immediately comes to mind for many librarians is bibliographic data, but the reality of course is that librarians deal with a much larger body of data that is affected. It includes all types of metadata (METS, EAD, MARCXML, to name a few) and all types of digital content including text (DAT, HTM, HTML, LOG, RTF, TXT, XML), video (ARC, BMP, GIF, JP2, PNG, TIF), and audio (MP3, WMA). So, there is a very high probability this kind of service will bring major reductions in costs not only in the creation of the data, but in the maintenance of it as well.

6. **Cloud computing is green.** One additional advantage that is sure to have appeal to both librarians and the vendors that serve them is: "If you are worried about the environment, you will be happy to know that cloud computing is the greenest approach to computing out there" (Linthicum, 2009: Chapter 2).

7. **Analytics.** A further benefit of moving data into the cloud and enabling some level of sharing is the ability to utilize analytic tools with that data. This enables new levels of collaboration, coordination, and agility that are not easily replicated with today's systems without massive amounts of additional work. Data in the cloud makes it possible to analyze user trends and potential click-streams to understand how users utilize systems and see how those same systems can better anticipate and serve users. In addition, libraries will more easily be able to compare data collections for development, sharing, and/or licensing. Analytics, when coupled with cloud computing, enable the engine for new automated library services that can be deployed across the web to wherever users have information needs that libraries can meet.

49

As a result, libraries and vendors both will realize some major new benefits under cloud computing. In addition the utilization of this technology will enable libraries to develop new services and capabilities, some of which are discussed at the end of this chapter in "The Future of Cloud Computing."

These kinds of features resulted in Gartner (2010) going on to say in its Hype Cycle Special Report that it believes cloud computing will have a "significant impact." That impact will be quite measurable. A recent projection stated: "by 2012, 80 percent of Fortune 1000 companies will pay for some cloud computing service, and 30 percent of them will pay for cloud computing infrastructure" (Rhoton, 2009: Chapter 1). Even today, many library automation vendors are offering and supporting many customers at some level of the cloud computing environment. Out of over 9,000 product installations that Ex Libris has today, nearly 1,500 are utilizing some version of the cloud computing environment. In fact, all of the major integrated library system (ILS) vendors already offer one model of cloud computing, that is, software as a service (SaaS) solutions.

Moreover, there are efforts underway at this writing that will bring libraries even further into the cloud computing environment. These include Ex Libris's next-generation library services framework, Alma, and OCLC's Web Scale Management Services. Each offers new and radically different capabilities based on the cloud computing model. One attribute in both models is the use of Software Object Architecture (SOA). "Cloud computing and SOA are different concepts, but they are related. SOA is a pattern of architecture, whereas cloud computing is an instance of architecture" (Linthicum, 2009: Chapter 2). Ultimately, this architecture will become an important part of the evolution of cloud computing and will substantially contribute to the benefits derived from it.

Cloud Computing Configurations

For a better understanding of where some of these benefits will be derived, it's important to understand the configurations of cloud computing that are possible in the library context. Describing the various configurations necessitates a two-dimensional matrix. At one dimension, there are public, hybrid, and private clouds. In the second dimension, within these types of clouds, there can be infrastructure as a service (IaaS), platform as a service (PaaS), or software as a service (SaaS). "Amazon Elastic Compute Cloud (EC2) is a classical example of Infrastructure as a Service. Google App Engine is generally considered to be a Platform as a Service. And Salesforce represents one of the best known examples of Software as a Service" (Rhoton, 2009: Chapter 2).

Vendors of library products might well be utilizing a combination of these second-dimension configurations. For instance, a common example would be for a library automation vendor to use IaaS as part of a larger cloud computing product offering. Other examples would be SaaS offerings of open source ILS products using Amazon EC2 services or some of the aggregated indexes of articles that are currently available to libraries.

As librarians, it is important to know the configurations being utilized in a cloud computing–based product offering. As with anything, there are benefits and potential complications that need to be understood as a result of a multilayered, multiprovider solution. Asking detailed questions is key. What are the offering options? What components are based where? What companies will provide valuable information concerning what can be expected from the service level agreements (SLAs) as well as the overall scalability and availability of the offering being offered? For instance, if a supplier uses Amazon EC2 services to provide SaaS solutions such as an ILS or a data service, it would virtually ensure that scalability, redundancy, and availability are extremely high. At the same time, it would be important to understand how the SLA provided and signed by the library's solution provider also ensures that Amazon EC2 will meet or support the terms of that SLA. Likewise, if the solution provider says it provides the cloud-based solution from top to bottom, the library staff should probe into whether or not they truly have the same levels of scalability, redundancy, and availability as that available from firms that focus on those aspects.

Before leaving this overview of cloud computing and why it's important, it is equally important to remember that "[c]loud computing is anything but a mature technology" (Rhoton, 2009: Chapter 29). Consequently, there are numerous areas where librarians and vendors will need to work together to bring that maturity to the technology. You'll find a list of these areas in a later section of this chapter.

51

Disadvantages, Real and Perceived, of Cloud Computing

As with any emerging and rapidly evolving technology, there are questions yet to be answered and concerns expressed and the general feeling that not everything is likely to be as wonderful as the hype surrounding it would lead you to believe. The most commonly cited concerns when discussing cloud computing with librarians include security, control, branding, and service.

Security

Librarians worry about security of cloud computing applications for several reasons. All of these should be examined and addressed as part of the decision to move to the cloud. Most of these concerns seem to center around the library's data, the organizations holding it in the cloud, and its physical storage and safety as well as whether the security is sufficient to prevent unauthorized access by third parties.

A frequent question is what happens to the library's data if its vendor is bought and/or goes into bankruptcy?

This can be complicated because, in the library field, many times it is thought that nonprofit entities, if they offer a comparative, cloud-based service, give the customer extra security in this realm. There may be a belief that there is less risk of it going through organizational changes that would create substantial likelihood of these types of risks being encountered. But the comparison is more complicated than that. A comparison of the organizational entities must include questions about how many products/services have been purchased and/or launched and then subsequently abandoned or otherwise then ceased to be offered to the market in a relatively short time frame.

The comparison must also include the financials of all the organizations being considered, to ensure financial viability in terms of revenue growth and in terms of comparing profitability (those that are for-profit) against revenue in excess of costs for a nonprofit entity. All organizations bring some level of risk to this consideration. Measuring those risks and making informed choices based on those measures is the only responsible way to proceed.

Another area of major concern is the privacy of the patron data. The reasons are obvious, as exposure of patron data causes major uproars and public embarrassment for the institution and may well violate laws in cases where FERPA (Family Educational Rights and Privacy Act) compliance is mandated. So ensuring the vendor will handle the patron data appropriately is essential. From the vendor's point of view, this can be further complicated if the company operates on a global basis. Depending on where the data resides in the cloud, laws such as the USA PATRIOT Act (Uniting and Strengthening America by Providing Appropriate Tools Required to Intercept and Obstruct Terrorism Act, or "Patriot Act") may mean organizations not based in the United States will not want their data stored on systems that would fall under the reach of the Patriot Act. For the vendor, this means co-locating data centers in multiple countries, usually on different continents, so as to also address redundancy and availability requirements at the same time.

When it comes to measuring the risk to the data itself, there are audits available that can be used by both librarians and vendors in order to provide assurance that a responsible and well-managed operation is being run. There are a number of existing security audits, such as SAS70 and ISO/IEC 27001, that can be used by cloud computing providers, and asking to see those is one step to take (although providers may want only to indicate if they've passed those audits, as disclosing the details in full can reveal details of their security setup they may feel would compromise their secure environment). In addition, "[t]he Trusted Cloud Initiative, the product of an alliance between the CSA (Cloud

Security Alliance) and Novell, will be a third-party, vendor neutral standard for cloud security and compliance that's designed to offer additional security certification requirements for cloud providers as well as educational tools" (Colaner, 2010: 22–23).

Control

Librarians need to be concerned that when moving to the cloud they maintain enough control to support the "value-add" of their library and services within the final solution. Some call this the ability to highlight the unique while integrating the common. Data when moved to the cloud where it becomes a service inherits the disadvantage of becoming more of a commodity. Commodities become widely available and typically at a low cost. So, this forces librarians to think where they'll add value to that data in order to provide differentiation. This can be done with cloud computing–based systems via:

- **Software configuration options.** While it is important that software can be quickly installed and put into production quickly, librarians seek configurability of the system in order to meet unique needs. This is a critical way to provide differentiation to their end users. This can be supported in numerous ways ranging from the data that can be loaded (can the library load local and unique data?) through to the software options (for instance, can the library configure relevance ranking on *all* data, facets used, displays, etc?). For vendors, trying to provide the same level of flexibility systems had when they existed in individual installations can prove difficult. In the end, the new benefits derived from this architecture need to be balanced against the loss of configuration options to make an informed decision on which course is best for the library.
- **Software extensions.** Vendors can find it hard to provide enough configuration options to make the system, using shared code and data, flexible enough to meet all the needs of the customer base. In order to do this, extensions and the ability to configure those extensions will become important. Open platforms are one model, and others address the same concern.

Yet another area of control that is of concern to both librarians and vendors is recognizing that many customers innovate on a regular basis and may want access to their data at levels that would permit that innovation. Providing this can prove challenging for the vendors while simultaneously maintaining a secure and stable environment for their other customers.

In analyzing the concerns surrounding control, even though libraries are clearly more comfortable with products and data in the cloud than they used to be, the final decision on using cloud solutions will hinge on deciding if the business needs clash with the unique materials of the institution. In the end, it will require a very institutional decision, and the library administration must be sure they are philosophically comfortable with that decision.

Branding

As more and more data moves into the cloud and the software using that data becomes cloud based, it becomes harder and harder for the end user to know exactly where the information appearing on the screens is originating. As this happens, libraries will want and need to brand the information they serve. By so doing, it will establish both the authority and authenticity of the information and at the same time remind the end user of the value of the library in delivering appropriate information to meet their needs. Branding may be done via logo displays or, depending on the type of data object being delivered, style sheets and/or placing the logo in the image or background behind the information display. There are no easy answers here, but clearly this issue is becoming one of increasing importance and one where smart and creative solutions will quickly gain wide market acceptance.

Service

Both librarians and vendors realize that for librarians to turn additional service/support over to the vendor, an element of trust is needed. This should be backed up by an SLA that details what the service expectations will be, how they will be met, and in what time frames. This is fair and good, as expectations should be clearly documented by both parties to ensure that the measurements are fairly applied and evaluated.

One area of service that is hard for both the vendor and librarians to control is that of network/bandwidth availability. Most cloud-based solutions will not be based on private networks, and, as such, a backhoe or competing services on the network can have a major impact on overall system performance. As one librarian noted about bandwidth concerns: "It's hard to compete with YouTube on campus," and, of course, this is a very valid point. There are technologies available, however, that can be used to protect bandwidth for important and major functions on the campus, and their use may become necessary in the future.

Additional Concerns

In the final analysis of advantages and disadvantages, "the most important consideration is not whether a potential solution satisfies the definition of cloud computing but rather whether it adds value" (Rhoton, 2009: Chapter 1). Because of the requirement of libraries to be far more efficient and effective with their resources in the current economic environment, the cloud computing model, combined with new functional capabilities that derive from both the architecture and the software capabilities developed, has the potential to add substantial new value.

Finally, let's note what cloud computing is not:

Cloud computing is not the savior of IT. It is nothing but a way to deploy your enterprise architecture in a way that has the potential to be more productive and cost effective. In essence, it is a tool, not a way of life. It is not magic, it is not even new, but if approached correctly, it could be a path toward efficiency. (Linthicum, 2009: Chapter 2)

It would be hard to say it better than this.

Areas Where Librarians and Vendors Must Work Together Closely

The cloud computing environment will create areas where both librarians and vendors will need to work together for the future of cloud computing to achieve its full potential. In particular, there are two key areas important for this collective process: standards and/or best practices and legislation.

Standards and/or Best Practices

For cloud computing to ultimately reach its full potential, standards will need to be developed and adopted. "One of the biggest challenges to cloud computing is the lack of standards that govern the format and implied functionality of its services. The resultant lock-in creates risks for users related to the portability of solutions and interoperability between their service providers" (Rhoton, 2009: Chapter 2).

Lack of standards will clearly not be acceptable to libraries and ultimately to vendors. Unfortunately, it is well known in the library profession that standards can often be lowest common denominator solutions because vendors, not librarians, dominate the standards process. In addition, in rapidly evolving fields such as cloud computing, moving to standardization too early in the life cycle of a technology can have negative consequences. For instance, it can both stifle innovation and, at the same time, commoditize solutions, reducing vendors' return-on-investment prematurely. Neither is good.

The Open Cloud Manifesto website (http://www.opencloudmanifesto.org) provides some very sound principles to be utilized:

1. Cloud providers must work together to ensure that the challenges to cloud adoption (security, integration, portability, interoperability, governance/management, metering/monitoring) are addressed through open collaboration and the appropriate use of standards.
2. Cloud providers must not use their market position to lock customers into their particular platforms and limit their choice of providers.
3. Cloud providers must use and adopt existing standards wherever appropriate. The IT industry has invested heavily in existing standards and standards organizations; there is no need to duplicate or reinvent them.

4. When new standards (or adjustments to existing standards) are needed, we must be judicious and pragmatic to avoid creating too many standards. We must ensure that standards promote innovation and do not inhibit it.

5. Any community effort around the open cloud should be driven by customer needs, not merely the technical needs of cloud providers, and should be tested or verified against real customer requirements.

6. Cloud computing standards organizations, advocacy groups, and communities should work together and stay coordinated, making sure that efforts do not conflict or overlap.

Legislation

A more recent trend that is troubling to both librarians and vendors is the increasing intervention by local, state, and/or federal governments to put into place legislation with the intent to protect user data. An unfortunate, and likely not well understood, consequence of this legislation could be a greatly slowed down adoption rate of cloud computing while these issues are sorted out in the marketplace and courts.

In the United States, the Patriot Act is widely seen as an issue in the adoption of cloud computing solutions. The government's ability to access data without the data owner even being informed will cause many organizations, particularly corporate libraries, to take a more cautious approach wherein data is stored on machines owned and controlled by the organization.

The *New York Times* reported on September 19, 2010, that "cloud-based breakthroughs face a formidable obstacle in Europe, however: strict privacy laws place rigid limits on the movement of information beyond the borders of the 27-country European Union" (*New York Times,* 2010).

There will likely be other examples of this type in the future, and this kind of prescriptive legislation is the result of legislators not fully understanding that which they're trying to legislate. As a result, in the end, they'll cripple their constituents. Other countries, unhindered by these inflexible approaches, will enjoy the benefits of cloud computing earlier and will be more agile and will move ahead in what is a highly competitive global environment. Neither libraries nor the educators they serve can afford this risk. It would be far wiser for libraries and vendors to proactively and jointly educate administrators and legislators about what can be done today that addresses security issues so that better and more appropriate legislation results.

The Future of Cloud Computing

The future of cloud computing as it looks today is best described by saying, "You should go as far as you can see, for you will be able to see farther when you get there." This is because the technology and the environment are changing rapidly and the future will be very dependent on the many internal and external dynamic factors discussed in this chapter, including social networking, analytic capabilities, and standards and legislative environments.

Even so, given cloud computing today, there are several things likely in the not-too-distant future. Through the use of data clouds, cloud computing, analytics, and mathematics, the value of librarianship will be turned into a new vehicle of information processing that can be readily and widely deployed across the web in a scalable fashion. "There is a growing need for filtering, sorting, categorization and analytics to help users manage the vast repositories of both structured and unstructured information and to easily find and extract the information that is of interest" (Rhoton, 2009: Chapter 29). As a result, cloud computing has the potential to become a vehicle for the reinvigoration of librarianship.

Clouds will achieve interoperability, not only between like systems, but between all types of systems, and this will lead to a more seamless integration of library services into numerous environments such as course management, online education, and certainly worker re-education and training programs.

On the flip side of these positives, librarians need, as a group, to realize they should "expect some demographic effects of cloud computing. By virtue of its location independence there may be increases in off-shoring. There may also be impact on employment as workers need to re-skill to focus on new technologies and business models" (Rhoton, 2009: Chapter 1). As services move into the cloud and become deployable across the web, this is a very real potential risk. As with so much of technology today, the new, well-paying, and lasting jobs to be created will require that workers in the librarian profession engage in getting up-to-date training and education and to employ that education in developing leading edge information services.

In a recent issue of *EDUCAUSE Review,* David Lewis, Dean of the IUPUI University Library, described the future of libraries this way:

> Ten years from now, the historic corpus of printed books will likely have been converted to digital files. . . . Print copies will be stored in long-term print repositories. . . . Ten years from now, digital book readers will be common, and print-on-demand machines will be better and cheaper. . . . Finally, ten years from now, everyone will expect that all documents should be instantly available anywhere and in all the forms—digital or paper—that might be useful. (Lewis, 2010: 11)

This is indeed a possible scenario. It is one viable way for libraries to benefit and to be part of the fabric of that coming environment if they're operating in a cloud computing environment.

This chapter started with a quote by Arthur C. Clarke and so it will conclude with another. According to The Quotations Page (http://www.quotationspage.com), in an address to the U.S. Congress in 1975, Clarke said "I'm sure we would not have had men on the Moon if it had not been for Wells and Verne and the people who write about this and made people think about it."

Hopefully this chapter will contribute to librarians thinking about cloud computing and leading libraries toward a future that utilizes and benefits from the same.

References

Colaner, Seth. 2010. "Cloud Computing Security Considerations." *PC Today* 8, no. 9: 22–23.

Gartner. 2010. "Gartner's 2010 Hype Cycle Special Report Evaluates Maturity of 1,800 Technologies." Gartner, Inc. October 7. http://www.gartner.com/it/page.jsp?id=1447613.

Lewis, David. 2010. "The User-Driven Purchase Giveaway Library." *EDUCAUSE Review* 45, no. 5: 10–11.

Linthicum, David. 2009. *Cloud Computing and SOA Convergence in Your Enterprise: A Step-by-Step Guide.* Reading, MA: Addison-Wesley Professional. Kindle e-book.

New York Times. 2010. "Cloud Computing Hits Snag in Europe." *New York Times,* September 19. http://www.nytimes.com/2010/09/20/technology/20cloud.html.

Oblinger, Diana. 2010. "Stewards for Higher Education: Looking at Clouds and the Top-Ten IT Issues." *EDUCAUSE Review* 45, no. 3 (May/June): 4.

Rhoton, John. 2009. *Cloud Computing Explained: Implementation Handbook for Enterprises.* Recursive Press. Kindle e-book.

Chapter 6

Cloud Computing for LIS Education

Christinger R. Tomer and Susan W. Alman

Introduction

The future of libraries and archives may well be determined to a significant degree by the technological competence of the librarians and archivists who run them. Cloud computing and its capabilities provide educational programs in library and information science new and potentially powerful choices in supporting the technological components of their programs. There is a need for Library and Information Science (LIS) programs to develop a consortium using cloud computing as an integrating and sharing mechanism to build a virtual learning and computing laboratory.

The technological component of LIS education has long been constrained by the high costs of information technologies and institutional priorities that tend to discourage experimentation and emphasize administrative concerns such as security. Notwithstanding a general increase in the attention devoted to information technology in basic courses, the vast majority of LIS students enrolled in ALA-accredited programs learn relatively little about library and archival systems, such as integrated online library systems or digital repositories, and even fewer of them acquire hands-on experience with these or other relevant systems.

This technological deficit is a significant, if not readily acknowledged problem of LIS education and one that may ultimately threaten many programs, given the growing importance of technology-oriented skills in the professional marketplace. Cloud computing alone may not constitute a solution to the problem—the acuity and technical competencies of LIS faculty are presumably the most important factors in determining the technological competence of future librarians and archivists. The potentially favorable economies and adaptability of the cloud computing environment, particularly when combined with what has been learned in other disciplines through experiments in the development of virtual laboratory capabilities, offer opportunities for LIS programs to render major improvements in the technical infrastructure supporting teaching and learning about learning technologies, in consortial or independent modalities.

Owing to the capabilities of cloud computing, LIS programs have new and potentially powerful choices in supporting the technology components of their educational programs. The aim of this chapter is to identify and explore briefly the opportunities afforded by cloud computing, culminating in a series of specific recommendations for the support of LIS education.

Advantages and Disadvantages of Cloud Computing

The advantages of cloud computing include potentially much greater efficiency, enhanced flexibility, and a more simplified approach to the organization and management of computing and data centers. Specifically, the benefits include (1) reduced costs (because the costs of using cloud technology are paid incrementally and often without the significant, initial investments that are required by so-called "on premise" computing); (2) increased storage capacities (because cloud-based storage is almost always elastic); (3) flexibility (because virtual machines can be installed or removed from service within a matter of minutes); and (4) increased access (because cloud-based instances can be made available to anyone with an Internet connection).

The most notable disadvantages of cloud computing are its reliance on network connectivity, legal ambiguities (particularly where ownership of data and privacy are concerned), and peripheral communication with an array of devices and systems, including printers and personal storage media. Most of the controversy over cloud computing has been focused on issues of access, user privacy, and security. However, these are pervasive issues, and there is little evidence that shifting computing to the cloud-based services exacerbates any of the attendant problems. Personnel requirements are also often cited as a disadvantage because familiarity with cloud technologies among IT professionals is by no means universal.

In the context of LIS education, all of the factors cited above apply if cloud computing is being considered as the basis for a more general approach to computing. Virtual machine (VM)-based general computing services running in the cloud would furnish the basis for e-mail, personal file storage, and the source of productivity applications such as word processing, presentation software, spreadsheets, and databases. In the more specific context of using cloud computing to establish virtual computer and learning laboratories for support of the LIS education, at least some of the legal ambiguities that attend cloud computing in more general settings presumably do not apply because personal data is unlikely to be stored on such instances. However, there may be other issues, depending on the types of data incorporated by instructors or students in an academic exercise, such as building a prototypical collection of materials on a digital repository system.

Building a New Technological Environment for Teaching and Learning about Library and Archival Systems

Cloud computing is important in the context of LIS education for two reasons. First, the embrace of cloud computing by many organizations, including OCLC, OhioLINK, SirsiDynix, and the Library of Congress, suggests that this mode of computing will have a significant impact on the configuration, the economics, and perhaps the personnel requirements of library computing in the years to come. A key issue associated with cloud computing in almost any setting today is the problem of qualified personnel, and it may be expected that as libraries, archives, and information centers move into the cloud, this will be an issue for them as well. So, providing access to the cloud infrastructure for the purposes of teaching and learning can be viewed as an important step toward a remedy for the personnel problem, assuming, of course, that programs in LIS education can indeed provide the appropriate education and training.

The second reason is that cloud computing offers new opportunities for prospective librarians and archivists to gain direct, hands-on experience in the use of various systems, including integrated online library systems, digital archiving and asset management systems, digital repositories, learning management systems, content management systems, metadata harvesters, web-based link resolvers, and online publishing systems. When it is coupled with open access operating systems and applications, cloud computing may also afford LIS students their first opportunities to work extensively with the code base of many systems and toward the improvement of such systems.

The technological element of LIS education has long been constrained by a lack of adequate resources, a long-standing tendency to react rather than innovate, a failure to recognize the transformative effects of information technologies and changing requirements of librarianship where information technology is concerned, the reluctance of vendors to contribute to the educational infrastructure, and a host of other problems in making educational scenarios relevant to the circumstances of professional practice. LIS education has long been afflicted by the now clearly misguided view that technology is peripheral in its relationship to librarianship's central concerns. Michael Gorman's well-known concerns about LIS education are relevant in this context, and, under a view first articulated in the early 1990s by Malinconico, what most librarians need to know about information technologies should be defined by what is required in order to collaborate effectively with computer scientists and information technologists (Malinconico, 1992). This view that librarians do not need to understand fully the information technologies with which they deal in professional practice has been reinforced by the facts that many library educators know surprisingly little about information technology in general or computing and networking in particular and that perhaps even more of them are largely disconnected from the realities of professional library practice. As a result, there has been little inclination to examine how speci-

61

fically the technological component of LIS education affects the development of new librarians and archivists, much less to pursue innovations in the curricular uses of information technology in LIS education. In a related vein, Aharony (2008) has observed that "LIS schools in the United States are not adequately prepared for the rapid changes in Web technology and use," and LIS programs "have not yet internalized [sic] the importance of the new, changing and dynamic innovations that are taking place in their environment."

The laboratories available to the students in most LIS programs are configured to support an array of basic computing requirements through the presentation of a standardized configuration distributed over a local area network. The focus of such facilities has been on providing students with access to the Internet and the World Wide Web, e-mail, and productivity applications, while largely ignoring information processing and its vast implications for librarians and archivists. What most LIS students have lacked is access to the administrative interfaces of library and archival systems. It should have been clear that librarians need the knowledge and skills necessary to control their technological environments toward creative ends and that the training that they receive needs to take place in an environment that allows access to systems sufficient for teaching, learning, and experimentation; however, most of the students have learned remarkably little about the technologies that have transformed library operations in the course of the previous generation.

There are presumably a number of ways in which this state of affairs might be improved. Of them, the most appealing is the notion of combining the idea of the virtual laboratory with the potential efficiencies and flexibility of cloud computing.

The idea of implementing a virtual laboratory through the Internet for teaching and learning can be traced to the early 1990s (Aburdene, Mastascusa, and Massengale, 1991). In recent years, the effectiveness of web-based remote laboratories and virtual laboratories has been evaluated, and at least several investigations have indicated that student learning is not adversely affected (Koretsky et al., 2008). As a result, and owing to the increasing importance of online education, interest in virtual laboratories as instruments of teaching and learning has been growing at a rapid rate.

The advent of cloud computing has served only to expand interest and accelerate the implementation of virtual computing laboratories. In some instances, the idea of the virtual computer has been sparked by the realization that the combination of increasing ownership among students of laptop computers and ubiquitous access to networks via Wi-Fi now precludes the need to maintain physical laboratory facilities at the levels required over the past two decades. In other instances, the notion of building a computer lab in the cloud has been a response to the growth of online degree programs and the computing needs and requirements of the students enrolled in online programs. In yet other cases, the virtual lab has come into existence because it affords unprecedented possibilities for collaboration and resource sharing. Perhaps most important of all, the flexibility of the cloud computing model and the ease with which virtual machines can be built allows course designers to build systems that are designed to meet the requirements of specific courses (Seay and Tucker, 2010). For example, at North Carolina State University, the combined use of cloud computing and virtualization has enabled the university to expand the number of the production images available for use from approximately 20 to more than 600, thereby vastly increasing the array of resources and configurations available to faculty and students (Shaffer et al., 2009).

The idea of virtual laboratories is not unknown in LIS education. While it does not fully qualify in technical terms, distributed access to the Internet Public Library (IPL) by various LIS education programs for instruction and training has set an important precedent, whereby collaborative technologies are used to increase the array of resources available for teaching and learning and provide shared access to them. The IPL (http://www.ipl.org) originated in a graduate seminar at the University of Michigan in 1995. What became the IPL was defined at the outset by two ideas: to ask some interesting and important questions about the interconnections of libraries, librarians, and librarianship with a distributed networked environment, and to learn a lot about these issues by actually designing and building an Internet-based reference resource/service. In 2006, responsibility for the IPL was transferred to a consortium that is led by Drexel University, with the University of Michigan and Florida State University as major contributing partners.

The precedent established by the IPL's "virtual learning laboratory" has been reinforced lately by LibLime and OCLC, each of which has used cloud computing and virtual machine technologies to provide LIS faculty and students with access to archetypical systems. In the case of LibLime, it has created and maintains instances of its enhanced version of Koha, the open source integrated library system (ILS), for use in LIS education programs, whereas OCLC provides access to CONTENTdm, its digital archiving platform, as part of a broader initiative in support of LIS education. See LibLime (http://www.liblime.com/), Koha (http://koha.org/), and Library and Information Science Education Program (http://www.oclc.org/ca/en/community/education/lis/) for more information.

The significance of access to what are effectively educational versions of CONTENTdm and Koha is that for the first time LIS students in significant numbers have the opportunity to work with and learn about systems that are effectively representative of the platforms that define digital libraries and archives. In addition, virtual machine images of other key LIS systems, such as DSpace, Evergreen, and Islandora, are now available for downloading and installation. This means that key components of a virtual learning laboratory providing access to a series of relevant systems and resources for LIS education are already available, and it is now mainly a matter of how and under what specific circumstances such a laboratory should be built.

There are plenty of options available. LIS programs could band together using cloud-based services as an integrating and sharing mechanism and build a virtual computing and learning laboratory designed to serve the requirements of the participating programs, much like the IPL is shared by the programs that underwrite its ongoing costs. The programs participating in such a consortium would still have the option to supplement these shared services through private clouds and/or on-site systems, or they could pursue the development of a virtual laboratory capability on an independent basis.

In any of these instances, it seems reasonable to imagine that students in particular would have access to computing and networking resources not available to them on the basis of locally provided and traditionally configured computing services, that the technological aspects of LIS education would be substantially, if not uniformly improved, and that continuities without parallel in LIS education could be achieved. For example, students in a course on digital libraries could work with digital archiving systems like Archon and ICA-AtoM to learn about design, interoperability, and administrative requirements of those systems, whereas students in a course on metadata might work with the same systems in order to achieve an operational understanding of how archivists describe digital objects. Of equal importance, a more uniform approach to technology education might establish a meaningful basis for defining and assessing technological competency within the library and archival professions.

The key issue in building a virtual lab is selecting the systems and applications that will be supported. Because many vendors have been reluctant to allow their systems and applications to be released for educational use—OCLC is an obvious exception—most of the options entail the use of open source software. But there are decided benefits to working with library and archival systems that have been developed in the open source environment. Licensing issues and compliance requirements tend to be minimal, which means, for example, that systems such as EPrints or DSpace or Koha can be built and configured as virtual machines and then deployed under a variety of circumstances without the consent of the developers.

Another significant benefit is that the open source systems that have been developed by and for the library and archival communities are typically based on either the so-called "LAMP" architecture—Linux, Apache, MySQL, and PHP—or a Java-based framework often incorporating Apache Tomcat. Those architectures are sufficiently standardized to make installation, configuration, and deployment comparatively simple tasks (Morelli and de Lanerolle, 2009). For example, in the domain of digital archiving, Archon and ICA-AtoM are based on the LAMP architecture. EPrints, probably the most widely used of the digital repository systems, is also LAMP based, whereas DSpace and Fedora Commons, the other prominent digital repository systems, are based on Java and Apache Tomcat. See Archon (http://www.archon.org/), ICA-AtoM (http://ica-atom.org/), EPrints (http://www.eprints.org/), DSpace (http://www.dspace.org/), and Fedora Commons (http://fedora-commons.org/) for more information.

What Should Be Included in a Virtual Learning Laboratory Program?

The heart of a computing lab supporting the education of librarians should be the integrated library system (ILS), and here there are several options (which afford the opportunity to run systems in parallel so that students can actively compare the design and functions of the respective systems). As noted earlier, Koha is available via LibLime, or it can be installed independently. Of the other open source ILSs, Evergreen, which was developed by a group of public libraries in Georgia, is arguably the most important, owing mainly to the interest it has generated in the library automation and public library communities and because it incorporates technologies, most notably the Open Service Request Framework and the XMPP protocol, and design features that have not been employed in other library systems (Scott, 2010). A third open source ILS that might be included is OpenBiblio (http://obiblio.sourceforge.net/). OpenBiblio is not as complex or robust as Koha or Evergreen, but its simplicity makes it a desirable environment in which students learning how to program in the LAMP environment could work with ease.

What other types of applications and systems should be included in a virtual computing laboratory for LIS education? At the University of Pittsburgh's School of Information Sciences, the faculty offering the MLIS degree took up this question in 2010 and recommended that, in addition to CONTENTdm, a set of open source applications, including the applications discussed in this chapter, should be included in what was referred to as a "digital sandbox." Contributions to the list of applications were made by Leanne Bowler, Kip Currier, Debbie Day, Ellen Detlefsen, Sherry Koshman, Geof Bowker, Janet Ceja, Daqing He, Tim Schlak, and Leigh Star. The recommendations focused on content management systems (Table 6.1), library, archive, and repository systems (Table 6.2), and software from the Public Knowledge Project, including Open Journal Systems (Table 6.3). The Public Knowledge

65

Table 6.1. Recommended Content Management Systems

SYSTEM	DESCRIPTION/URL
Drupal	Widely used content management system. http://drupal.org/
Joomla	Content management system as well as a model–view–controller (MVC) web application framework. http://www.joomla.org/
MediaWiki	Wiki package originally used on Wikipedia. http://www.mediawiki.org/
Plone	Content management system built on top of the open source application server Zope and an accompanying content management framework. http://plone.org/

Project (http://pkp.sfu.ca/), which works to improve scholarly and public quality of research through open access, is based on a partnership among the University of British Columbia, the Simon Fraser University, and Stanford University.

Table 6.2. Recommended Library, Archive, and Repository Systems	
SYSTEM	**DESCRIPTION/URL**
Archivists' Toolkit	Archival data management system to provide broad, integrated support for the management of archives. http://www.archiviststoolkit.org/
Archon	So-called simple archival information system supporting EAD and MARC. http://www.archon.org/
CONTENTdm	Digital archiving system focusing on multimedia collections. Provided by OCLC. http://www.contentdm.org/
CWIS	Supports development of collections of data about web-based resources conforming to international and academic standards for metadata. http://scout.wisc.edu/Projects/CWIS/
EPrints	Widely used platform for building digital repositories; self-archiving capabilities. http://www.eprints.org/
Fedora	General-purpose, open source digital object repository system. http://www.fedora-commons.org/
Greenstone	Suite of software tools for building and distributing digital library collections. http://www.greenstone.org/
ICA-AtoM	Web-based archival description software based on International Council on Archives (ICA) standards. http://ica-atom.org/
Islandora	Combines the Drupal and Fedora software applications to create a digital asset management system with support for collaboration at several levels, including metadata and narration. http://islandora.ca
Koha	Koha was the first open source integrated library system. It was created in 1999 by Katipo Communications for the Horowhenua Library Trust in New Zealand. http://koha.org/
Omeka	Web publishing platform for the display of library, museum, archives, and scholarly collections and exhibitions, combining features of content management, collections management, and archival digital collections systems. http://omeka.org/
OpenBiblio	An open source integrated library system, with an extensible, context-sensitive help system. http://obiblio.sourceforge.net/index.php/Main/OpenBiblio

Table 6.3. Recommended Public Knowledge Project Software

SYSTEM	DESCRIPTION/URL
Open Conference Systems	An open source conference management system that can create and manage the complete web presence for an academic conference. http://pkp.sfu.ca/?q=ocs
Open Journal Systems	An open source journal management and publishing system that's purpose is to make open access publishing a viable option for more journals. http://pkp.sfu.ca/?q=ojs
Open Harvester Systems	An open source metadata indexing system that allows you to create a searchable index of the metadata from Open Archives Initiative (OAI)–compliant archives. http://pkp.sfu.ca/?q=harvester

Conclusion

The future of librarianship and the archival profession may well be defined to a significant degree by the technological competence of librarians and archivists. But that future is at issue, in part because LIS educators have commonly assumed that it was sufficient for the technological component of LIS education to engender awareness, as opposed to detailed, substantive knowledge and proficiency. In reality, librarians need to master the technologies that define the twenty-first-century library in order to exert appropriate controls and use those technologies in ways that clearly and creatively serve the interests and needs of library users. Moving into the cloud and building the virtual learning laboratories that provide future librarians with access to the technologies they will use and need to understand is an important step in that direction and one that LIS education can ill-afford to forego.

References

Aburdene, M.F., E.J. Mastascusa, and R. Massengale. 1991. "A Proposal for a Remotely Shared Control Systems Laboratory." In *Frontiers in Education Conference,* 589–592. Twenty-First Annual Conference—Engineering Education in a New World Order Proceeding, West Lafayette, Indiana.

Aharony, Noa. 2008. "Web 2.0 in U.S. LIS Schools: Are They Missing the Boat?" *Ariadne* 54. http://www.ariadne.ac.uk/issue54/aharony/.

Koretsky, Milo D., Danielle Amatore, Connelly Barnes, and Sho Kimura. 2008. "Enhancement of Student Learning in Experimental Design Using a Virtual Laboratory." *IEEE Transactions on Education* 51 (February): 76–77.

Malinconico, S.M. 1992. "What Librarians Need to Know to Survive in an Age of Technology." *Journal of Education for Library and Information Science* 33: 226, 228–232.

Morelli, Ralph, and Trishan de Lanerolle. 2009. "FOSS 101: Engaging Introductory Students in the Open Source Movement." In *Proceedings of the 40th ACM SIGSCE Technical Symposium on Computer Science Education* (Chattanooga, Tennessee, March 4–7), 311–315. New York: ACM Press.

Scott, Dan. 2010. "Easing Gently into OpenSRF, Part 1; and Easing Gently into Open-SRF, Part 2." *Code{4}Lib Journal* 10 (June). http://journal.code4lib.org/articles/3284 and http://journal.code4lib.org/articles/3365.

Seay, Cameron, and Gary Tucker. 2010. "Virtual Computing Initiative at a Small Public University." *Communications of the ACM* 53 (March): 75–83.

Shaffer, Henry E., Samuel F. Averitt, Marc I. Hoit, Aaron Peeler, Eric D. Sills, and Mladen A. Vouk. 2009. "NCSU's Virtual Computing Lab: A Cloud Computing Solution." *Computer* 42, no. 7: 94–97. doi:10.1109/MC.2009.230.

Part II

TECHNOLOGIES

Chapter 7

Library Discovery Services: From the Ground to the Cloud

Marshall Breeding

Introduction

In recent years libraries have turned to a new generation of interfaces more in tune with the expectations of today's users shaped by their experiences of the current web. Against the context of incredibly powerful search tools, intuitive navigation, and socially engaging and visually appealing virtual destinations on the web, the incumbent generation of online catalogs falls short in the way that they present the collections and services of the library. The past five years have seen a continual advancement of new products, both proprietary and open source, working toward ever more modern user-friendly features and broader scope of search. These new discovery services have become increasingly expansive and virtual, tapping ever more deeply into the concepts and technologies of cloud computing.

71

In this chapter, the term "discovery services" is used to describe this new genre of end-user library interfaces. Other terms commonly associated with this genre include "next-generation library catalogs" and "discovery interfaces." The term "discovery services" is applied generally, including services installed on the library's own servers and those offered through software as a service arrangements.

The concept of discovery services isn't brand new. These products have been available in some form since about 2004. Libraries can consider these discovery interfaces not as bleeding-edge technologies but as relatively well-established and maturing tools that have steadily improved the interfaces offered to their users.

The initial, ground-level round of products, often characterized as next-generation library catalogs, modernized the interface but remained mostly focused on local library collections. Subsequent offerings and new product versions have continually elevated their scope of search, adoption of social networking concepts, and improved integration with the broader enterprise of library products and services.

The products and services available today fall in a continuum ranging from those focused more on local content physically held in the library to those that progressively address the diffuse cloud of content representing a broad view of library collections that includes the body of all the electronic content libraries consider within their scope of interest. Libraries will differentiate their selection of a discovery service, or how it's implemented, based on their strategic approach to how they want to position their collections to their users.

This new genre of library discovery services aims to go beyond the capabilities of the traditional online catalog delivered as a module of the integrated library system (ILS) and to present a more modern interface to library users. These products have evolved to expand the search of scope far beyond the aspects of library collections managed by the ILS, encompassing materials managed by other systems. The latest and most ambitious set of products extend the reach of discovery even further, layering in access to the vast collection of individual articles represented within a library's subscriptions to electronic resources. These new products aim to deliver an experience of libraries on the web that reflects a more user-centric approach and that better represents library collections that include print, electronic, and rich media.

This chapter aims to provide a general understanding of discovery services, how they fit into the larger context of library technologies, and some of the trends that have shaped the current landscape. No attempt is made to review or provide detailed information on the specifics of the individual products within this genre.

End-User Discovery Separated from In-Library Automation

One of the major changes to library automation in recent years involves a parting between the software and systems that directly interact with end users from that used by library personnel for internal operations. Today a wide variety of discovery services are available that complement, or even replace, the online catalog module delivered as part of the ILSs that formerly stood as the all-in-one automation software for libraries. (Note: Outside the United States, the term "library management system," or LMS, is used instead of ILS.)

Discovery systems and the ILS perform distinct functions. The ILS provides automation support for the work performed by library personnel, whereas discovery interfaces address services the library offers to its users. Discovery services provide a presentation-layer interface that allows users to find materials of interest in library collections and obtain access to those items. The methods of access differ depending on whether the materials selected are physical formats, such as books, periodicals, or DVDs, or whether they are available digitally.

In this decoupled environment, libraries have flexible options regarding discovery service and their ILS. Given the broad disenchantment with online catalogs, most of the companies offering ILS products have shifted their development efforts to the creation of their discovery service products.

Discovery services provide the opportunity, but not the necessity, of decoupling the ILS from end-user presentation. Although a variety of discovery service

72

products have been available for a number of years, the majority of libraries continue to rely on traditional online catalogs. We can expect the proportion of libraries implementing discovery services to increase over time. Contributing factors include the lack of ongoing development of ILS online catalog modules, aggressive marketing of discovery services products, bundling of discovery services with the ILS, as well as increased interest by libraries in improving their offerings facing end users. Limiting factors include the lack of financial or personnel resources to implement any new technology products, waiting for product offerings to further mature, and long selection and procurement cycles.

The ILS: No Longer Comprehensive Automation

The role of discovery services needs to be understood in the overall picture of library automation components. Discovery services coexist with, and depend on, the ILS. An ILS typically includes several modules that address different aspects of library operations—all tied together through common databases, with interrelated business logic and shared interfaces. Core modules would include:

- cataloging for the description of library materials;
- circulation to manage the loans, returns, renewals, fines, late notices, and related activities;
- acquisitions to facilitate the selection, ordering, and procurement of new materials; and
- serials control designed to deal with the special requirements of periodicals and serials, managing subscriptions, check-in, routing, and other features.

73

Library personnel operate each of these modules through an interface that allows them to perform all the functions needed for their work. These staff interfaces address the detailed functionality of the system and may require specific training for personnel to take advantage of the more complex behind-the-scenes tasks involved in operating the library.

Integrated library systems include an interface designed for library users, often called an "online public access catalog" (OPAC), or simply "online catalog." These online catalogs vary in specific features but generally include the ability to search all the material managed within the ILS and to perform various self-service features:

- Use authenticated sign-in (username/password)
- View/change profile information (address, phone number, e-mail address, etc.)
- View materials currently checked out
- Renew items
- Place holds on material
- View outstanding fines or fees

- Pay fines or fees
- Add/export items to citation management systems
- Save queries for future use
- Send alerts for notification of new materials

Online catalogs, although they increasingly embodied very detailed functionality, involve complex interfaces that often require some explanation, training, or documentation in order to be used effectively. A user might, for example, need to select field limiters or form advanced queries using Boolean logic in order to receive results narrowed to a specific area of interest. As discovery services aim to replace traditional library catalogs, they must subsume its features but hopefully are delivered in a more palatable form.

Originally created as comprehensive business applications to support all aspects of library operations, the integrated library system in recent years has largely persisted in a focus on print materials. As libraries expanded their collections to include growing proportions of digital media and electronic resources, additional products have emerged such as digital collection management platforms, OpenURL link servers, and electronic resource management systems to supplement the ILS. In the same vein that these new products emerged to help libraries manage other formats of materials internally, a new breed of discovery interfaces emerged to support access to this expanded view of libraries to end users.

Discovery services can replace the online catalog of the ILS, but they do not replace the ILS itself. Discovery services aim to not just displace the online catalog of the ILS, but to provide an end-user interface for all the other systems and services that manage a library's content offerings. They radically modernize the interface and expand the scope of content addressed.

Expanding Scope through Federated Search

Prior to the development of the types of discovery services available today, libraries were able to offer some expansion of search scope to library users through federated search utilities. As libraries made ever larger investments in electronic content, the need became apparent to provide some assistance to users in accessing these resources. Initially, libraries simply offered lists of the products available on their websites. The number of electronic resources eventually reached the point where it was not realistic to expect a typical library user to work through these lists and search each product individually.

Federated search products emerged to address the need to provide better access to these growing collections of electronic resources. These products operated by providing an interface that would allow the user to formulate a query, which would then be cast simultaneously to several different target resources, collect the results from each, and then present a unified list of materials. These products, because they relied on real-time connections with the target resources, were dependent on variables such as network connectivity issues, performance of the remote servers, and especially the quality and quantity of results returned by each target resource. These federated search products initially made use of standard search-and-retrieval protocols such as Z39.50 but eventually expanded to also use more efficient XML gateways or other technologies that improved the power and performance possible through this search architecture.

Federated search products popular in the library arena include the following:

MetaLib from Ex Libris (announced July 2000)

Research Pro from Innovative Interfaces

WebFeat (released about 1998)

360 Search from Serials Solutions (released in January 2005 under product name Central Search)

MasterKey and **Pazpar2** from Index Data, a firm specializing in open source library software (MasterKey is a complete federated search product. Pazpar2 is middleware that can be integrated into other products.)

MuseSearch from MuseGlobal (released 1992; several of the federated search products rely on technology license from MuseGlobal)

Although federated search products such as these provide some ability to expand the scope of search for library resources, they did not attempt to supplant the online catalog of the ILS. Libraries would continue to offer their online catalog for searching their local collection; federated search utilities generally provide a way to consolidate search for electronic resources but do not subsume functionality of the online catalog.

Although federated search products serve as useful tools in assisting users with access to electronic content, they are not commonly positioned as replacements for the online catalog of the ILS. These products paved the way for discovery interfaces, a more complex genre of products that modernize the traditional online catalog and expand the scope of search.

Discovery Service versus Federated Search Resource Allocation Differences

Participating in a comprehensive index involves a different access model than federated search. Federated search involves a high volume of activity in real time between libraries and the servers of the target information products. Once selected and activated in a federated search platform, target servers will be bombarded with queries from many users from many libraries. Given the relative inefficiency of federated search, only a small number of documents from any given information resource may be accessed relative to the volume of queries submitted. These queries take place in real time and compete with the use of these services through the native interfaces.

In the consolidated search model of discovery services, the content owners provide all the content of a given product through an initial transfer, with subsequent transfers for newly added content. End users then perform searches against the discovery service, accessing the target servers only once an article has been selected. The wholesale and incremental harvesting that supports consolidated search discovery services can be performed at the convenience of the information provider during off-peak times. In addition to the benefits associated with more powerful search capabilities for end users, the consolidated index model offers a more sustainable technical model for information providers compared to federated search.

Discovery Interfaces: Replace and Expand OPAC Functionality

While content from the library's local collection as managed in the ILS represents only one aspect of what might be covered within a discovery interface, it requires a great deal of special attention. For electronic materials, the ideal scenario involves allowing the user to view the full text online, which can be accomplished fairly easily through various authentication and linking tools. Dealing with the physical materials held in the library requires a much more complex set of interactions. Ideally, the discovery service replaces the online catalog, though with expanded scope and more modern interface features. To serve as replacement for the traditional online catalog, the discovery service needs to incorporate its functionality related to the library materials managed within the integrated library system. To deliver this functionality, a relatively involved set of interactions must take place between the ILS and the discovery service.

This new genre of discovery services generally avoids the real-time query approach embraced by federated search products in favor of a search model based on wholesale harvesting and indexing. The genre of discovery services has generally embraced the data model of the Open Archives Initiative, where the entire contents of any relevant repositories of content are harvested and placed into a new consolidated index. Once in this new central service, users can search across all the content quickly; the new service can offer features beyond that of the original repositories.

The first round of discovery products made great strides in delivering a much more modern interface than the incumbent online catalogs. Some of the improvements seen in these products include the following:

- **Relevancy ranked result lists.** Traditional online catalogs list results alphabetically by author or title or chronologically by publication date. These kinds of ordered lists can be difficult for users to work through, especially when containing large numbers of results. Search engines on the web usually return results according to relevancy rankings where items of highest interest appear at the top, followed by those of decreasing importance. Tuning relevance to work well in a library setting can be challenging, given that different criteria of importance may apply depending on the interests of the user. Most discovery services offer relevancy ranking by default, with options to sort by other categories.

- **Faceted navigation.** This involves terms and categories presented as part of a search interface that allows the user to make a series of selections to incrementally narrow the results to hone in on items of interest. The facets are generated dynamically from the query results, usually with the number of items displayed associated with the term or category.
- **More intuitive navigation.** Discovery interfaces are generally quite attuned to usability issues, aiming to make dramatic improvements beyond online catalogs that gained a reputation for unintuitive and quirky interfaces, designed more for librarians and expert searchers than for the general public.
- **Enhanced visual display.** Rather than rely on purely text-oriented descriptions, discovery services make more frequent use of graphics and icons, such as cover images of books and DVDs, to improve the visual appearance of the interface.
- **Expanded scope of search.** Online catalogs provide access only to the resources managed by the ILS; discovery services have the capability to include many other sources of library-related content, such as that from institutional repositories and collections of digitized images or manuscripts. More recent products expand the scope of search to the articles represented in library subscriptions through large consolidated indexes of preharvested content.
- **User-supplied rating and reviews.** In tune with Web 2.0 concepts, discovery services allow users to supply reviews, rate materials, and make recommendations to other users.

Such features are commonplace among the popular nonlibrary web destinations. The first wave of discovery services helped libraries catch up to expectations of their users established by their experiences with other information-oriented websites that were sorely lacking in the majority of online catalogs.

Connecting Discovery Products

In a decoupled environment, finding ways to efficiently connect discovery products to the other components used by a library becomes a paramount concern. Discovery systems must interoperate with ILS and other systems used to manage or provide relevant content. A variety of protocols and practices have become well established for allowing discovery services to operate with an ILS.

Discovery interfaces generally follow a data model that involves wholesale harvesting of relevant content from the ILS and other related systems, supplemented by the ability to interact with the ILS interactively as the interface requires real-time status or to support end-user services. In practical terms, the complete bibliographic database is exported from the ILS, loaded, and indexed by the discovery service. The process of exporting and re-indexing may involve additional processing steps to facilitate the creation of facets, to control relevancy weightings, to determine presentation, and to make other transformations. In addition to the basic bibliographic record, other data elements such as location codes, authority references, and circulation status may also be transferred. Following the initial wholesale transfer of data from the ILS to the discovery service, frequent updates will be scheduled to keep the indexes current. How often to perform incremental updates depends on how rapidly new materials are added to the library's collection but in most cases would take place daily.

In addition to the data harvested from the ILS, the discovery interface requires other information in real time, such as whether an item is on the shelf, checked out, or on hold for another user. Such status information can be obtained as needed through a real-time request from the discovery service to the ILS, using any of a number of techniques, such as through a standard protocol such as NCIP or SIP2 or through other APIs.

Some of the discovery systems simply rely on the web-based online catalog when detailed information is needed regarding the current status of an item. The discovery interface would deep link into the online catalog for a specific item, taking advantage of its native ability to display its complete status information, as well as invoke user services such as placing holds. While simpler to accomplish, the transitions between pages delivered by the discovery service and those of the online catalog can introduce confusion to the user. A more elegant, though technically complex, approach brings all this functionality directly into the discovery service.

Discovery services include a set of services for users tied to their personal profile. Such features might include the abilities to save search queries, mark items for later consultation, send alerts of new materials, and set up a profile of preferences or interests. It may also be possible to link users' profiles in the discovery interface to their account in the ILS, making it possible to view items charged, place holds, renew items, or pay fines within the interface of the discovery service. This more sophisticated level of integration may not yet be available in all the discovery services, and it's still common for users to have to deal with the activities managed by the ILS and those managed by the discovery service separately.

As discovery services began to proliferate, the need emerged to find standard ways to connect them with ILSs. The Digital Library Federation, now part of the Council on Library and Information Resources, charged a group to develop a standard protocol in this arena. The Integrated Library System Discovery Services Task Group, chaired by John Mark Ockerbloom, was formed in 2007 and developed a set of protocols that support graduated levels of interoperability. The lowest of the four levels, dubbed Basic Discovery Interface, uses Open Archives Initiative Protocol for Metadata Harvesting (OAI-PMH) for transfer of data from the ILS to the discovery service and passes control back to the online catalog of the ILS for end-user services. Level 4 describes a robust level of interoperability where the discovery interface handles all aspects of search and relevant services (Breeding, 2008, a summary of the ILS-DI proceedings and outcomes; Ockerbloom, 2008, the full report of the task group).

Discovery: Mix and Match with the ILS

While the ILS divides its functionality into different modules, they cannot generally be broken apart. It's not practical, for example, for a library to describe materials with the cataloging module from one product, perform circulation functions with another, and manage the business aspects of procurement through the acquisitions module of yet another. Such a best-of-breed approach of assembling an automation environment from the best modules has not been possible with the ILS products offered to date. New products created outside of the bounds of the ILS, such as OpenURL link resolvers, electronic resource management systems, and—most recently—discovery services, have followed a strategy of interoperability rather than being tied to any specific ILS.

All of the discovery interfaces currently available have been designed to operate with any of the major ILSs. Libraries may elect to adopt a discovery product from the company from which they purchased their ILS or from a competitor or implement one of the open source offerings. The end-user discovery arena allows a mix-and-match approach that has not previously been a practical alternative with the other core modules of the ILS.

As an ILS vendor approaches discovery products, they are motivated to create offerings that will appeal to the libraries that use their own products but also to libraries that use a competing ILS. As interest wanes in traditional online catalogs, ILS vendors focus their development efforts on the development of discovery services instead. These discovery service products are offered to their existing library customers as add-ons to complement or replace their online catalogs. Discovery services offered by ILS vendors include the following:

Encore from Innovative Interfaces (introduced May 2006)
Primo from Ex Libris (February 2006)
LS2 PAC from The Library Corporation (October 2008)
Enterprise from SirsiDynix (June 2008)
Visualizer from VTLS (January 2008)
BiblioCommons, launched by Canadian BiblioCommons (2008)

OCLC, a global membership organization, but also involved with a number of ILS products, began offering **WorldCat Local** as a discovery service designed to displace the need to operate the online catalog of the library's ILS.

Another set of discovery services have been created by commercial companies outside the fold of ILS vendors. These products include the following:

AquaBrowser Library, initially developed by Medialab Solutions of Amsterdam, the Netherlands, found use by libraries in Europe beginning about 2001 and was distributed in North America by The Library Corporation beginning in September 2004. R.R. Bowker acquired Medialab Solutions in June 2007; in 2009 control of AquaBrowser shifted to Serials Solutions, a sister company under common ownership of Cambridge Information Group.

Summon, a discovery service offered by Serials Solutions, was launched in early 2009. Serials Solutions has been involved in providing a slate of products surrounding management and access to electronic content but does not offer an ILS. Serials Solutions offerings now include two discovery services, AquaBrowser Library, with more of a focus on local library collections, and Summon, which it characterizes as a web-scale discovery service that also encompasses articles and other electronic content.

In addition to the offerings of these organizations, all offered as proprietary solutions, open source alternatives have also been created, including these:

VuFind, originally created by the Falvey Library at Villanova University in 2007, has found extensive use by other academic and public libraries worldwide. This discovery service relies on open source components such as Apache SOLR and Lucene and uses the PHP programming language.

Blacklight, created at the University of Virginia, finds use by other libraries, such as Stanford University Libraries, in addition to its home institution. Blacklight also uses Apache SOLR and Lucene and the Ruby and Rails development framework.

eXtensible Catalog, a project of the River Campus Libraries of the University of Rochester with funding from the Andrew W. Mellon Foundation, has created a number of tools that facilitate the deployment of discovery interfaces and is working toward a Drupal-based discovery service.

SOPAC, or the Social OPAC, originally created by John Blyberg at the Darien Library in Connecticut, emphasizes user interactions, such as reviews, ratings, and other Web 2.0 concepts. The open source Drupal content management system provides the underlying foundation for SOPAC.

Discovery Aims for the Cloud

Since about mid-2009, the realm of discovery interfaces has made a dramatic shift toward much more comprehensive scope, attempting to represent all aspects of library collections through a single search with unified results. Today, many of the library discovery services aim to provide comprehensive and powerful search for the library arena that Google and its competitors offer for the broader web.

Cloud infrastructure providers, such as Amazon, use the term "web-scale" to describe a computing architecture that expands to deliver the capacity required for the levels of use associated with popular web destinations. Such a platform must deliver extremely powerful technical performance, not constrained by a more limited quantity computing and storage that might be available in an organization's local data center. Web-scale implies almost infinite capacity that won't top out, even if a site spikes in use as it gains in global popularity.

It has become common for producers of library systems to characterize their offerings as "web-scale." This marketing term may carry different technical meanings, but it's intended to convey a sense that the scope and extensiveness of their product compares to that of the overall web. In the library realm, the term "web-scale" tends to be applied rather loosely, tagging onto the qualities of the global cloud computing arena in terms of both infinitely expandable capacity and scope.

Web-scale discovery implies that the scope of search spans the entire universe of relevant content. The specific interpretations differ. It may mean all the content that a given library makes available to its users, all the content offered by libraries collectively, or all the literary or scholarly content that exists.

OCLC uses the term "web-scale" extensively, even to the point of using it in the name of its strategic library management product. Its Web-Scale Management Service extends the technical infrastructure underlying WorldCat to provide all the functionality needed to automate the internal operations of a library, obviating the need to run an ILS locally in an individual library or even one shared by members of a consortium. OCLC's vision for library automation involves a single shared platform used by its members throughout the world. This latest and most ambitious genre of discovery products aims to deliver a comprehensive search that includes all aspects of a library collection, including the content managed in the ILS, other local collections managed in other systems, and the contents of the electronic resources to which a library subscribes.

As noted earlier, the initial wave of discovery products provided a platform that delivered access more effectively to locally managed resources but made use of federated search to provide some degree of access to subscribed content. The web-scale products aim to bring articles into the scope of search with the same features and performance as local content. A variety of products can be considered part of this new arena of web-scale discovery services. These include:

Summon from Serials Solutions. This product aims to index all of the content relevant to the library, all easily accessible through a single search box. Summon, launched in early 2009, was the first commercial discovery service to provide a massive article-level consolidated index and primarily targets academic libraries. Serials Solutions has engaged in partnerships with a broad array of publishers and providers to obtain content to populate the Summon index.

Primo Central from Ex Libris includes a large aggregated index of article-level e-journal content, e-books, and other electronic materials. Ex Libris has made partnerships with the major publishers and providers of content licensed by research libraries to populate the Primo Central index, which it maintains and hosts. Through Primo Central, libraries can extend their implementation of Primo to include electronic resources as well as those from local repositories.

EBSCO Discovery Service from EBSCO Publishing builds on the EBSCO-host platform to provide a comprehensive search environment that includes materials managed in the library's local ILS, other publishers' content, as well as any of its own resources to which the library subscribes.

WorldCat Local from OCLC builds on the massive WorldCat database of bibliographic records. OCLC has also made arrangements with publishers and aggregators of e-journal content to extend WorldCat to provide more comprehensive searching. Through a variety of other arrangements, OCLC has also loaded metadata from institutional repositories, digital image collections, and other content available through OAI-PMH.

Encore Synergy from Innovative Interfaces, unlike the others in this group, does not involve the creation of a large consolidated index as part of its search model. Rather, Encore Synergy relies on web services invoked in real time to layer in selective articles in response to user queries.

Building the Aggregated Index

One of the key strategies for these web-scale discovery platforms involves the creation of a massive index including all the material represented in the electronic resources to which libraries subscribe. The creation of such an aggregated index entails making arrangements with the publishers and providers of content products to gain access to the metadata, or even full content, of their offerings. Producing such an index involves both developing business relationships with the producers of library-oriented information products and the work of creating a very large-scale technical infrastructure and loading and continually updating the index.

Library discovery services bring to the fore issues regarding the various roles and interests of the organizations that produce information products to which libraries subscribe. Most offer feature-rich products that include end-user interfaces for searching as well as delivery of the underlying articles. As library discovery services come into play, libraries bring the search features into their own environment, still relying on the provider to provide access to the underlying content. Yet, even when the library provides its own discovery interface to article content, there will be many circumstances in which a library user might need to work with the more specialized native interface of the information product rather than the more generalized interface of the library's discovery service, designed to work across content from many disciplines.

The nature of the agreements made involves resource providers offering content to discovery providers for indexing purposes only and allowing users of the discovery services to continue to access content from the publisher's site. This arrangement improves the likelihood that library users will find and access the

82

content from that publisher. Such increases in use amplify the value of the content, providing motivation for content providers to cooperate with discovery service providers. Some content providers continue to be reluctant to partner with discovery services, concerned that wholesale harvesting of their content might increase the risks of unauthorized access. Content providers also express concerns that their content loses some degree of branding when accessed through a more generic discovery service rather than through their own custom interface. Any problems with the discovery interface may also reflect negatively on the providers of the content. The growing portfolio of partnerships between discovery service developers and content providers gives evidence of increased cooperation in this arena.

In the competition among discovery service products, one of the most important differentiating factors involves the completeness of the comprehensive index. Ideally, each of the discovery services would obtain content from all of the companies and organizations that provide some sort of information product to libraries. In reality, however, not all the publishers and providers cooperate with any or all of the discovery service providers. Some discovery providers have been able to make arrangements with providers of aggregated databases of articles, gaining access to very large numbers of articles through a single business partnership. In some cases the producer of an aggregated information product may choose not to cooperate with a discovery service. In those cases, the discovery service provider can approach each of the individual publishers involved to gain access to the articles in the e-journals covered in an aggregated product. In evaluating the comprehensiveness of a discovery product, it can be difficult to assess what content is represented through deals with large aggregators and what has been gained by indexing content provided by individual publishers.

Aggregated indexes can involve both citation data and full texts of articles. Many, if not most, of the native interfaces of the information products to which libraries subscribe support searching on both citations and full text. Google Scholar indexes the full texts of articles. Given that most search environments involving journal articles support full-text searching, end users naturally expect this level of access rather than searching only citation data. Ideally, a discovery service based on a central aggregated index would have both high-quality citation metadata and the full texts of all of the articles from all the publishers and providers. The current state of the products, however, involves high proportions of citation-only searching. The technology platforms of the products generally support full-text searching, but many of the business arrangements between content and discovery providers currently involve citation data. We can expect higher portions of full-text searching in the discovery services over time.

The evaluation of a discovery service needs to involve an analysis of the content indexed relative to the library's current subscriptions. The overall volume of indexed content may differ from the relative proportion of titles covered to which the library actually subscribes. Because end-user searching usually will be scoped to those resources to which the library subscribes, it's not so much the total number of articles indexed that matters most, but rather the best coverage of active subscriptions.

These arrangements with content providers almost always specify that the content will be exposed only to mutual subscribers. Users taking advantage of a discovery service will see results from a given resource only if their library subscribes to that resource. An important part of the configuration process of a discovery service for a library involves setting up the profile of subscriptions. This profile will filter search results to not display results from resources that a user cannot access.

Unlike online catalogs, which almost always can be searched by the general public regardless of affiliation with the institution, discovery services may require authentication in order to display results from a library's licensed resources. Some implementations of discovery services prompt all remote users to sign on prior to searching. Others may allow searching by users who have not signed in but will show only resources that allow free access, such as the library's local holdings from its ILS, open access journals, local repositories, and the like. Through IP-based authentication, in-library and on-campus computers can be configured to search licensed resources without users signing on through their personal account.

The creation of the aggregated centralized index also involves a great deal of technical work on the part of the discovery service provider. This discovery model requires a highly scalable platform capable of loading and indexing many hundreds of millions of items. The platform will need to index citation and full-text content as delivered by the information resource providers. In addition to the initial data loads, the index must be kept up to date with incremental additions from each product represented. For products including time-critical content, such as current news sources, new content may need to be added daily, or even more frequently.

The maintenance of a consolidated index for a discovery service represents a great deal of labor intensive and technically complex work in addition to the business negotiations involved in acquiring the content. Given the vast amount of business, procedural, and technical work involved, much less the creation of an appropriate highly scalable technology platform, it is not surprising that only a few of these discovery services based on consolidated indexes have been created and that they come out of commercial organizations able to devote significant resources. While it would be possible for a library or consortium of libraries to create such an index, so far all of these projects have emerged almost exclusively from the commercial sector.

These discovery products based on large aggregated indexes also incorporate the content from the local library. In addition to the content obtained from the external providers of electronic resources, these indexes also harvest the content from the ILSs of the libraries that use the service and any other local collections of interest. This combination of content from local and remote resources results in the ability to present a single search box that returns unified results that span all the different aspects of a library's collection.

This new generation of discovery services based on comprehensive centralized indexes appeals primarily to research and academic libraries with large investments in electronic resources. Public libraries whose operations center more on the circulation of physical materials may care less about discovery products with expansive coverage of scholarly articles and look more to products that provide stronger services related to local collections and deeper levels of social engagement.

Discovery Taps the Cloud

The discipline of library discovery services receives considerable inspiration from cloud computing. Discovery services aspire to provide the same success in providing access to library collections that Google and other search engines achieve for the broader web. Social networking, e-commerce, and other contemporary web destinations likewise help shape their form. Discovery services play an important role in bringing libraries up to the expectations of their ever more web-savvy customers.

As we have seen, the realm of discovery services has expanded from a focus on local materials to a more expansive approach to library collections. Consistent with this shift and with the general technology trend away from locally maintained hardware and software toward more abstract cloud computing models, these products are increasingly deployed through software as a service (SaaS), especially those based on a centralized aggregated index. The massive size and the rigorous labor-intensive process of maintaining these indexes make these products ideally suited for SaaS.

Discovery services are not, however, tied to any single technology model. Many libraries have implemented discovery services through local installations on their own tangible computing equipment. In step with the trends toward increased movement toward cloud computing, discovery services gravitate toward the cloud. This product genre, with its lofty goals of reinventing the ways that libraries present their collections and services on the web, stands to benefit from the scalability, extensibility, and flexibility offered through the various models of cloud computing. Moving forward, we can expect increasing synergies between the advancing genre of library discovery services and cloud computing technologies.

References

Breeding, Marshall. 2008. "Progress on the DLF ILS Discovery Interface API: The Berkeley Accord." *Information Standards Quarterly* (Summer): 18–19.

Ockerbloom, John Mark (chair). 2008. "DLF ILS Discovery Interface Task Group (ILS-DI) Technical Recommendation: An API for Interoperability between Integrated Library Systems and External Discovery Applications." Digital Library Federation (Now CLIR). December 8. http://www.diglib.org/architectures/ilsdi/DLF_ILS _Discovery_1.1.pdf.

85

Related Resources

Breeding, Marshall. 2007. "Front-End Focus." *Smart Libraries Newsletter* 27, no. 3 (March): 1.

——. 2007. "Next-Generation Library Catalogs." *Library Technology Reports* 43, no. 4 (July/August).

——. 2007. "VuFind: A Next-Gen Catalog from Villanova." *Smart Libraries Newsletter* 27, no. 9 (September): 1.

——. 2008. "Beyond the Current Generation of Next-Generation Library Interfaces: Deeper Search." *Computers in Libraries* 28, no. 5: 39–42.

——. 2008. "SirsiDynix Launches Its Faceted Search Product." *Smart Libraries Newsletter* 28, no. 8 (August): 3.

——. 2009. "The Advance of Computing from the Ground to the Cloud." *Computers in Libraries* 29, no. 10 (November/December): 22–26.

——. 2009. "BiblioCommons Prepares for the Next Stage of Roll-Out." *Smart Libraries Newsletter* 29, no. 8 (August): 1–4.

——. 2009. "EBSCO Sets Strategy for Discovery." *Smart Libraries Newsletter* 29, no. 9 (September): 1–3.

——. 2009. "OCLC Partners with EBSCO to Expand Access to Articles in WorldCat Local." *Smart Libraries Newsletter* 29, no. 5 (May): 1–3.

——. 2009. "Summon: A New Search Service from Serials Solutions." *Smart Libraries Newsletter* 29, no. 3 (March): 1–3.

——. 2010. "Encore Synergy Launched for Article Discovery: A New Search Model." *Information Today NewsBreak,* May 3. http://newsbreaks.infotoday.com/NewsBreaks/Encore-Synergy-Launched-for-Article-DiscoveryA-New-Search-Model-66962.asp.

——. 2010. "Guide to Discovery Layer Interfaces." *Library Technology Guides.* Accessed November 1. http://www.librarytechnology.org/discovery.pl.

——. 2010. *Next-Gen Library Catalogs.* New York: Neal-Schuman.

Dempsey, Lorcan. 2007. "Web Scale." January 7. http://orweblog.oclc.org/archives/001238.html.

Index Data. 2010. Company website. Accessed November 1. http://www.indexdata.com/.

NGC4LIB. 2010. Electronic discussion list. Established by Eric Lease Morgan of Notre Dame University in June 2006. Archives. Accessed November 3. http://dewey.library.nd.edu/mailing-lists/ngc4lib/.

Open Archives Initiative. 2010. Accessed November 1. http://www.openarchives.org/.

Serials Solutions. 2010. Summon. Accessed November 10. http://www.serialssolutions.com/summon/.

SOPAC: The Social OPAC. 2010. Website. Accessed November 10. http://thesocialopac.net/.

Tennant, Roy. 2005. "Lipstick on a Pig." *Library Journal,* April 15. http://www.libraryjournal.com/article/CA516027.html.

VuFind. 2010. Website. Accessed November 1. http://www.vufind.org.

Chapter 8

Koha in the Cloud

Christopher R. Nighswonger
and Nicole C. Engard

Introduction: The History

Twelve years ago, before cloud computing was even defined, a small library in New Zealand was trying to decide how it was going to survive the possibility of the impending Y2K issues its integrated library system was destined to have. The Horowhenua Library Trust (http://www.library.org.nz) was still using the integrated library system it had purchased in 1988, and the system was starting to show its age.

While the librarians were pretty sure that their system would in fact survive Y2K, the company managing their library system would not guarantee that their old system would live through the turn of the millennium. The librarians were able to convince the Trust that they needed the funds to change systems. They started traditionally with "Plan A," which meant sending out a request for proposal. When no off-the-shelf product met the stated objectives, the next step was "Plan B," build a system specifically for the Horowhenua Library Trust.

The then director decided to contact a new development firm to start fresh, this time with two visions in mind. First, the system had to be released as open source so that if the firm ever went away they would be able to get help with upgrading. Second, the system should run on low-end systems over sometimes unreliable Internet connections. Katipo Communications Ltd. (http://katipo .co.nz), a web development firm, stepped up to the challenge and agreed to the terms laid out by the library.

As a web development firm, Katipo tackled the project like it did all its projects, by coming up with a way to make the system run via the web. Coming from a different industry, it didn't have any predefined notions of what an integrated library system should look like or how it should function. While this sounded like a shortcoming, it actually made it so that the developers were able to listen to the librarians and create a system that specifically met their needs; one of these was that the system "used up-to-the-minute technologies" (Ransom, Cormack, and Blake, 2009), such as web-based programming languages and databases. The

87

members of the Horowhenua Library Trust named their integrated library system Koha. The word "koha" is the Māori word that means "a gift that comes with expectations." Horowhenua chose this name because it was giving Koha (the software) back to the world as a gift with the expectation that it would then be improved on by others and shared back (Ransom, Cormack, and Blake, 2009).

In January 2000, Koha 1.0 was released as open source to the world, and the Horowhenua Library Trust was the first library to go live on a completely cloud-based (although back then it was known as "web-based") open source integrated library system. Thus Koha (http://koha-community.org) was born.

Over the years Koha gained a following of developers, librarians, and library enthusiasts to help keep it up with the times. The Horowhenua Library Trust's gift to the library world was growing, and libraries worldwide were adopting this new system. For the first time libraries not only had the power over the direction the software grew, but they were able to use the software without having to upgrade their machines with every major new release simply because the code lives in the cloud.

Koha and the Cloud

Koha is an application that is ideal for running on a cloud of any sort, public or private. As with any application, a number of factors need to be considered when deciding whether to invest in an internal infrastructure to implement a private cloud or to outsource all of those details and go with a public cloud as the hosting platform for Koha. As most of these factors have already been discussed elsewhere in this book, they will not be rehashed again here. However, because a significant number of libraries do not own or maintain enterprise class data centers, the public cloud becomes a very cost-effective alternative, and, given the nature and purpose of Koha, it falls high on the list of applications contending to be hosted in that environment. Three aspects new to cloud computing should be especially appealing to small to midsized libraries:

1. *The illusion of infinite computing resources available on demand,* thereby eliminating the need for Cloud Computing users to plan far ahead for provisioning.
2. *The elimination of an up-front commitment by Cloud users,* thereby allowing companies to start small and increase hardware resources only when there is an increase in their needs.
3. *The ability to pay for use of computing resources on a short-term basis as needed* (e.g., processors by the hour and storage by the day) and release them as needed, thereby rewarding conservation by letting machines and storage go when they are no longer useful. (Armbrust et al., 2009: 1)

This chapter discusses the reasons why Koha is best suited for a public cloud interface by dividing these reasons into three categories: deployment and administration, scalability and cost, and application exposure.

Koha in the Public Cloud: Deployment and Administration

When viewed from the standpoint of deployment and administration, Koha is an ideal application for installation in the cloud. The entire application and its required dependencies can be installed and operational in less than an hour via a remote SSH session. SSH (Secure SHell) is a network protocol that allows data to be transferred and exchanged using a secure channel between two (securely or insecurely) networked devices. This means that you can connect to a server in the cloud from your home computer via a secure connection. Given that many cloud infrastructure as a service (IaaS) vendors offer prefabricated server (or instance) images, which contain most of the major dependencies of Koha such as Apache, MySQL, and Perl already installed, libraries see additional time savings during installation, increasing the overall "time to market" of the application. Further time savings can be realized if libraries utilize prepackaged server and/or virtual machine images for Ubuntu (http://mizstik.com/projects/koha-livecd/) or Debian (http://kylehall.info/index.php/projects/koha/koha-virtual-appliance/) compiled by Koha developers worldwide.

The administrative benefits of a public cloud deployment of Koha are significant as well. The most immediate administrative benefit is seen in the elimination of the need for in-house hardware support and maintenance. There are other administrative gains as well. Because Koha's core code along with all of its associated modules and software dependencies reside on a single server platform, application-related administrative and support activities are reduced to a single location, which is available literally from anywhere in the world where the cloud is accessible.

The ever-vital area of backup administration is also enhanced by the deployment of Koha on a public cloud. Earlier the concept of server (or instance) images was mentioned. These images offer the additional benefit of a simple, direct, and rapid backup and disaster recovery mechanism. These represent some of the increases in operational efficiency that can be realized by utilizing a cloud-hosted instance of Koha.

Koha in the Public Cloud: Scalability and Cost

Both cost and time savings are again realized by a cloud deployment of Koha in the area of scalability. Most public cloud platform service providers offer billing plans based on actual usage of the service. Libraries may capitalize on this option to maximize their cost savings by having in place a capacity plan projecting a schedule of the resource capacity requirements of their Koha installation based on user demand and load trends. This plan can be converted into an automated schedule for dynamic scaling of cloud resources, which, in turn, always guarantees the min-

89

imum necessary resource usage, thereby minimizing associated costs. Dynamic scaling of resources also provides basic insurance against Koha outages caused by a sudden lack of resources, making a more satisfactory experience for library patrons. This feature of cloud hosting can also be used by a consortium of libraries to allow for theoretically unlimited growth as additional libraries come on board, thus reducing the burden of long-term growth projection during initial planning and deployment of Koha. Whatever the case, the cloud provides maximum flexibility for libraries looking to use Koha.

Koha in the Public Cloud: Application Exposure

Running Koha in the cloud results in maximum application exposure. This integrated library system is among the few integrated library systems that are completely web-based applications. This simply means that no special software needs be obtained and installed on the part of the individual accessing either the Online Public Access Catalog (OPAC) or the staff interface (a fact that allowed Horowhenua to run the application on any machine in its library). This feature unites with the ubiquitous nature of the public cloud to provide the highest level of exposure. In such an installation, both Koha's OPAC and its staff interface can be accessed from anywhere the public cloud can be accessed (meaning from any computer with access to the Internet). One author summarizes Enterprise Resource Planning (ERP) benefits of deploying web-based SaaS applications (such as Koha) in the public cloud as: "no client software install, no client software maintenance, real-time data, access from anywhere, [and] cross platform compatibility" (djohnson, 2010). While this aspect may be true both of in-house hosting and traditional web hosting services, the ability of cloud platforms to perform both dynamic scaling and load balancing ensures a nearly unlimited capacity to accommodate users, which in turn allows unhindered, unrestricted exposure.

Another benefit of deploying Koha in a public cloud environment stems from a combination of the cost savings realized and the open source nature of Koha. A large portion of libraries choosing to implement Koha as their integrated library system solution do so because of the ability to access the source code and modify and improve the application to better serve their needs. In a traditional, in-house hosting of Koha, a percentage of a library's annual budget will go toward the expenses of supporting and maintaining the infrastructure necessary to support the application. This consumes financial and/or personnel resources that could be invested in improvement of Koha. For most libraries choosing to host Koha on a public cloud platform, there will be some significant level of cost savings, which can then be reinvested in Koha development with a more lasting return on investment resulting.

Putting Koha in the Cloud

A number of things are involved in hosting Koha on a public cloud platform. Probably the first consideration and decision that must be made is whether to tackle the project with in-house personnel or to outsource the entire project to a support company that can provide a complete, turnkey cloud-hosted package. This decision will probably be driven largely by the desire and/or ability of the library to hire the personnel necessary to provide in-house support of a Koha installation. Larger libraries with established IT (information technology) departments will probably be in a better position to go the in-house route, although very often one person can install and support a Koha instance. If the choice is made to completely outsource, the library should be sure to mark up the contract to ensure that its exact expectations are spelled out in order to avoid real or de facto vendor lock-in. The services of a lawyer should certainly be retained if the markup is extensive.

If the decision is to use in-house personnel, there must be the vetting and choosing of a cloud service provider. The number of companies offering cloud services is ever increasing. Careful consideration should be given not only to various service plans, service level agreements (SLAs), and their associated costs, but also to documented, past service levels (i.e., uptime, etc.). The latter is the most important factor apart from cost. Service level history should be heavily weighted in the selection process of a service provider, as it provides the most objective prediction of future performance. Once a service provider has been selected, an appropriate service plan must be chosen from among those available. As mentioned earlier, user demand and load must be carefully considered and a service plan selected that will offer the best compromise between budget and resource need. Plans that allow for dynamic scaling of resources should be preferred.

Other considerations and decisions involved in hosting Koha on a public cloud platform include installation, support, and maintenance of Koha. These things can be accomplished with a minimum of personnel. (This would not, of course, include staff who perform day-to-day operations such as cataloging and circulating.) It may be that libraries that already include an IT department may already employ the necessary individual(s) to deploy and support a Koha cloud installation.

A library undertaking either in-house or hosted installation should select an individual who has a strong background in the administration of Unix-type platforms. Consideration should also be given to experience in database administration as well as some level of exposure to programming with an emphasis in Perl, as this is the language Koha is written in. This latter qualification becomes more important if the library plans to do its own Koha development and bug fixing.

Conclusion

The time of the desktop-based library system is coming to an end. Many products are upgrading to cloud-based alternatives for many of the reasons discussed here. With Koha, however, libraries get the added benefit of using an open source application with a vibrant developer community behind it.

When deciding which cloud-based hosting option (private or public servers) is best for a library it is important to remember to weigh all the options and consider the skills of those on the library staff. It's also important to remember to consult and work with those who have been using and improving Koha for the past decade.

References

Armbrust, Michael, Armando Fox, Rean Griffith, Anthony D. Joseph, Randy H. Katz, Andrew Konwinski, et al. 2009. "Above the Clouds: A Berkeley View of Cloud Computing." Electrical Engineering and Computer Sciences, UC Berkeley. February 10. http://www.eecs.berkeley.edu/Pubs/TechRpts/2009/EECS-2009-28.pdf.

djohnson. 2010. "Web-Based, SaaS, and Cloud ERP Benefits." ERP Software at Your Service. July 22. http://erpcloudnews.com/2010/07/Web-based-saas-and-cloud-erp-benefits/.

Ransom, Joann, Chris Cormack, and Rosalie Blake. 2009. "How Hard Can It Be? Developing in Open Source." *Code4Lib Journal,* no. 7 (June 26). http://journal.code4lib.org/articles/1638.

Chapter 9

Leveraging OCLC Cooperative Library Data in the Cloud via Web Services

Karen A. Coombs

Introduction

When most technologists discuss cloud computing, they focus on hardware or software in the cloud. The purpose of this chapter is to discuss the advantages of data in the cloud and data as a service, in particular, library data as a cloud-based service. Libraries have been pooling and sharing data over a networked infrastructure since the early 1980s. This started out as the ability to draw on a single shared and maintained repository for catalog records, which could be downloaded from a shared repository and into a local repository. This in turn helped to build a repository of library holdings data that libraries could use to facilitate sharing of collections. Since that time, the types of data that libraries need to share have grown exponentially beyond bibliographic records and library holdings. Today, libraries also need to share electronic subscription information and information about the libraries themselves.

Unfortunately, most systems in which this library data is stored are black boxes composed of proprietary technologies, which makes it difficult for libraries to get any data out of most library systems. Even if a library has the local expertise to get the data out of their systems, they then must make it available in a scalable standards-based way to others. Not only does this require expertise in metadata standards (both in and outside of libraries), web service protocols, and best practices, it also requires a significant investment in hardware.

What libraries really need is a shared infrastructure that is capable of making library data flexible and repurposeable. Cloud-based infrastructure lends itself well to this scenario because cloud-based infrastructure is inherently meant to be shareable. To allow developers to interact with them and build applications, these systems are also inherently open and standards based.

Because of its shared metadata repository, Online Computer Library Center (OCLC) is in a unique position to create cloud-based data services that can expose

93

library data in standards-based useable formats and in a scaleable fashion. By making library data available in this way, OCLC enables members of the cooperative to share their data and facilitates reuse of library data throughout the cooperative. In addition, this infrastructure allows the cooperative to reach library users in their own spaces and as part of their daily workflows.

Overview of OCLC Web Services

WorldCat Search API

The WorldCat Search API provides programmatic access to bibliographic and holdings data in the WorldCat database. The web service is available to libraries that subscribe to WorldCat and participate in OCLC cataloging. OCLC also negotiates agreements with commercial partners who wish to use this metadata in their applications. One example of this is Red Laser, an iPhone application that will be discussed later in this chapter.

The WorldCat Search API is made of five different types of requests: search requests, requests for an individual record, requests for citations, requests for library catalog URLs, and requests for holdings. Search requests to the WorldCat Search API can take two forms: OpenSearch or SRU. OpenSearch is a simplistic protocol used on the web for keyword searching. Results from OpenSearch requests can be returned in two different formats: Atom or RSS. Both of these formats contain basic record metadata including title, author, OCLC number, ISBN, and summary.

In contrast, SRU is a more complex and feature-rich type of search request. This protocol allows fielded searching, Boolean logic, and limits. Results from this type of request can be returned in Dublin Core formats or MARCXML. The Dublin Core output utilizes a metadata mapping for MARC to Dublin Core that produces simple Dublin Core records, while the MARCXML output is more complex and rich.

WorldCat Search API can also be used to retrieve single bibliographic records in MARCXML based on identifier: OCLC number, ISBN, or ISSN. The API can also be used to request citations for a particular record, based on OCLC number. The service is capable of providing citations in Modern Language Association (MLA), American Psychological Association (APA), Harvard, Turabian, and Chicago styles. Citations come back in HTML format, which can easily be embedded into an existing web page.

Another type of request that can be sent to the web service is one for the library catalog URL(s) for a given item at a given library or libraries. This type of request requires an identifier (OCLC number or ISBN) and an OCLC symbol or symbols. If any of the libraries have the item, then the request will return a response with basic information about the library, including the catalog URL. If the library doesn't have the item, then the request will return a no holdings message in the response.

The last type of request that can be made to the WorldCat Search API is one for holdings information. This type of request requires an identifier (OCLC number, ISBN, and ISSN) and a geographic location be sent to the API. Geographic location can be defined based on latitude and longitude, zip code, city and state, or IP address. If no geographic location is provided, then the API assumes that it should retrieve holdings closest to the IP address of the application making the request.

A library holdings request will return a list of libraries with the item requested along with basic information about those libraries, including their name, address, and a link to the item in that library's catalog. Holding requests also allow users to choose the format in which the data they are retrieving will be returned. Currently holdings requests support output in both XML and JSON formats.

xIdentifier Services

The xIdentifiers services are a suite of services based on the WorldCat database that associate, group, and relate items together. There are three different services that make up the xIdentifier services: xISBN, xOCLCNum, and xISSN. The xISBN service associates ISBNs together. As a result it can be used to show different editions and formats of the same work based on an ISBN that has been submitted.

xOCLCNum

xOCLCNum is a very similar service; however, rather than submitting an ISBN to the service to retrieve related editions, developers can ask for related editions based on OCLC number or LCCN (Library of Congress Classification Number). This service is particularly helpful for materials that don't have an ISBN. This service also contains information on whether or not a particular publication is available as free full text from HathiTrust or Open Content Alliance. Queries to the service can be limited to these particular full-text collections and if full texts exist for the item requests or any other edition of the item, then a URL to that full text will be returned.

xISSN

The xISSN web service is slightly different from the other two identifier services because it relates together serial publications. As many librarians know, serial publications, journals in particular, can change titles over time. They can also be split into different publications, or two publications can be merged together into a single publication. In addition, journals can be made available in a variety of formats: print, electronic, microfiche, and microfilm. The getHistory request type can be used to find these relationships based on an ISSN. Submitting an ISSN to this request type retrieves basic metadata about that publication including the ISSNs for all the formats, along with any related publications such as preceding and succeeding titles. A getMetadata request to the web service will return whether or not a journal is peer reviewed and a URL for the table of contents feed for that particular publication.

WorldCat Identities

WorldCat Identities is a web service based on data in WorldCat that provides personal, corporate, and subject-based identities (writers, authors, characters, corporations, horses, ships, etc.). The service has four types of requests: direct linking by LCCN, OpenURL, Name Search, or SRU Search. Direct linking by LCCN is the simplest way to use WorldCat Identities. Simply send a request containing the LCCN and a single Identity record will be returned. Identity records contain a rich amount of metadata, including the identity's name, authoritative name, alternate names, dates of works related to identity, most popular items about and by an identity, subject headings associated with an identity, and Wikipedia link for the identity. Linking by OpenURL is the next simplest way to access data in WorldCat Identities. A typical OpenURL request will contain an OCLC number and the name of the identity. Typically OpenURL requests will result in a single Identity record. However, if more than one Identity record matches, then the service will return the matching records in a result Name Search response format. Name Search is another type of request that can be made to WorldCat Identities. This type of request takes a name parameter and searches for Identity records matching that parameter. The service returns results in a simple XML format that contains the established form of the Identity, URI, dates, date span of publications, and type of identity. Results are returned ranked based on frequency of use of and closeness of match to name submitted.

In addition to the simpler Name Search request type, Identities also makes available a full-fledged SRU service that allows developers to search the service based on specific fields such as family name, first name, birth and death dates, and LCCN. SRU Searches can be performed on the entire Identities database or on subsets such as personal name Identities, corporate name Identities, and subject Identities. SRU requests return results in the SRU format with embedded Identity records. This response format contains a level of detail that is not often required by most applications using Identities data.

Terminology Services

Terminology Services is an experimental web service from OCLC Research that makes a variety of controlled vocabularies available via SRU. Some vocabularies available within the service include:

- FAST
- GSA Form and Genre Terms
- Library of Congress AC Subject Headings
- Library of Congress Subject Headings

- Medical Subject Headings (MeSH)
- Thesaurus for Graphic Materials: TGM I
- Thesaurus for Graphic Materials: TGM II

Each vocabulary can be searched via its own SRU interface. Results include:

- Concepts/headings
- Preferred terms
- Alternate terms
- Broader and narrow terms
- Related terms
- Notes
- Classification/category number

Results can be returned in a variety of formats, such as MARCXML, MADS, and SKOS. One way in which the service can be used is to find preferred terms. Another possible use of the service is to find broader and narrow terms related to a particular term. The VuFind Recommender Module, discussed later in this chapter, takes advantage of the service in this way to show broader and narrower terms.

WorldCat Registry

The WorldCat Registry is a database of libraries, museums, and cultural institutions worldwide. Data from the WorldCat Registry is freely available for noncommercial use. The database contains basic metadata about every institution, including its name, address, and phone number. In addition, the Registry contains more detailed information specific to libraries, such as the library catalog software, URL for the library catalog, OpenURL resolvers, and whether or not the library makes Wi-Fi freely available.

The WorldCat Registry can be accessed in three ways: direct linking, search, and OpenURL resolver lookup. Developers can direct link to a registry entry based on either Registry ID or OCLC symbol. Registry requests return information about the library being requested in an XML format. The level of detail of the information returned depends on whether the serviceLabel is set to content or enhancedContent. Content returns the basic public metadata about the library, while enhancedContent returns all the public metadata about the library.

The Registry can also be searched via SRU. The SRU interface provides a number of indexes including institution name, library type, city, state, country, and postal code, which developers can use to search for libraries matching the criteria submitted. The service would then return a list of libraries matching the criteria submitted in XML format. The XML response to this request returns basic information about the libraries, such as library name, street address, city, state, and zip code.

It is also possible to look up OpenURL resolvers using the Registry web service. Resolvers can be looked up based on IP address or the "requestor" value,

97

which will look in the request's http header for IP address and submit this as the IP address to search upon. These queries will return an XML response containing information on the OpenURL resolvers associated with the submitted IP address.

Integrating WorldCat Data in Other Tools

There are several projects which have used these web services in order to incorporate WorldCat data into other interfaces and tools. Some of the more notable projects using these web services include:

- IDS Gift Deselection Manager
- VuFind Recommender Module
- LibX

IDS Gift Deselection Manager

The Information Delivery Services Project (IDS) created the IDS Gift Deselection Manager to help libraries manage their gifts and facilitate deselection of materials. The tool is a Microsoft Windows application that allows library staff to scan the bar code on a donated book and bring up metadata about this item based on information in the WorldCat Search API. In addition to seeing basic metadata about the item, the Gift Deselection Manager allows staff to see which libraries hold the item. Libraries can set up the Gift Deselection Manager with a set of libraries with which they conduct resources sharing. The WorldCat Search API then is searched to see which of these libraries hold the gift item. Based on the available information and decision criteria the tool provides a best guess as to whether or not the gift should be added to the library collection (see Figure 9.1).

Additionally, the tool also allows libraries to submit a batch of OCLC numbers that the library holds through an automated deselection process. The deselection process is based on a number of criteria determined by the library, including what level the library is collecting in that particular area and what other libraries own the item. WorldCat Search API is used in this process to determine holding information. By using holdings data from the WorldCat Search API the Gift Deselection Manager is able to help libraries make quick and efficient decisions regarding their collections, saving staff time and allowing gifts to be processed in a timely fashion.

VuFind Recommender Module

The VuFind Recommender Module is an add-on for the VuFind next generation discovery tool. The module adds "recommendations" to the user interface based on user input and cooperative identity and vocabulary data in the cloud. The first type of recommendation that the module offers is based on data from WorldCat Identities. When a user searches for an author within the VuFind interface the author search is sent to Identities to find matching records. When the search results screen is returned it displays the results of the search as well as a section

Figure 9.1. IDS Gift Deselection Manager

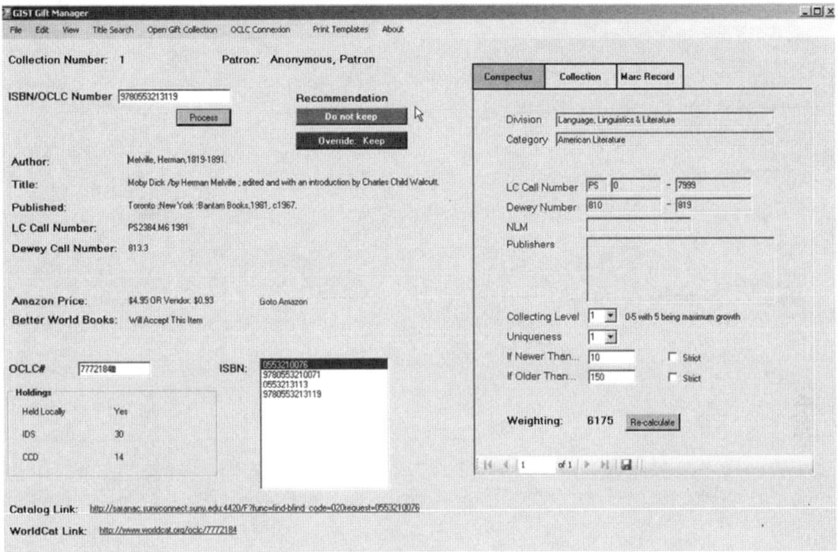

called "Authors Related to Your Search" at the top of the page. Within this section are identities that matched the search sent along with subjects related to those identities. This enables users to see other possible names the author uses as well as possible subject headings they might want to search (see Figure 9.2).

In addition to making recommendations for author searches, the VuFind Recommender module makes subject recommendations. When users perform a subject search VuFind returns a results page with the results of that search as well as a "Subject Recommendations" section. With this section VuFind displays possible related subjects. These subjects are drawn from the Terminology Services web service. VuFind performs an SRU search of the Library of Congress Subject Headings database within Terminology Services and returns related, broader, and narrower terms in the Subject Recommendations section. By returning these subject recommendations, VuFind is able to direct users to other possible searches that might meet their needs and help them refine their searches.

LibX

LibX is a tool that helps libraries create a custom browser toolbar that facilitates access to their library's collections. LibX uses a number of OCLC web services both to help libraries create a customized toolbar and to link users to library materials. When librarians choose to create a LibX edition they are asked to provide a basic set of information including the URL for the library catalog and OpenURL resolver. In the library catalog tab of the LibX edition creation screen, users can

Figure 9.2. VuFind Recommender Module—Authors Related to Your Search

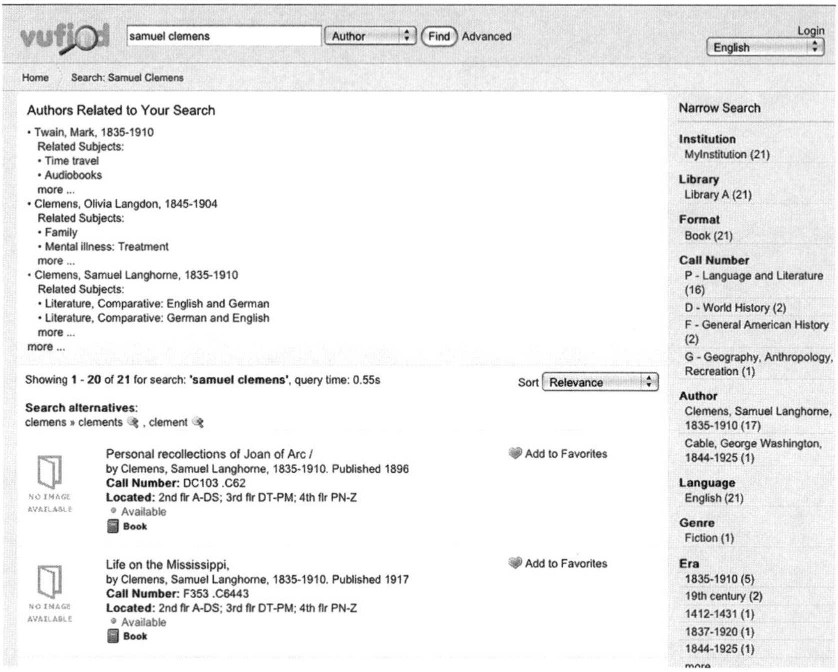

Figure 9.3. LibX—Library Catalog Configuration

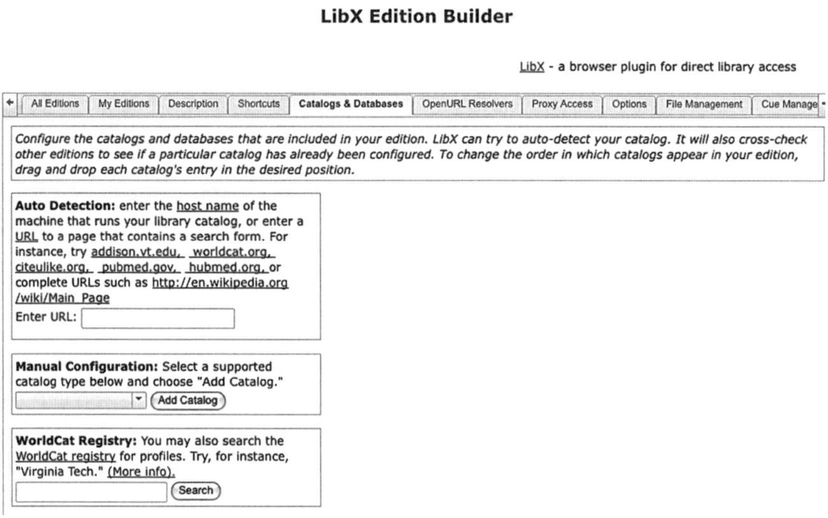

search the WorldCat Registry for the appropriate catalog URL for a given library and select it (see Figure 9.3). In addition, in the OpenURL tab users can input a hostname or IP address in order to search the Registry for the library's OpenURL resolver.

LibX also leverages the xISBN web service to help users find resources. If LibX finds an ISBN within a web page it autolinks it and adds basic metadata about the book (title, author) from the xISBN web service to a tooltip. It also helps users search for different editions of the book with a different ISBN that the library might hold.

Shared Solutions to Simple Problems

In addition to these larger applications a number of libraries have used OCLC web services to create simple scripts that enhance the functionality of their user interfaces. Three examples of this are:

1. Peer Reviewed Journal script
2. Cite This
3. Libraries Nearby with this item

Peer Reviewed Journal Script

The Peer Reviewed Journal script is a JavaScript that is intended to add peer review indicators to a user interface. The idea for the script originated with Karen Coombs who wrote the script as a demonstration for the Seattle Mashathon. The basic idea behind the script is to harvest the ISSNs from a web page and send them to the xISSN web service to determine whether or not the journal is peer reviewed. If the journal is peer reviewed then a Peer Reviewed indicator is added to the user interface, which for the initial prototype was Serial Solutions E-Journal List (see Figure 9.4).

Based on Coombs's work, the IDS project created a version of the script called "Peer Reviewer" that can be downloaded from the project website (http://idsproject.org/Tools/PeerReviewer.aspx). A number of variations of the original prototype are being used at several libraries.

Cite This

Another simple solution that several libraries have adopted based on OCLC web services is the Cite This tool. One of the best examples is Miami University

---

Figure 9.4. Peer Review Indicator Prototype

Paleontological journal (0031-0301) *Peer Reviewed* <u>Citation Linker</u> <u>Other access options</u>
from 02/01/2007 to present in <u>SpringerLink</u>

Library, which embeds a "Cite This" button into their library discovery tool (see Figure 9.5).

The "Cite This" button takes an OCLC number from the interface and sends it as a Formatted Citations request to the WorldCat Search API. WorldCat Search API then returns formatted citations for the given OCLC number, which the user interface displays within a pop-up window. Bryn Mawr Library's catalog has a similar feature (http://tripod.brynmawr.edu/record=b3437799~S10). Additionally, variations of this idea are being used in several libraries, including University of Houston, Virginia Tech, Colorado School of Mines, and Universal College of Learning. Most of these libraries link back to WorldCat.org for citation rather than directly embedding links within the user interface, but the basic idea is the same. Another variation is the "Cite Me" Facebook application, created by Bruce Washburn of OCLC Research (http://www.oclc.org/developer/applications/citeme-facebook-app). This application allows Facebook users to search WorldCat for materials and get back results in various citation formats.

Figure 9.5. Miami University Library Cite This Button

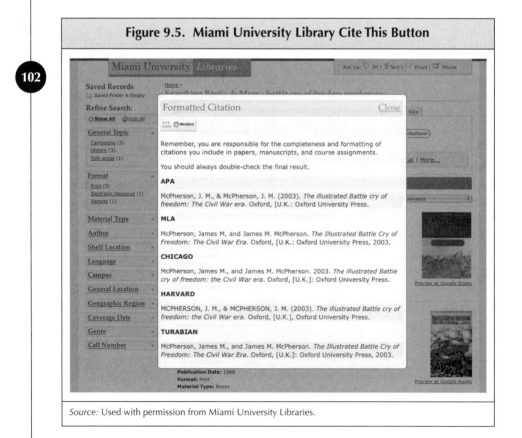

Source: Used with permission from Miami University Libraries.

Libraries Nearby with This Item

The third simple idea based on OCLC web services that has been popularly proto-typed and adopted is the idea of showing other libraries with holdings. These ideas take three basic forms: (1) a simple list of libraries nearby as shown in the Wageningen University Library's catalog; (2) a Google Maps mashup of libraries nearby as prototyped by both Mark Matienzo (http://matienzo.org/project/worldcat/examples/mappingholdings) and Karen Coombs (http://www.librarywebchic.net/mashups/worldcat_map/worldcat_holdings_map.php) and implemented by Brandeis University Library; or (3) a count of results for a particular search in libraries worldwide as shown in North Carolina State University Libraries and University of North Carolina Libraries discovery tools (see Figure 9.6).

All of these use the WorldCat Search API to get information about global library holdings, and, while each puts its own particular spin on the idea, the basic concept of connecting users with materials at other libraries can be seen in each.

WorldCat Data in the Mobile Environment

One area where there has been a considerable amount of development using cooperative data in the cloud is mobile applications. Most of these applications have been built by third parties who want to incorporate data about libraries and their holdings into their applications in order to enhance the experience of their users. Many are shopping-centric applications for iPhone. However, some Android applications have been built as well. Five mobile applications of particular note are:

1. BookMinder prototype
2. iBookshelf
3. CampusBooks
4. Red Laser
5. Pic2Shop

Figure 9.6. Results from Libraries Worldwide

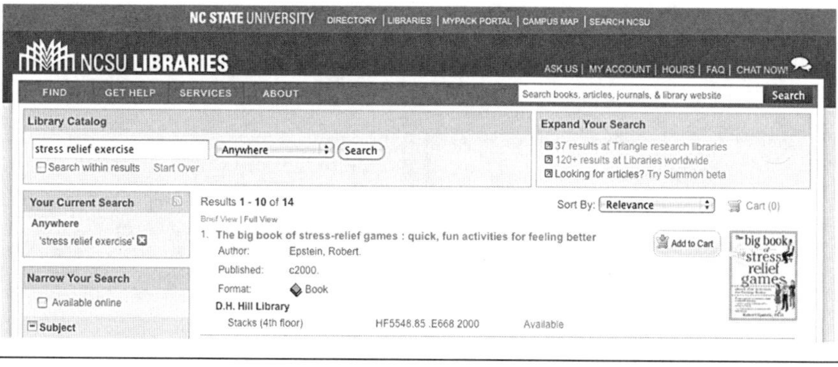

Source: Used with permission from NCSU Libraries.

BookMinder Prototype

The BookMinder prototype is an Android application developed by Bruce Washburn at OCLC Research. The idea behind the application was to give users a way to scan a bar code and add that item to a personal library on their Android device. Once an item was added to a user's personal library the user would be able to see libraries nearby with that item. Further information on the prototype is available on the OCLC Developer Network website (http://www.oclc.org/developer/applications/bookminder-android-app).

iBookshelf

iBookshelf is an iPhone application quite similar to the BookMinder prototype. Users can scan a bar code or search for a title and add it to their personal library. Users can organize their books, track if they have loaned them to other people, and rate books. The application allows users to find libraries near them with a particular book based on information in the WorldCat Search API. Information about that library and its location is then available to the user (see Figure 9.7).

Figure 9.7. iBookshelf Application

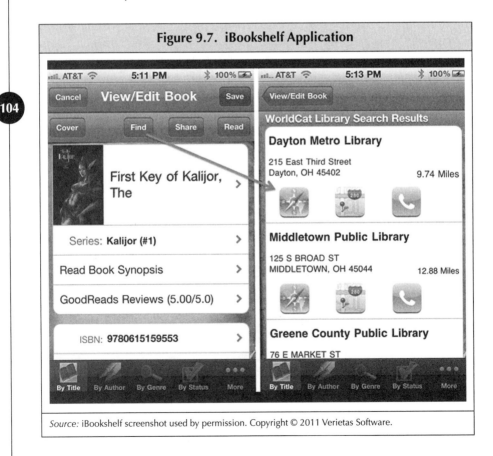

CampusBooks

CampusBooks is an application for both iPhone and Android that allows users to scan a bar code or enter a title, author, keyword, or ISBN in order to search for books online, compare prices, and find books in local libraries through the World-Cat Search API. Once users finds the item they want they can contact the local library through information provided by the WorldCat Registry API, such as address, phone, and URL (see Figure 9.8).

Red Laser and Pic2Shop

Red Laser and Pic2Shop are also both bar code scanning and shopping applications. Each allows users to scan the bar code on an item and then see the closest and most cost-effective ways to obtain that item. Red Laser was an early adopter of the WorldCat Search API, which allows it to show its users libraries that have the item available and details regarding that library.

Figure 9.8. CampusBooks Application

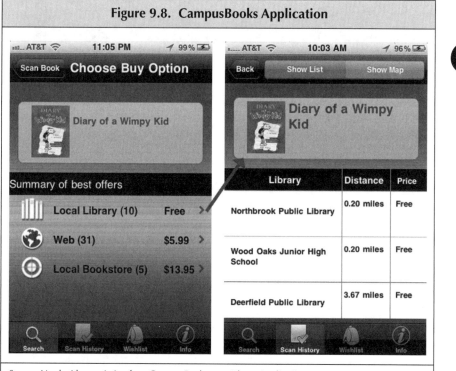

Source: Used with permission from Campus Books.com IPhone Application.

Figure 9.9. Pic2Shop Application

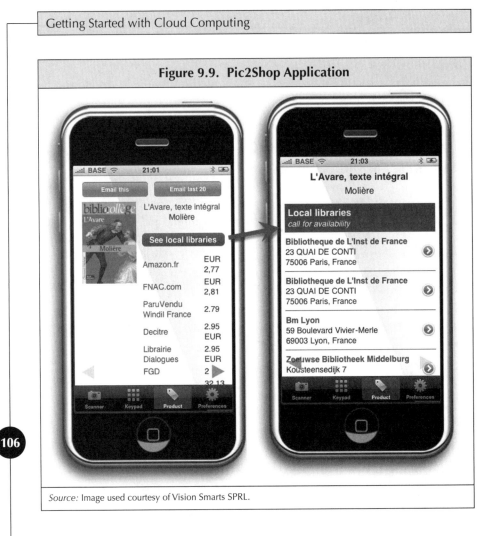

Pic2Shop has also adopted the WorldCat Search API in order to connect users with libraries. This application is downloadable globally and shows results for libraries worldwide (see Figure 9.9).

Conclusion

Data services in the cloud allow library data to be repurposed and leveraged in new ways. For example, OCLC's cloud-based data services provide multiple services based on the data in WorldCat. WorldCat Search API, WorldCat Identities, and the xIdentifier services are all fundamentally built on WorldCat data. However, each service represents an optimized and enhanced view of the WorldCat data for a particular purpose.

Furthermore, as is evident from the variety of applications discussed in this chapter, cooperative data in the cloud offers several distinct advantages. It creates a shared infrastructure to distribute library data to members of the cooperative, nonprofit organizations, and third-party partners. Because of this infrastructure, developers are able to use library data in new ways and build innovative applications that meet the diverse needs of library users. Additionally, because the data lives in the cloud, libraries do not need to maintain their own infrastructure and data repositories for distributing this information. Cloud-based systems also allow library data to be reusable and create a scenario where libraries can have a central repository for efficiently maintaining and sharing data. Using this infrastructure, libraries can integrate library data into new systems and more effectively go where their users are.

Shared cloud-based data services have a final advantage. Because they are open and standards based, cloud-based library data services create an environment where code and applications can more easily be shared among libraries. OCLC has already seen examples of this in practice. Demonstration code built by OCLC Developer Network staff and made available under an Apache 2 license has been used and modified by other libraries. One example is the Peer Reviewed script mentioned earlier. The potential power of this sharing and reuse of code is that libraries don't necessarily need to have developers on staff in order to take advantage of the cloud-based data services. OCLC is working on facilitating this type of collaboration, application development, and sharing via the OCLC Developer Network, a community of developers building applications on OCLC's cloud-based data services. These community-built and contributed applications will allow more libraries to take advantage of cooperative data and services in the cloud and better meet the needs of their library users.

Resources

Developer Network Application Gallery. http://www.oclc.org/developer/applications.

Terminology Services Documentation. http://www.oclc.org/developer/documentation/terminology-services/using-api.

WorldCat Identities Documentation. http://www.oclc.org/developer/documentation/worldcat-identities/using-api.

WorldCat Registry Documentation. http://www.oclc.org/developer/documentation/worldcat-registry/using-api.

WorldCat Search API Documentation. http://www.oclc.org/developer/documentation/worldcat-search-api/using-api.

xISBN Documentation. http://www.oclc.org/developer/documentation/xisbn/using-api.

xISSN Documentation. http://www.oclc.org/developer/documentation/xissn/using-api.

xOCLCNum Documentation. http://www.oclc.org/developer/documentation/xoclcnum/using-api.

Chapter 10

Building Push-Button Repositories in the Cloud with DSpace and Amazon Web Services

John Davison

Introduction

The Digital Resource Commons (DRC) is a multi-institution academic repository for archiving, discovering, and sharing unique academic materials produced by the University System of Ohio and Ohio's private colleges. The DRC uses DSpace open source software to store an ever-expanding set of digital collections. At the present time, the DRC hosts more than half a million items from 39 institutions and serves more than three million page views annually to visitors from all over the world. This chapter focuses on the experiences of the DRC in the Amazon cloud from June 2009 to December 2010.

The DRC development team has created a freely available, preconfigured version of their repository software that will allow other organizations to replicate the DRC's cloud-based procedures for building digital collections and take advantage of Amazon Web Services (AWS) to reduce the technical barriers to digital object storage and preservation. Hosting these repositories in the cloud environment removes the need for expensive hardware investments and simplifies site management, allowing more organizations to preserve their unique digital heritage. This chapter will outline some of the uses and advantages of cloud-based repository services and will describe how others can use the DRC software to quickly create digital collections.

Necessity Is the Mother of Cloud Computing

After building several instances on OhioLINK servers and promoting the repository throughout the state, the DRC faced an extended delay in resource procurement. The team was faced with an unexpected and difficult problem: how to

109

continue building critical mass for the project while financial and technical road-blocks prevented its parent organization from allocating additional computing resources. The answer was to use the cloud to divorce application architecture from underlying hardware and build a repository framework that masked the service's complexity from the end user. At the same time, virtualization allowed the DRC team to create a process with push-button simplicity. Relying on the Amazon cloud to provide the hardware on a pay-as-you-go basis, the DRC was able to quickly create new institutional repositories for eight members: Kent State University, Kenyon College, Xavier University, Ohio Wesleyan University, Ohio University, the University of Cincinnati, and the two education-related groups The Digital Archive of Literacy Narratives and the College & University Disability Access Collaborative. The majority of member organizations are part of the Ohio-LINK library consortium, but the DRC is broadly tasked to include nonmember educational and historical communities such as The Archives of the History of American Psychology and the Rutherford B. Hayes Presidential Center.

One of the key indicators of success is the inability to distinguish cloud-based instances from internally hosted ones. At the same time, each repository is seamlessly integrated with its parent institution's branding, and federated searching is possible across all repositories. DSpace instances can be brought online for new members in less than 10 minutes, and they can begin submitting content immediately.

This chapter serves as an introduction to the DRC's cloud-based repository development, providing details for creating an AWS account and step-by-step instructions to launch instances of the DRC software. Additional administrative steps are briefly outlined to assist the reader in moving toward a production-ready repository. Possible future options for cloud computing, open source repository software, and the DRC project are also discussed.

The Mission of the DRC

The DRC is a first-of-its-kind service: a statewide federation of centrally hosted individual repositories, branded to match each member organization's main website, and administered remotely by liaisons from each institution. Its marketing tagline is, "Your Files, Our Server, Your Site." As part of the University System of Ohio's plan to create a single, integrated technology infrastructure for higher education in the state (Fingerhut, 2010), the DRC is in a position to host a broad range of content, including faculty scholarship, historical archives, unique photographic collections, and research datasets. The DRC has made a concerted effort to provide a presentation layer for a wide range of media types, including audio from oral history projects, video from educational demonstrations, and multimedia animations. Additionally, the DRC has become the repository of choice for several million dollars in grant-funded digitization projects across the state. In recognition of these efforts, the American Library Association's Office of Information

Technology Policy has named the DRC a 21st Century Cutting-Edge Technology Service for 2011.

Progress through Careful Planning

There was an understandable suspicion of building a trusted digital object storehouse in something as poorly understood and remote as the cloud, but there were enough indicators in the institutional repository community to give the project credibility, including an Andrew W. Mellon planning grant to create DuraSpace, an organization committed to the preservation and long-term availability of digital collections (Morris, 2008). DRC developers kept this skepticism in mind and built a system with multiple fail-safe checkpoints. As a result, a DRC instance in the cloud is flexible enough to withstand failure at any one of three different levels (operating system, application, storage) and be replaced by an identical copy within minutes.

All applications are installed into block level storage volumes and are completely isolated from the underlying virtual machine, known as an Amazon Machine Image (AMI). Data snapshots can be connected to a stock AMI to produce an exact copy of the current repository. Not only does each repository exist in production, but this method of cloud virtualization allows for immediate and identical cloning—a hallmark of digital preservation. Because each cloud instance is a separate virtual machine, there is no way one client can gain access to another client's data. This allows the DRC to grant liaisons much greater access to and control over their site's operations (Cunningham, 2009).

Faced with a backlog of demand for new instances, the DRC was able to continue creating repositories without making a single capital expenditure or new hire and without waiting for the outcome of budget haggling over multimillion dollar IT investments. More than 10,000 digital items were added to the system, most of them submitted remotely by institutional liaisons. These items were immediately available to users. By creating or migrating DRC instances in the cloud, institutions were able to proceed with their digitization projects without losing grant funding or having to renegotiate the timeline for completion of projects.

Similar deployments in Amazon's cloud can be scaled for any type of library or library consortium, from a small library experimenting with software but lacking the resources to invest in the necessary infrastructure, to large library systems that need an agile and cost-effective way to respond to new projects or unexpected demand. Without the burden of up-front expenditures on hardware, each DRC cloud instance operates full-time for 8.5 cents per hour, or around $60 per month. Using the Amazon Reserved Instances prepayment plan can cut this price in half. The use of Micro instances, announced in September 2010 and designed for smaller applications, low traffic volume, or test environments, is billed at a mere two cents per hour. Starting in November 2010, the Amazon free usage tier allows new accounts to use 750 hours of micro instances free each month for one year.

111

Building a Push-Button Repository

There are only a handful of steps necessary to bring a cloud repository online. The DRC team has installed and preconfigured most aspects of a standard DSpace installation. This includes all software prerequisites such as the Java JDK, Apache Ant and Maven build tools, a PostgreSQL relational database, and the servlet container Tomcat. Since DSpace is an open source project, there are numerous ways to integrate other tools into the build process to meet specific needs. Developers interested in expanding on the example provided here are encouraged to visit dspace.org for additional details.

For the typical user, all of the initial software installation issues have already been performed, leaving only the following steps before a fully operational repository is available. An AWS account will need to be created; registration with the Amazon virtual machine provisioning system, known as Elastic Compute Cloud (EC2), must be completed; a security key needs to be created; the DRC stock example must be selected; and lastly an instance of the virtual machine must be launched. These actions are outlined in greater detail below.

Step One: Set up an AWS Account

The first step to building a cloud-based repository is account creation and verification. This is a straightforward process requiring a valid e-mail address, credit card, and phone number. In fact, an existing Amazon.com account can be used to access AWSs, making registration easy for anyone who's ever ordered a product from Amazon.com (see Figure 10.1).

All of the steps below are shown in the AWS Management Console, a browser-based administrative GUI; however, site management can also be performed with the exceptionally good Firefox plug-in, Elasticfox. Because AWS is an application programming interface, developers will no doubt find value in the command line EC2 API Tools.

Step Two: Register to Use EC2

After signing up, the next step is to register to use the EC2 environment. EC2 is the Amazon cloud function that allows for creation of on-demand virtual machines. Launching the AWS Management Console (https://console.aws .amazon.com/s3/home) will automatically detect new users and present a sign-up button (see Figure 10.2). At this point valid credit card information is needed, and the last step is identity verification by telephone to activate the account. The AWS Management Console will now display all of the options for creating and managing Amazon virtual machines under the tab labeled EC2 Dashboard.

Step Three: Create Security Keys

The security for building and accessing instances is governed by an RSA secure key pair process. Amazon holds the public key, and whenever users want to per-

Figure 10.1. Amazon Web Services Sign In

form an administrative function, they provide the matching private key. Security key pairs can be one of the more confusing aspects of AWS for new users, but they are relatively easy to create in the Management Console. For this example, use the name "EC2 Account." Under the Networking & Security section, click on the Key

113

Figure 10.2. The AWS Management Console Dashboard

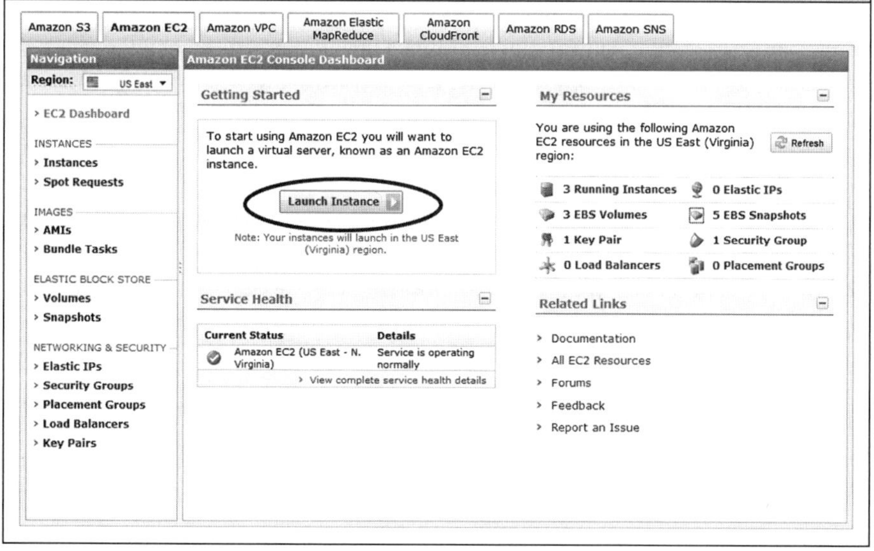

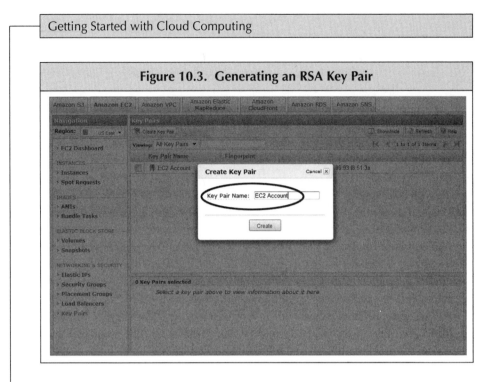

Figure 10.3. Generating an RSA Key Pair

Pairs link on the left-hand side. Generating the RSA key pair will download a file with a .PEM (privacy enhanced mail) extension (see Figure 10.3). Because this file provides the needed credentials to access all aspects of instance management, take care to protect it.

Step Four: Select the DRC Software

The next step is to locate the DRC AMI and launch a new instance from it. An AMI is similar to a gold master disk and contains the preconfigured operating system and application software for building a new repository. Clicking the launch button will bring up the Request Instances Wizard. The Community AMIs tab provides a list of all available machine images. Searching for the term "Digital-ResourceCommons" will bring up the latest version of the DRC public image. In such a rapidly developing environment, the DRC team will have added more features to the AMI prior to publication, so the AMI ID will likely change. Also, multiple versions of the DRC AMI with specialized functionality may be available (see Figure 10.4). For illustrative purposes the example in Figure 10.4 uses a reference installation of DSpace version 1.6.2 and provides access to both the XML user interface and the Java Server Pages interface.

Step Five: Set Preferences

Highlight the stock DRC AMI, and press Select. The Request Instances Wizard will advance to the next window and provide options to select the number of new instances to launch (for this test, only one), the availability zone to locate them in,

Figure 10.4. Searching for the DRC AMI

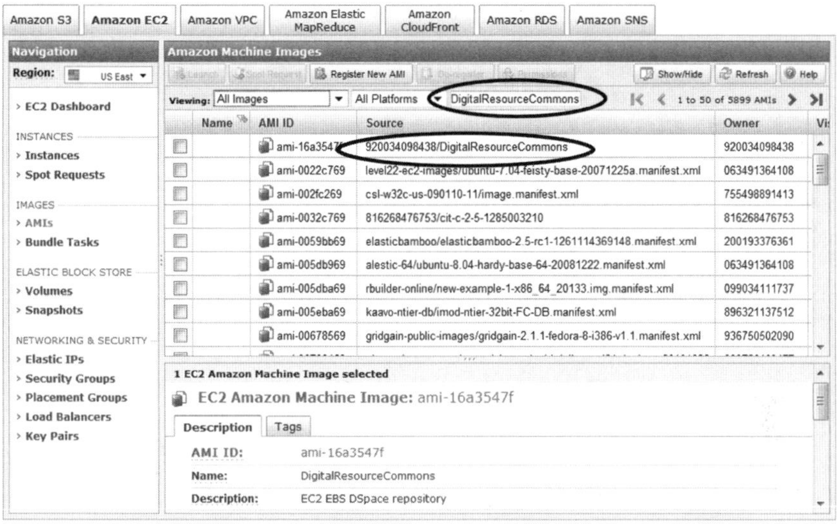

and the Instance Type. By launching multiple instances of an application in different availability zones, it is possible to insulate operations from failure in a single location. For this example, select No Preference. Choose the smallest instance type, the Micro with 613 MB of RAM. Make sure the "Launch Instances" radio button is selected and press Continue (Figure 10.5).

The next screen of advanced instance options can be left at default values for Kernel, RAM disk, and CloudWatch. Press Continue. The wizard will now ask for an instance name. Type "DRC Repository" in the Value field and continue. Verify the EC2 Account key pair generated earlier is being used. There is no need to change the default security group for this exercise. Review the options screen, and launch the new instance (see Figure 10.6).

Step Six: Launch the Repository

Launching a new virtual machine takes a moment, typically not more than a few seconds. Under the Instances link, there should now be a new entry labeled DRC Repository. Clicking this will provide a tabbed set of information panels. The first one, Description, includes the information needed to connect to the machine: the Public DNS entry. It should take the somewhat unconventional form of an alphanumeric value followed by ".compute-1.amazonaws.com." Copy this from the management console to a text editing program for easy access (see Figure 10.7).

Figure 10.5. Instance Details

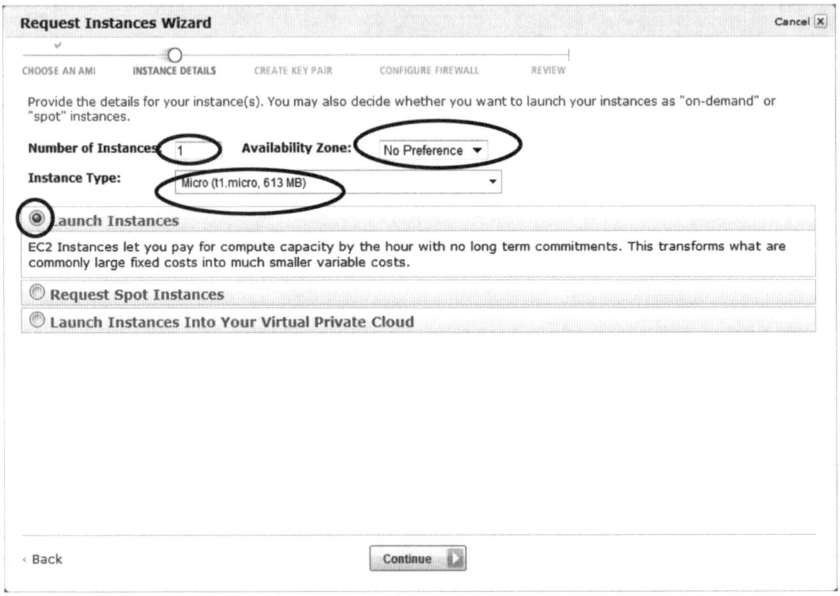

Request Instances Wizard   Cancel X

CHOOSE AN AMI   **INSTANCE DETAILS**   CREATE KEY PAIR   CONFIGURE FIREWALL   REVIEW

Provide the details for your instance(s). You may also decide whether you want to launch your instances as "on-demand" or "spot" instances.

Number of Instances: 1   **Availability Zone:** No Preference ▾

Instance Type: Micro (t1.micro, 613 MB) ▾

◉ **Launch Instances**

EC2 Instances let you pay for compute capacity by the hour with no long term commitments. This transforms what are commonly large fixed costs into much smaller variable costs.

◎ **Request Spot Instances**

◎ **Launch Instances Into Your Virtual Private Cloud**

‹ Back   Continue ▷

Figure 10.6. Review Options and Launch

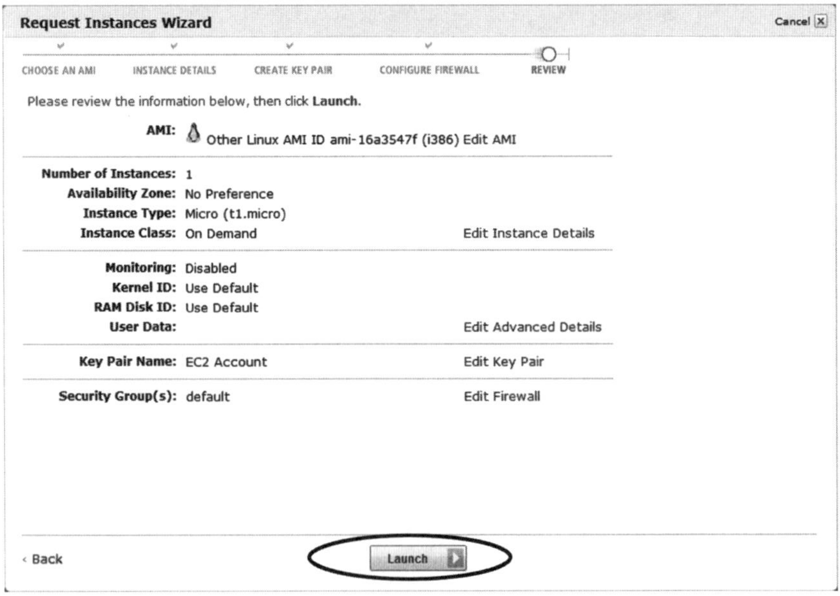

Request Instances Wizard   Cancel X

CHOOSE AN AMI   INSTANCE DETAILS   CREATE KEY PAIR   CONFIGURE FIREWALL   **REVIEW**

Please review the information below, then click **Launch**.

AMI: ◊ Other Linux AMI ID ami-16a3547f (i386) Edit AMI

Number of Instances:	1	
Availability Zone:	No Preference	
Instance Type:	Micro (t1.micro)	
Instance Class:	On Demand	Edit Instance Details
Monitoring:	Disabled	
Kernel ID:	Use Default	
RAM Disk ID:	Use Default	
User Data:		Edit Advanced Details
Key Pair Name:	EC2 Account	Edit Key Pair
Security Group(s):	default	Edit Firewall

‹ Back   Launch ▷

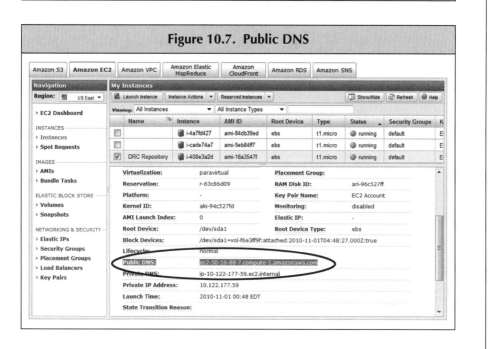

Figure 10.7. Public DNS

Step Seven: Open Firewall Ports

The last step in the Management Console before connecting to the new virtual machine is to open two ports in the firewall. Add two entries in the Security Groups section of Networking & Security, one for Secure SHell (SSH) connections and the other for the Tomcat web application container. Security Groups are the method for managing AWS firewall settings and as a security precaution are turned off by default. Highlight the default group. A list of connection methods will display. From the Custom drop-down list choose SSH. Entries for Protocol, Port, and Source will fill in automatically. As an added security measure, it is possible to restrict the range of IP addresses that can access any particular connection method, so SSH could be restricted to a single machine or range of IP addresses if desired. Next add a connection for Tomcat, the Java application container running the DSpace repository software. Select the Custom connection method, TCP protocol, and type 8080 for both the From and To ports. The source IP should be 0.0.0.0/0 to make the website available to the world (see Figure 10.8).

Step Eight: View the Site in a Browser

The AWS Management Console configuration is complete. It's now time to use the Public DNS entry and a web browser to view the page. In the browser address bar, type the Public DNS name followed by the port (:8080) and the interface

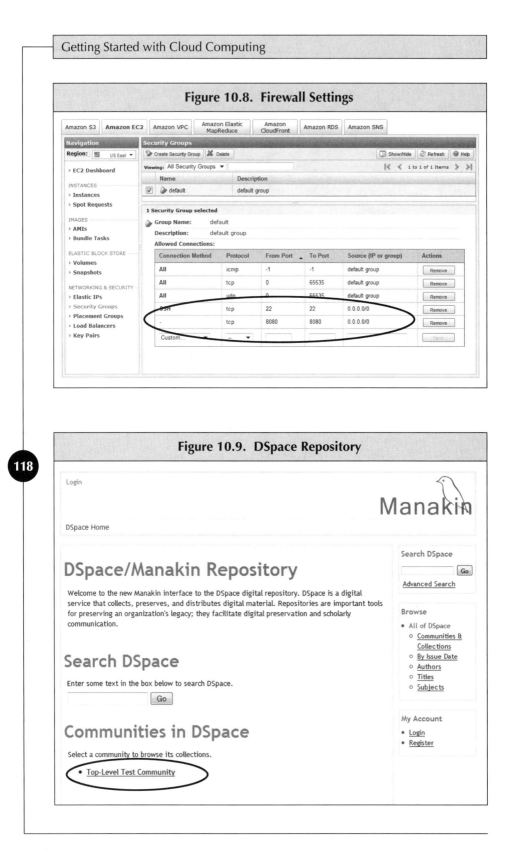

Figure 10.8. Firewall Settings

Figure 10.9. DSpace Repository

directory (xmlui), e.g., ec2-##-##-##-#.compute-1.amazonaws.com:8080/xmlui. The browser window should now display the stock DSpace Repository. The DRC team has created a top-level test community, a test collection, and placed a DRC promotional flyer in the collection (see Figure 10.9). This collection has permissions opened for anonymous submission and can be used right away with the ID "DRCAdmin" and password "DRCAdmin."

Next Steps: Your Repository on DSpace Software

Now that the repository is running, additional tests include creating communities and collections, adding digital objects in a variety of formats, creating new member accounts, and any number of other functions exposed through the DSpace administrative interface. If this DRC AMI will be live for any length of time, however, anonymous permissions should be revoked from the test collection and the DRCAdmin password changed as a precaution. Because it's a flexible open source application, DSpace is highly configurable, but not all options are exposed to a web browser. To perform batch submissions, alter the site branding or any of the other back-end functions; a secure shell tool such as PuTTY can be used with the RSA key to open a command line connection to the machine as the root user. Another important element of site customization is the DSpace Configuration file stored in the /usr/local/dspace/config directory and named dspace.cfg. This file contains a large number of user-definable options. Additionally, AWS has a Static IP service that will assign a persistent numeric address to the instance. This will allow a DNS entry to be created for the site, so the URL can take on the familiar pattern of a domain name.

119

With more experience, a repository manager can make significant changes to the way the software operates by editing any of the three tiers of the DSpace software. The Style Tier governs branding, the Theme Tier controls content display, and the Aspect Tier manages the core functions of the site. Simple changes can be made to the Style Tier using HTML and CSS. The Theme Tier is slightly more complex and as a result exposes more functionality to customization. Using XML, XSLT, and CSS, changes can be made to site layout and content display. Using Java, the Aspect Tier can be manipulated to add new features to the software (Donohue, 2010b).

DSpace is in the midst of a fundamental change designed to improve functionality. For example, site branding has made great strides over the past several software releases. This was achieved through standards-based XML-XSLT processing and cascading stylesheet development of the DSpace XML user interface (Phillips et al., 2007). This same flexibility allows the DRC to be fully customized for each OhioLINK institution. The merging of the DSpace Foundation and Fedora Commons in May 2009 is also part of this fundamental reorganization. With the two most recognized repository platforms moving toward greater interoperability, future releases will include best-of-breed functionality from both camps. Efforts are already underway to build a DSpace release that runs on top of a Fedora repository. This, along with the DuraCloud-hosted service, is widely seen as a major step toward building an entirely modular repository platform able to more easily leverage cloud computing options (Donohue, 2010a).

Next Steps for the DRC: Push-Button Micro Collections

The DRC has a large operational task to accomplish—the training and integration of additional member organizations. But beyond the daily requirements of running a repository with limited funding and skeleton staffing, the DRC is committed to continue cloud-based software development. In particular, the AMI offerings should include several DRC modifications to DSpace. The DRC team will integrate these changes into multiple AMIs, giving access to media format enhancements, such as video on-demand and large-scale image pan and zoom.

Equally important is the creation of a self-service provisioning application in the cloud, referred to as software as a service (SaaS). Leveraging the newly announced AWS Free Tier, the DRC is testing the development of an on-demand collection creation process that would spin up a new repository whenever requested by an authenticated remote user. This instance would be customized based on the particular media type being submitted and would exist only as long as needed to complete a collection. Providing self-directed access to the repository and to collection creation greatly expands the pool of collection submitters and allows DRC liaisons to shift from being the primary generators of content to being gatekeepers over content workflow. With additional development, submission schemas could be created with a choice of several preconfigured options depending on the user's field of research or their metadata requirements.

The importance of a web service API to this process is critical, because it exposes Amazon's web offerings to a browser-based interface. End-users become the focal point and are empowered to make IT service requests to support their collection creation needs. The entire AWS architecture layer performs a "disappearing act" and the end user is presented with "an interface to the cloud in such a way as to make self-service possible" (MacVittie, 2010).

The DuraSpace community has created an example of this sort of on-demand application with their AWS-based Fedora Repository test drive site. A user provides only an e-mail address and is sent the URL to a free instance of Fedora software for an hour-long experimentation session. In this case, however, it's only a "test drive" of the repository software, with all content submitted disappearing after the session ends (Fedora Reference Repository, 2010). For the vision of a SaaS repository to be complete, the central DRC would harvest the collection's metadata and bitstreams through the use of the OAI-ORE protocol before terminating the instance (Maslov et al., 2010).

The results of the DRC cloud project thus far have been a cost-effective, agile response to seemingly insurmountable delays in hardware provision and staffing; a rapid development of technical proficiency that can be shared throughout the state and with the DSpace community at large; and a compelling model for more independent institutional control and access to site administration. Interested parties can follow the work of the DRC Development Team at the *Files in This Item* blog (http://fiti.ohiolink.edu).

References

Cunningham, Lewis. 2009. "Using and Managing AWS—Part 3: AWS Security." May 17. http://clouddb.info/2009/05/17/using-and-managing-aws-part-3-aws-security/.

Donohue, Tim. 2010a. "DuraSpace Recommends DSpace & Fedora Integration Initiative." DuraSpace (blog), July 8. http://expertvoices.nsdl.org/duraspace/2010/07/08/duraspace-recommends-dspace-fedora-integration-initiative/.

———. 2010b. "Making DSpace 1.5.x Your Own." Accessed October 5. http://www.slideshare.net/tdonohue/making-dspace-15-your-own-customizations-via-overlays.

Fedora Reference Repository. 2010. DuraSpace (website). Accessed October 10. http://testdrive.fedora-commons.org/ref-repo.php.

Fingerhut, Eric. 2010. "Strategic Plan for Higher Education 2008–2017." Accessed October 2. http://www.uso.edu/strategicplan/.

MacVittie, Lori. 2010. "Infrastructure 2.0 + Cloud + IT as a Service = An Architectural Parfait." *Two Different Socks* (blog), September 15. http://devcentral.f5.com/weblogs/macvittie/archive/2010/09/15/infrastructure-2-enables-cloud-enables-it-as-a-service.aspx.

Maslov, Alexey, James Creel, Adam Mikeal, Scott Phillips, John Leggett, and Mark McFarland. 2010. "Adding OAI-ORE Support to Repository Platforms." *Journal of Digital Information* 11, no. 1. http://journals.tdl.org/jodi/article/view/749.

Morris, C.M. 2008. "Can Anything as Ephemeral as a 'Cloud' Provide Permanent Storage?" *Content Sausage* (blog), November 12. http://blogs.nature.com/uc0af3996/2008/11/12/can-anything-as-ephemeral-as-a-cloud-provide-permanent-storage.

Phillips, Scott, Cody Green, Alexey Maslov, Adam Mikeal, and John Leggett. 2007. "Manakin: A New Face for DSpace." *D-Lib Magazine* 13, no. 11/12. http://www.dlib.org/dlib/november07/phillips/11phillips.html.

121

Untethering Considerations: Selecting a Cloud-Based Data Access and File-Sharing Solution

Heidi M. Nickisch Duggan and Michelle Frisque

Introduction

Many librarians need to access files and data stored on their office hard drives from remote locations, even when they don't have access to their campus or library networks. In some cases files need to be accessible regardless of computer operating system. Staff librarians often also need to share files of all sizes with one or more colleagues and collaborators, not all of whom are part of the same institution. A number of excellent no- to low-cost cloud-based solutions are on the market that provide library staff with an easy way to securely access, share, and work on files from anywhere to ensure that the most recent version of each file is automatically available on any other computer that they use.

Variables to Consider

There are a number of variables to consider while selecting and implementing a cloud-based solution for file synchronization. Factors such as what data staff need to have remote access to and how much space is required, who needs access, whether the files require a private or a collaborative space or both, and if the product is priced affordably will guide the product selection itself. The library's computer support department will have concerns and questions regarding product administration and management, installation and user training, platform support, and restoration. The various IT units of the broader organization are sure to have requirements regarding encryption and other technical and legal compliance issues. Aspects librarians should consider when evaluating and selecting a cloud-based file storing/sharing solution include web-based, client-side, and hybrid solutions; administration and management of the system; ease of use; compliance; encryption; pricing structure; data restoration options; file type support; vendor support; and user recommendation.

Web-Based, Client-Side, and Hybrid Solutions

When choosing the file sharing system that best fits the library's needs, it is important to think about how and from where users will want to access their files. In most cases, librarians select a cloud-based file sharing solution because they want staff to be able to access files from anywhere, on or off campus, using a variety of devices.

Some file-sharing solutions are web-based solutions, meaning that no software needs to be installed on the user's computer(s); instead, users upload files they want to save or share to a website. To access the files later, users log into the website and download the files they want. A client-side solution requires the installation of a client on all computers staff will use to save and later access their files. Many solutions will offer both options: the ability to access user files from a website and through the locally installed client. When selecting which option best fits the library's needs, consider the following questions:

- What types of operating systems are used in the organization or wherever library staff will access their files (i.e., Windows, Mac, Linux, other)? It is critical to select a solution that will work on the various operating systems staff will be using to access their files.
- Will staff be able to install and configure client software on each device they will use to access their files? If not, does the solution offer a web-based solution for accessing and uploading files? Consider that library staff may not want to—or be able to—install a client on all of the computers they use, particularly ones they use once or infrequently.
- Is there an app for the various mobile devices staff use, and what features are and are not included in the app that are included in the web-based application and/or the client? While many file sharing services do have apps for mobile devices many of the apps are missing features that are available on the client that is installed on the desktop computer or laptop. Carefully investigate what options are and are not available in the mobile app, particularly if that functionality is important to the users.
- How are files saved to the file sharing site? How are updates to the files saved to the site? When considering which solution to use, consider how easy it is to save new files as well as update existing files. One benefit of a centralized file sharing system is the ability to access files from anywhere, so make sure to select a system that best fits with the staff's workflow. For instance, many of the client-based solutions allow for automatic data

syncing so that once users save a file in a specific location on their computer it is automatically synced to all of their other accounts. The web-based solution usually requires that users remember to upload the most recent version of the document.

• Synchronization is a useful feature that allows seamless access to the most current version of a document regardless of the computer on which it was last edited. If the solution selected has an option to sync files automatically, does the solution sync the entire file each time it is modified, or does it sync only the changes that are made to the file? Syncing only the changes to a file uses less bandwidth than saving the entire file each time a change is made. Can the users manually customize the bandwidth limits if they determine that the default settings are slowing down their Internet connection? If the users edit a file when the computer is not attached to the Internet, do they have to manually sync the files, or will the solution sync the changes automatically once an Internet connection is reestablished?

Administration and Management of the System

Many libraries have multiple users at the institution who use or will use a file sharing system, so librarians should consider selecting a system that has a centralized administration tool. A centralized administration and/or management tool allows the organization to identify at least one and sometimes more than one administrator responsible for managing all of the organizational user accounts and space allocation from a central location, usually a website. Administration and management tools usually include the following features: ability to create user accounts, deactivate accounts, reallocate accounts to another user, customize the amount of storage each user account receives, reallocate storage among users based on their changing needs, purchase additional storage, pay using a centralized billing feature, and so on. While most of these features are standard, each system offers different options, and the product evaluators should check the features of each option under consideration to ensure the product includes all of the features they require.

Ease of Use

A primary consideration for any organization deploying a new product is how easy it is for end users to learn and use as well as how easy it is for system administrators to manage. In the case of file access and synchronization, evaluate how straightforward it is to save, synchronize, organize, access, and share files. Doing some preliminary testing with the user base will let the computer support staff know whether users find the interface intuitive or whether they will need to provide training and a more gradual rollout of the product. The more difficult a product is to use the less likely staff will adopt the service. If the product cannot easily be installed, customized by the user, and implemented or it requires a system

125

administrator to set up and maintain, then computer support personnel will need to be available and prepared to support the end users.

Compliance and Rules and Regulations

An organization may restrict the types of files that can be stored or shared via the cloud. For instance, some organizations have policies that require all information be stored only on the organization's servers. Other organizations may allow some types of data to be stored on a third-party vendor server while other types of data must be stored on a local server. Data many organizations may not want stored on a third-party server include information that is governed by federal law like the Health Insurance Portability and Accountability Act of 1996 (HIPAA) or the Family Educational Rights and Privacy Act (FERPA). Librarians should check organizational policies to determine if there are any restrictions related to storing data on nonorganizational servers they need to abide by and should also read the vendor's policies, terms, and conditions to make sure that the service is in compliance with their organization's rules related to storing and sharing files with third-party vendors.

Encryption

When storing data using a cloud-type service, ensure that the data is encrypted when it is synced and stored on the vendor's servers. Most vendors automatically encrypt the data that is synced and stored on their servers, but some organizations may require an additional level of encryption using specific third-party encryption software. If the library's parent organization requires the use of encryption software like PGP Data Protection or Symantec Endpoint Encryption, make sure the file sharing solution selected supports third-party encryption.

Pricing Structure

Pricing structures vary by product, and it is often simpler and more cost effective to purchase products that have an organizational pricing model rather than paying for each individual account. Consider whether the product is available as a one-time purchase, is subscription based, or is part of a larger package. The fee structure may also vary by number of users, storage space required, or other criteria. Many vendors will accept institutional purchase orders, but some will require a personal or company credit card.

Options for Restoration of Data

A benefit of cloud-based file sharing is that the files are stored in the cloud so if a catastrophic event occurs to a file on a computer, a backup is safely stored in the user's account in the cloud. Consider the relevant significance to the library of the following questions to best determine which data storage/retrieval features are most important:

- How easy is it to recover a file that has been deleted? For how long are deleted files stored in the system?
- Is it possible to restore previous versions of a file? How long are previous versions of the document available? Some file sharing solutions keep every saved change of the file for up to 30 days. Some keep only a fixed number of saved changes of the document, and yet others keep the changes indefinitely, sometimes for an additional fee.
- Does file restoration require an administrator's support, or can the user complete it with ease?
- Will the system allow the restoration of more than one version of the same file?
- Does the product provide the ability to customize any of these settings for each user, or is that accomplished at the group level? If the library has an organization subscription, can these settings be customized in the administrative tool?
- If the organization has an institutional account, can the administrator restore deleted files as well as restore previous versions of existing files, or can this be done only at the individual account level?

File Type Support

While cloud-based file sharing tools allow users to access their files from any computer, most solutions will let the user edit the file only if the appropriate application is installed on the computer currently being used. For instance, to edit a .docx file the computer must have a software application installed on the computer that allows the editing of a .docx file, for example, Microsoft Word or Pages for Mac. Some of the cloud-based file sharing options are providing online tools that will allow users to edit their documents online even if the user's computer does not have the software installed on it. Although in most cases the cloud-based software application is not as robust as the desktop-based application, it does provide another option for editing documents when users are away from their desktop. Another option some cloud-based file sharing tools include is a viewer so that the user can view most file types online, even if the software is not installed on that computer. This feature is especially helpful on mobile devices.

Vendor Support

Even with solutions that are easy to use, there are times that the administrator or individual users may need additional support in troubleshooting issues with the cloud-based file sharing solution. Things to consider when thinking about future support issues include:

- Does the vendor have online documentation? Before selecting a solution, read some of the documentation to make sure it is easy to understand.

- Does the vendor have an active user group or forum that staff or the system administrator can consult to get help from other users?
- Can the library's support staff contact the vendor directly for support? Is the vendor's contact information easy to locate on its website? What is the library's support staff's preferred communication channel and does the vendor offer that option (i.e., e-mail, chat, phone)? Is there an additional fee related to any of these services? Does the vendor offer fee-based support packages that will provide the level of service you want? Is the price reasonable?

References from Other Users

Don't underestimate the value of other users' experiences and recommendations about a product. Contact other librarians who have used the product and ask them for their experiences. It is helpful to have the computer support staff from each institution communicate directly with one another.

Examples of Cloud Storage Solutions

For most libraries, the primary requirements for implementing a cloud-based file synchronization and backup service include seamless syncing of files and data across multiple computers, secure omni-locational access to files and documents, and a platform-independent solution (i.e., supported on multiple operating systems and mobile devices). Other considerations may include ease of implementation and use, compliance with standard encryption formats and requirements, cost, space, security, file types recognized, formatting of web-available documents, and versioning. Several solutions are available on the market; four possibilities a library may want to consider include Box.net, Dropbox, Google Docs, and Windows Live SkyDrive.

Box.net

Box.net (http://www.box.net) is a cloud-based file sharing tool libraries should investigate if the primary need is to support and maintain a large number of user accounts. Of all of the options explored in this chapter, this one is the most robust. Box.net has several different plans for organizations to consider. The Personal option is for individuals and is free. It includes 5 GB of web storage and any single file cannot be larger than 25 MB, although additional storage can be purchased. The Personal account option does not support syncing; instead, files need to be uploaded to the Box.net website. Files and folders can be shared with others via a web link. To make collaboration easier users can create wiki-style documents that allow multiple people to edit and comment on documents directly online.

The Box.net Business and Enterprise solutions include all of the features available to the Personal account as well as many others. The greatest benefit of the Business and Enterprise solutions is that they support syncing files from the desktop to Box.net. Users also have the option to access files via the Box.net website. The Business and Enterprise solutions also allow users to track file version. Other features available to both the Business and the Enterprise solution include full-text search, statistics, administrative console, and Google Apps integrating. The Business option begins at a 500 GB space limit for a monthly per-user subscription and includes a 2 GB file size restriction.

The Box.net Enterprise solution includes all of the features available to the Personal and Business account. Additional features that are available only to Enterprise customers include custom branding, role-based access control, additional level of data encryption, bulk account creation and editing, an option for Active Directory/LDAP integration for account authentication, and dedicated support from Box.net.

Dropbox

Dropbox (http://www.dropbox.com) is a cloud-based syncing and backup product for any file size or type. It is a hybrid solution with both client and web access. Dropbox is free for up to 2 GB of storage, with up to 100 GB of storage available for a fee. Users can also increase their free storage by inviting friends to join Dropbox or by purchasing additional space, available on an annual basis. Dropbox for Teams allows shared storage for a workgroup and has an administrative console for centralized management of the accounts.

Installing and configuring Dropbox is relatively simple; users are generally able to implement Dropbox without extensive IT support. To get started each Dropbox user needs to create an account on the Dropbox website. Then they install the Dropbox client software on all of the computers they want to access their Dropbox files from. As part of the software installation process, Dropbox creates a "My Dropbox" folder (by default placed in the My Documents folder on a Windows machine and the Finder window on the Mac). All files and folders saved in the Dropbox folder are synced in the cloud, and then Dropbox synchronizes those files to any other computers (Windows, Mac, or Linux) or mobile device (iPhone, iPad, Android, and Blackberry) where Dropbox is installed with that account. The syncing is automatic, occurring on-the-fly whenever the computers or devices are connected to the Internet, which means users always work on the most recent version of the file. Dropbox also allows users to work on their files in their Dropbox account even when they are not online. Any changes made to a file in Dropbox sync to the Dropbox account as soon as the computer is reconnected to the Internet.

Dropbox is also accessible from a web browser via a computer or mobile device—even if the Dropbox client is not installed—so files are always at hand. The Dropbox website allows users to access files when they are not at their own computers or if they do not have the client installed. By logging in to the website, users can see all of their files and folders in the same hierarchy used on their hard

129

drives. However, to edit files, users need to download them to the computer they are working on and then save them when they are finished and upload them to the Dropbox website. For more information about a library's use of Dropbox, see Chapter 15 of this book.

Google Docs

Google Docs (http://docs.google.com) is another option that some libraries have explored. Previously, Google Docs supported only a limited number of file types, and the files had to be converted to an available Google Docs format (i.e., Document, Presentation, Spreadsheet, Form, and Drawing). Early in 2010, Google started allowing users to store up to 1 GB worth of files that are not converted to a Google Docs format for free and anything above that for a fee.

All files must be uploaded via a Google webpage to be stored in Google Docs. A few browsers, including newer versions of Safari, Chrome, and Firefox, support the ability to drag files from the user's desktop. When users upload files to Google Docs they can choose to retain the file type or they can convert the uploaded file into the corresponding Google Docs format. All documents that are converted to a Google Docs format can be edited online; however, some file types cannot be converted to a Google Docs format. Examples of files that can be converted to a Google Doc format include, but are not limited to, .doc, .docx, .odt., sxw, .rtf, .txt, .ppt, .pps, .xls, .xlsx, .csv, and .wmf. When users choose to retain the file format that is uploaded and do not convert it to a Google Doc format, they will need to either download the file to edit it or convert it to a Google Doc format to edit the file online.

Files uploaded to Google Docs can be organized in folders created by the user. Files that are uploaded to Google Docs use the same permissions system that is used for other native Google Docs documents. The permissions can be set at an individual file level or at the folder level. There are three ways to share files with others. The first option is the Public on the Web option, which allows anyone on the Internet to view the document without signing in. The Anyone with a Link option allows anyone with a special link to access the file. The Private setting is the most restrictive in that it allows access to a file only to individuals who have been explicitly granted permission. All users must have a Google account to log into these files. While the user can share an uploaded file, only files that are converted to a Google Docs format can be edited online.

Windows Live SkyDrive

Windows Live SkyDrive (http://explore.live.com/windows-live-skydrive), as the name suggests, was created by Microsoft. This product is more than just a file storing/sharing application; it includes other features like e-mail, video chat, a photo gallery, etc. The Windows Live SkyDrive tool allows users to store, access, and share documents and images. While users can store almost any file type within

SkyDrive, some file types have additional features. For instance, Microsoft Office files can be created, edited, and stored within Windows Live SkyDrive using the Office Web App suite available online within the Windows Live Suite. Images and video can also be edited using online software within the Windows Live suite.

Windows Live SkyDrive includes 25 GB of free storage. The Windows Live SkyDrive software allows users to synchronize and access files across multiple computers. Users can choose to sync individuals' files or specific folders on their desktop. Desktop syncing requires a client to be installed on the computer. It currently supports both Windows and Mac operating systems, and files can also be accessed online via the Windows Live service. Any files stored online in Windows Live SkyDrive can be shared with individuals and groups or may be kept private. All files can also be accessed via the Windows Live website. Windows Live Sky-Drive does not currently have the option to manage group accounts.

Conclusion

A cloud-based file sharing solution can be an easy to implement, no- to low-cost solution, providing library staff with an easy way to securely access files from anywhere and the ability to seamlessly share files with colleagues and collaborators. To select the most appropriate cloud-based file sharing solution, organizations should assess their users needs to make sure that they select the most appropriate solution for their organization.

Consider what data staff need to have remote access to and how much space that data requires, whether the files require a private or a collaborative space or both, and whether the product is priced affordably. The library's computer support department should also consider the impact of the administration and management of the selected solution, installation and user training, platform support, and data restoration. The various IT units of the broader organization might need to be consulted regarding the organizational requirements for encryption and other technical and legal compliance issues. Fully understanding the library's needs will help each library evaluate the various cloud-based file sharing solutions available so that the library selects the option that not only fits its needs of today but seamlessly supports its needs for the future.

Chapter 12

SharePoint Strategies for Establishing a Powerful Library Intranet

Jennifer Diffin and Dennis Nangle

Introduction

In the world of cloud computing, libraries have many options for setting up a remotely accessible intranet, which can become a collaborative space that is flexible to a library's organizational needs. Many factors should be taken into consideration, including, but not limited to, security, accessibility, and features. Microsoft SharePoint is one option to be considered. Regardless of whether the servers being used to store the information are in house or outsourced, users can collaborate with colleagues regardless of physical location through their web browser. SharePoint is available as part of the Microsoft Core Access License (CAL) Suite for institutions (Gilbert, 2010). However, as Gartner analyst Mark Gilbert (2010) has mentioned, one SharePoint flaw is the lack of documentation. This chapter will outline strategies that libraries can utilize to develop an efficient and effective intranet that combines social networking tools like blogs, wikis, and discussion boards with dynamic knowledge management functionality.

SharePoint in the Cloud

While many institutions may choose to host Microsoft SharePoint locally, it is also possible to opt for the hosted version of SharePoint, SharePoint 2010 Online, via Microsoft Online Services. Either option allows SharePoint to be used as a cloud collaboration platform that provides document sharing (McDonald, 2010). Using the hosted option is what is known as software as a service (SaaS): software applications are hosted and maintained by a cloud services provider (CSP) outside of the institution that is using the software (Salido and Cavit, 2010). An institution's IT department should consider several factors (i.e., convenience, cost effectiveness, flexibility, security, etc.) when deciding which option works best. An instance of SharePoint for a given organization could be hosted in one of three ways: a private deployment by a

133

single institution; a community cloud encompassing a group of institutions; or a public cloud that is open to all customers of the CSP (Salido and Cavit, 2010).

Defining SharePoint

SharePoint can be defined overall as a proprietary collaborative workspace, owned by Microsoft and manifesting itself differently depending on the type of license purchased and implementation method. A couple of terms that often surface in the SharePoint environment are "Sites" and "Pages." While any user with a basic familiarity of the Internet can recognize these terms, it is crucial to understand their key distinctions within SharePoint. A Site in SharePoint carries with it much of the expected functions of a website in the traditional sense: it is the main location under which several Pages of a similar category would be placed. However, SharePoint's various Site categories, which a user must select upon creating a SharePoint Site, significantly affect functionality moving forward. In SharePoint 2010, there are five categories of Sites available for hosting and managing information: Team Sites, Document Workspaces, Group Work Sites, Meeting Workspaces, and Blog Sites (Bates and Smith, 2010). Categories may vary based on the version of SharePoint and the individual installation at an institution. Within a Site, there can be one or more components (Libraries, Lists, and Pages) available to use to add content to the Site (Bates and Smith, 2010).

Most SharePoint Sites begin with a blank Page. Using the Internet terminology, this can be likened to a homepage. From here various types of Pages and other content can be created and added to the Site. The Page types available are Page (SharePoint 2010 only), Publishing, and Web Part. A SharePoint List is essentially a simple database or spreadsheet that contains information or data that is collected in rows. Each row is called a "list item" (Sagi, 2010). Many of the features discussed in the chapter are based on the SharePoint List functionality: Tasks, Announcements, Discussion Boards, Calendar, etc. These Lists are very flexible and allow staff to customize them to best suit the needs for which they are being used. A SharePoint Library is a particular kind of List where each list item is one file (image, form, document, video, etc., depending on type of SharePoint Library). Sagi (2010) provides an example of an institution that could use SharePoint as an intranet, with the home Site housing relevant information for organizational staff as a whole. Then, Sagi (2010: 7) explains further, it may link to "a subsite called Human Resources that stores forms such as travel requests, expense claims, and other forms. . . . The two sites may share some attributes . . . but they have separate contents—for example, different pages, libraries, and lists."

Implementation Strategy

Establishing the intended purpose of SharePoint before implementation is extremely important. To help ensure that SharePoint is high on the priority list, the implementation project's goals and objectives should be clearly defined; agreed on by the key stakeholders; and tied to the mission and goals of the institution and/or group that will be implementing SharePoint.

As implementation of SharePoint progresses, understanding the specific objectives that are trying to be achieved will have an impact on which features are implemented. Each objective may have several corresponding SharePoint features that may be useful, so it is important to communicate with staff how a particular feature is expected to be used. To reduce possible resistance among staff to adopting SharePoint, be sure to have a clear communication plan and offer training sessions that explain how using particular SharePoint features will improve on existing workflows and systems (Jamison, Hanley, and Cardarelli, 2011).

Social Networking within SharePoint

A major reason for creating an intranet is to provide a way for staff to share information and knowledge within a secure environment. Social networking is becoming an increasingly more significant component of information and knowledge sharing. While SharePoint 2007 allows some collaboration through blogs, wikis, and discussion boards, SharePoint 2010 builds on those features with the addition of several new social networking capabilities. Although it can be tempting for a library to turn on all of these new features just for the sake of appearing trendy, it is very important at the onset to consider for what purpose these new features will be used (as was discussed above). There are several areas that can be better leveraged with carefully implemented social technologies, such as access to expertise, relationship building, connecting people with needed information, mentoring and knowledge sharing, user-enhanced access to information, public and centrally located conversations, and attracting technologically savvy employees (Jamison, Hanley, and Cardarelli, 2011).

Some of the new social networking features available in SharePoint 2010 are My Sites, ratings, tags, notes, personal blogs, Team Sites (Wiki), and Enterprise Wiki Sites. My Site contains profile-building categories like Basic Information (with areas such as About Me, Skills, Interests, Ask Me About, Picture, Office Location, and Time Zone), Contact Information, Details, Status Updates, Preferences, visual directory lookup or browser, content library, and group memberships within SharePoint. As with much of SharePoint, it is up to individual institutions to decide which features will (or will not) be used and to define the purpose of each used feature. Many of these social networking features are meant to help staff find colleagues in the institution who may have knowledge about a specific topic and to encourage collaboration.

SharePoint Features

Wiki

Regardless of context (special, academic, public, etc.), most libraries face the issue of how to consolidate documentation. Is institutional knowledge evenly distributed and accessible with paper manuals or sporadic sticky notes in cubicles? By

135

fully exploiting the Wiki feature in SharePoint, libraries can create and easily maintain a consolidated knowledge base. SharePoint allows for easy editing and updating through the WYSIWYG (What-You-See-Is-What-You-Get) editor. Collaboration can be encouraged with the knowledge that any errors can quickly and easily be undone via the version history feature. Each time a Page is saved with new changes, SharePoint creates a new version of the Page in the background and keeps track of what changes were made. When viewing a previous version, all changes are marked in red for easy identification. Staff can be automatically alerted to changes through e-mail alerts. Access to certain Pages, such as those that contain passwords and private user data, can be controlled by permission levels. Sensitive information can still be added to the Wiki with the knowledge that it can be securely locked down.

With the SharePoint Wiki, text can be written concisely when libraries utilize visual aids. Most training manuals regarding library procedures function as a quick-reference tool as well as a supplement to the training process. Therefore, by frequently inserting screenshots libraries can replace exhaustive body text and increase the usability of their manual. Libraries can take advantage of SharePoint's Photo Library feature to enhance the visual component of their Wiki manuals. The role of the Photo Library function as it relates to efficient Wiki updating and insertion of screenshots will be discussed in greater detail later in "Other SharePoint Libraries."

Discussion Board

The proliferation of interdepartmental communication tools has certainly been beneficial to efficiency among coworkers. However, these diverse channels create "leaks" in important information; two employees discuss a procedural issue over IM but do not think to transfer the communication in a group e-mail or blog post. SharePoint's Discussion Board allows for a complete record of valuable departmental interactions that do not occur in a vacuum. Discussions are consolidated in one location in a threaded message format and can be stored for as long as they are needed. At the University of Maryland University College Library, the Document Management Team "uses the discussion board to build consensus on issues that require group decision making. Team members can respond to discussions while working on other tasks at their desks, eliminating the need for time-consuming meetings" (Diffin et al., 2010: 233). Staff members are notified of new discussions and responses through e-mail alerts.

Calendar

Utilizing the Calendar feature on a library's remotely accessible SharePoint Site contributes to open lines of communication. Library staff can update their schedules on-the-fly to account for absences and sudden schedule shifts, which immediately informs relevant departments through the e-mail alerts feature. Another use for the Calendar is tracking "project milestones and deadlines along with the inevitable team meetings and other more social get-togethers that are scheduled during the period of the collaboration" (Harvey, 2009: 311). Depending on the versions of the software that are being used, the SharePoint Calendar can be integrated with Microsoft's Outlook e-mail software. In remote situations, updating the SharePoint Calendar is often easier than updating the Outlook calendar via the web client.

Announcements

An effective replacement for e-mail blasts, the Announcements feature ensures immediate mass notification to an entire team, while also automatically preserving the information in a location more authoritative and secure than an individual's e-mail inbox. For a project, Announcements provide a quick and easy way to alert team members of changes or updates, as well as a way to provide encouragement and support (Harvey, 2009). Staff can stay up-to-date on their department's happenings through various channels, including customizable e-mail alerts and RSS feeds.

Document Library

The issue of document storage is a common struggle within library departments. While emerging solutions have initially been promising (e.g., shared networked drives and local intranets), these stand-alone systems remain static and are thus not conducive to collaboration. While the SharePoint Document Library seems like simply a storehouse of pertinent files, the cloud environment in which these files are stored allow for unprecedented collaborative efficiency and flexibility. Users can upload documents directly in SharePoint or through the use of a mapped network drive. Documents can also be "checked out," which officially locks them until they are "checked in" again. Workflows can be created to set up routing for document review. Each document has a unique and permanent URL, which makes sharing and linking to the document very simple. Like the Wiki, it has version history and granular permission settings. This ensures secure data storage and access in the cloud while allowing and encouraging collaboration. With version history enabled, restoring a previous version is as easy as a few clicks of the mouse. And the granular permission settings allow management to lock down documents to only staff who should have access to read or edit a particular document. There is also a Recycle Bin where deleted documents can be recovered.

Similar to implementing a Wiki in SharePoint, the Document Library's use should be planned before moving any documents into it. A few things to consider are naming conventions, retention policy, and version history control. At the University of Maryland University College Library, the Document Management Team originally simply moved all of their documents from a shared network drive into the SharePoint Document Library. They quickly realized the Document Library

137

would become just as messy as the old shared network drive if they did not step back and plan a hierarchy and structure for the documents. Many documents ended up becoming Wiki Pages based on this planning and restructuring (Diffin, Chirombo, and Nangle, 2010). Without these strategies, even with its high-level functionality, a library's SharePoint Document Library could become as ineffective as the systems that came before it.

Other SharePoint Libraries (Photo, Audio, Video, Form, etc.)

There are several categories of SharePoint Libraries, each of which has a specialized purpose, yet also many features similar to the Document Library. One of these is the Photo/Picture Library, which functions similar to the Document Library but adds image-specific features and integration into other SharePoint Pages (Bates and Smith, 2010). The potential for providing a smooth screenshot process in the Wiki documentation adds another important level to the SharePoint feature. In the Photo Library, when the user updates or replaces an image in one location it is automatically updated on every Page in which it is located. The ability to batch upload images through a mapped network drive greatly simplifies uploading images into SharePoint.

These other SharePoint libraries also build on the Document Library by providing a centralized repository to store a particular type of file or data. Even the Wiki discussed earlier is essentially a collection of Pages stored in a Wiki Page Library. Files stored in these individual SharePoint libraries (i.e., images, video, audio) can be used in other SharePoint areas like Wikis and Blogs. An academic, public, or special library could store marketing material in a SharePoint library that is tailored to the specific function of the media in question. When it is time to use the material, staff members know where to find it and know it is the current version.

Task List

Task-tracking systems tend to vary greatly, from formalized task lists in Microsoft Outlook and Project to a carefully arranged physical stack of sticky notes. While these approaches are effective, and certainly prove to be acceptable methods of managing tasks, SharePoint's Tasks feature brings a team element to project management. Library organizations are beginning to embrace a "clan culture . . . [which] provide[s] a more supportive environment for innovation and risk-taking" (Kaarst-Brown et. al., 2004: 42). This particular culture survives by individuals regularly collaborating to get work done. With this emerging team approach, it is imperative that project deadlines and details be uniformly shared with the group.

Teams can use SharePoint Tasks to efficiently keep team members aware of project progress. If a team has a SharePoint group formed, individuals can post a Task that is assigned to the team in general, with all members receiving alerts to various Task creations and progress updates. Having the ability to assign Tasks to groups of individuals can allow team members to use the Tasks List as a kind of asynchronous brainstorming room for projects.

Blog

Similar to the Tasks feature, employing the Blog function in SharePoint has the potential to serve as an effective multi-team sounding board, while still maintaining the capability to speak to more granular sub-teams and committees. People can create individual Blogs that they can use to keep others informed on specific topics or the progress of projects. Team Blogs are a great way for team members to discuss projects and post project updates. A more general library Blog can also be created to allow staff throughout the organization to contribute and provide feedback on topics of discussion. Each Blog entry can be assigned a category that can help staff find discussions that are of interest to them. Permission levels can be set to allow entries and/or comments by specific people or groups. An approval process can also be implemented that would ensure content is reviewed before being posted.

Conclusion

Microsoft SharePoint is a powerful collaborative tool that is certainly difficult to encapsulate in one chapter. However, the intended outcome is not to equip the reader with a comprehensive skill set in the technical features of SharePoint. Instead, use the strategies described to get the innovative wheels spinning based on the context of your particular library's intranet needs. SharePoint's open-ended approach of providing several customizable options to the user can be overwhelming. However, take advantage of this customization to tailor features that will speak directly to your organizational workflow. Refer to the References cited to learn more about carrying out specific technical functions within Share-Point.

139

While these features and functions work effectively on their own, SharePoint's greatest and most long-lasting strength is when it is used as a comprehensive solution. Simply using SharePoint as a Wiki or a documentation platform may overwhelm and complicate matters for staff members, as they may see SharePoint as just another website or login they have to remember. Using every feature within SharePoint to create a complete intranet solution will exponentially increase its success within an organization. Even if buy-in is not evident (or even possible) in every library department, start small and allow these successes to influence wider adoption.

References

Bates, Seth, and Tony Smith. 2010. *SharePoint 2010 User's Guide: Learning Microsoft's Collaboration and Productivity Platform.* Berkeley: Apress. http://common .books24x7.com/book/id_35235/book.asp.

Diffin, Jennifer, Fanuel Chirombo, and Dennis Nangle. 2010. "Cloud Collaboration: Using Microsoft SharePoint as a Tool to Enhance Access Services." *Journal of Library Administration* 50, no. 5: 570–580. http://www.informaworld.com/10.1080/01930826.2010.488619.

Diffin, Jennifer, Fanuel Chirombo, Dennis Nangle, and Mark de Jong. 2010. "A Point to Share: Streamlining Access Services Workflow through Online Collaboration, Communication and Storage with Microsoft SharePoint." *Journal of Web Librarianship* 4, no. 2: 225–237. http://www.informaworld.com/10.1080/19322909.2010.501278.

Gilbert, Mark. 2010. *Making SharePoint Deliver* (webinar). Gartner. http://mfile.akamai.com/23543/wmv/citrixvar.download.akamai.com/23543/www/900/613/5585308717325900613/1-5585308717325900613-12ac8ced095.asx.

Harvey, Greg. 2009. *SharePoint 2007 Collaboration for Dummies.* Hoboken: Wiley. http://proquestcombo.safaribooksonline.com/9780470413425.

Jamison, Scott, Susan Hanley, and Mauro Cardarelli. 2011. *Essential SharePoint 2010: Overview, Governance, and Planning.* Upper Saddle River, NJ: Addison-Wesley. http://proquestcombo.safaribooksonline.com/9780321700827.

Kaarst-Brown, Michelle, Scott Nicholson, Gisela von Dran, and Jeffrey Stanton. 2004. "Organizational Cultures of Libraries as a Strategic Resource." *Library Trends* 53, no. 1: 33–53. http://hdl.handle.net/2142/1722.

McDonald, Kevin. 2010. *Above the Clouds: Managing Risk in the World of Cloud Computing.* Cambridgeshire: IT Governance Publishing. http://proquestcombo.safaribooksonline.com/9781849280310.

Sagi, Ishai. 2010. SharePoint 2010 How-To. Indianapolis: Sams. http://proquestcombo.safaribooksonline.com/9780132487481.

Salido, Javier, and Doug Cavit. 2010. *A Guide to Data Governance for Privacy, Confidentiality, and Compliance. Part 5: Moving to Cloud Computing.* Redmond, WA: Microsoft. http://go.microsoft.com/?linkid=9740995.

Part III

CASE STUDIES

Using Windows Home Server and Amazon S3 to Back Up High-Resolution Digital Objects to the Cloud

Edward Iglesias

Introduction

The idea of digital preservation is nothing new. What is new is the need for libraries to preserve digital objects for an indeterminate period of time. Systems backups were always required. These were focused, however, on restoring immediate access after something went wrong. Digital preservation must look at longer goals. According to William Dougherty (2009: 599-602) in "Preservation of Digital Assets: One Approach," "Britain's National Archive holds the equivalent of 580,000 encyclopedias of information in file formats that are no longer commercially available." Digital preservation is more than just bringing a system back up, it is planning for a time when the very technologies currently in use will be obsolete and some future user with unknown technology must try and retrieve that data. Many large libraries and institutions are working on these issues at a monumental level. Projects such as Portico (http://www.ithaka.org/portico) seek to archive massive collections of e-journals. For preserving individual digital objects there are commercial products such as OCLC's Digital Archive (http://www.oclc.org/digitalarchive/). Other libraries have built custom solutions, such as the Florida Digital Archive (Caplan, 2010). This works well if you have the technical expertise in house to create custom solutions, but for a library like ours, another way was needed. To do this we created a system that allows us to archive digital objects securely both locally and to the cloud. We also designed a way to make sure that those objects could be found and retrieved in the same condition in which they were deposited.

143

Background

The Burritt Library at Central Connecticut State University is part of a consortial system of five libraries encompassing the four Connecticut State Universities as well as the State Library. We have approximately 12,000 students and around another 1,000 faculty members actively using the library. In addition to traditional holdings the library has extensive Special Collections in Polish as well as digital materials pertinent to the state of Connecticut and especially the city of New Britain.

I became the Systems Librarian at Central Connecticut State University in 2005. At the time several competing solutions were used to serve digital objects to users, and all of the originals were stored in folders on a networked drive. There was no set schema for finding any of the original objects so that folder names were the only indicator. There was also no set method of performing checks on data integrity. Within the Connecticut State University system each library is independently responsible for any digital objects outside of the shared integrated library system and a collection of art images stored in the LUNA system. We also had an EPrints repository for storing all of our student theses. Part of the Systems Librarian's responsibility is to administer the servers as well as chart a path forward. To help accomplish both tasks unifying the disparate sources of data became a top priority.

As a first step we migrated as many of the digital objects as feasible, the LUNA art images which are shared with another library, into CONTENTdm. CONTENTdm is OCLC's proprietary solution for archiving and display of digital objects, which in Burritt's case includes high-resolution scans, video, and text. In the case of text such as student theses the entire document is uploaded to the CONTENTdm server and displayed in its native format, such as PDF. The other types of data stored pose different challenges. High-resolution scans of special collections documents start out as very large TIFF images that are then converted to JPEG or JPEG2000 images for the web. The question then became what to do with the very large original TIFFs that were not being loaded onto CONTENTdm. A similar situation occurred with our Veteran's History Project, which includes interviews averaging two hours with WWII veterans. CONTENTdm only holds the metadata and points to our streaming server.

Selection Process

As a result of all this valuable digital information leftover, we decided to pursue a policy of archiving the "digital originals." This did not necessarily mean an object had to have been "born digital," but it was usually a result of hard work on the part of library staff. As an example, a work might exist in special collections and be scanned at a high resolution. The original was undoubtedly the work scanned, but the TIFF also had intrinsic value. The cost of work done had to be factored as well as the fact that derivative works might be gathered from it, and, in the case of the displayed object, this was of a much lower quality. Because these items had value, several solutions were proposed.

The first solution considered was to do nothing. The university's IT department maintained a generous network share of 100 gigabytes (GB) of storage. When the possibility of storing up to 4 terabytes (TB) with room to grow came up, the library was quickly given a lesson in the economics of backup. Because of legal issues as a state institution, Central Connecticut State University has very extensive and expensive backup procedures. On average it costs our IT department $10,000 a TB for backup. The network share was infeasible.

The next solution considered was OCLC's Digital Archive product. This was a natural fit because there was a tie into CONTENTdm. Digital Archive also had everything the library wanted, including built-in systems management, physical security, data security, and disaster recovery. Furthermore, the library would not have to invest in staff training because the procedure is very simple. Unfortunately, Digital Archive is also very expensive. The library simply could not afford the costs when dealing with the volume of data being considered.

The solution the library settled on was entirely home grown, using off the shelf components as well as a combination of low-cost proprietary and open source software. This was not without some controversy. I have long been a proponent of open source solutions and had originally proposed the use of a Linux box with scripts to do everything. Fortunately, the archivist, who has a good computer background, made a compelling case to try out a solution that seemed at first glance completely inappropriate: Windows Home Server.

145

Our Solution

Windows Home Server

Windows Home Server is an operating system introduced by Microsoft in 2007 and, as the name implies, was targeted at home users with several computers. Because of its ease of use and reliability it has gained a great deal of popularity and has an active community of developers who create add-ins. The vendor from which we purchased the server, Hewlett Packard (HP), provides some very polished plug-ins that assist in backup operations as well as system monitoring. Because these units were designed for home use they do not need as much attention as a traditional server.

The choice of Windows Home Server as a solution made sense on several levels. The first was cost. The HP box and 2 TB disks in a RAID array could be set up much more cheaply than a comparable Linux box. While something along the lines of FreeNAS using an old computer might have sounded tempting from an economic point of view, the Windows Home Server box was actually cheaper in the long run. Another issue was software. Although there are open source solutions available, none of them was as polished and easy to implement in the library's

IT environment as the Windows solution. The drive was able to be mapped easily, and remote desktop allowed for easy access to the server even from a Mac environment. A full-fledged Windows Server was never considered because of the complexity of administration and costs involved.

Amazon S3

Available software was another factor as the decision was made to use Amazon's S3 cloud computing environment. This choice was made because of S3's price and scalability. Software was also abundant for uploading, scheduling, and syncing of data. Another factor working in Amazon's favor was that we had a history of doing business with the company. This is no small matter for a state institution that can use only approved vendors. Finally, all of the scripts needed to run other solutions involving data integrity, XML transformations, and fixity checks were easily available and inexpensive or free.

Implementation

Once hardware decisions were made, we started figuring out a workflow plan to actually implement the process. Fortunately, we had access to a small Windows Home Server to test everything out on. Additionally, the Systems Librarian created a MySQL database based on the requirements for tracking that were specified in the workflow plan. In addition to the database an HTML interface was constructed and several MySQL clients tried out before settling on a solution.

At this point it became necessary to write a formal policy to be approved by the director on how and what would be stored to the cloud, who would pay for it, and who would do it. The library formed a working group that considered all of the impacts and wrote up a policy document that spelled out the details. Of particular importance was the continued funding of this project because there would be ongoing expenses involved that were sure to increase with the proportional increase in data. Additionally, the workflow plan was added to so that everyone involved in the process would know what the procedures were for depositing an item. Finally, staffing issues were addressed and a long-term commitment of resources was secured.

The workflow, shown in Figure 13.1, was modeled on OCLC's Digital Archive product. A focus was placed on:

- Systems management
- Data security and integrity
- Data backups

Process

Systems management consists of policies and workflows that ensure the data being stored is always findable by staff and in good shape wherever it is. The workflow

146

Figure 13.1. Workflow of Items Entered into Digital Repository

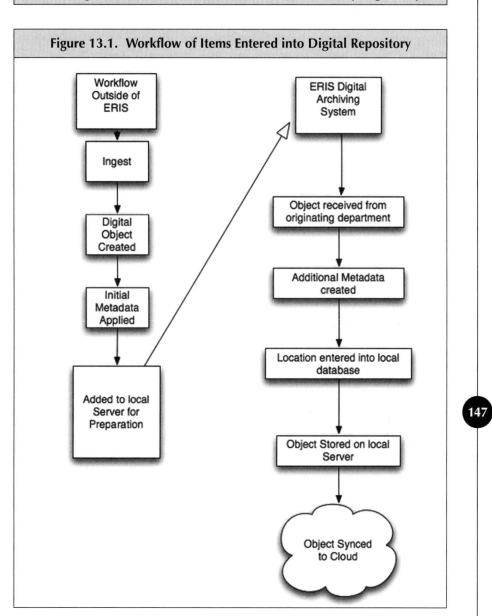

starts with a user placing an item or items on the server. This is usually a high-resolution TIFF. If it is only one or two items, then it is simply a matter of dragging the item to the mapped drive and placing it in the correct folder. This is an inbox folder that serves as a waiting area until the object can be processed by staff. If the items are large, consisting of more than 2 GB, then a removable hard drive is used to ease the strain on the network. The hard drive is then physically attached to the server and the items are transferred. Once the object is deposited on the server it is processed by staff. First a MySQL database is populated with data that shows when the item was deposited, who did the depositing, location, and checksum data.

To capture this data the Burritt Library uses the Library of Congress's BagIt system. BagIt is "a set of guidelines for creating and moving digital containers called bags" (http://www.digitalpreservation.gov/videos/BagIT0609.html). We use the free Library of Congress Transfer Tools available at http://sourceforge.net/projects/loc-xferutils/ to create "standardized digital containers," which include some sparse metadata and built-in inventory checking. This system works very well because anything digital can be placed in a bag and a manifest can be generated to ensure data integrity.

In addition to the checks run with BagIt the library uses JHOVE, the JSTOR/Harvard Object Validation Environment (http://hul.harvard.edu/jhove/), to ensure object level validation. While the BagIt format captures data at the level of bags the individual items in that bag are scanned with JHOVE, which provides information about the format of an object and its "well-formedness" and validity that ensures the data has not been corrupted. By employing a series of batch files, this process is more or less automated. JHOVE file format analysis is quickly and easily done at the command line. This becomes part of the Preservation Metadata or PREMIS. PREMIS is a data dictionary developed by the Library of Congress and "includes semantic units for Objects, Events, Agents, and Rights" (http://www.loc.gov/standards/premis/v2/premis-dd-2-0.pdf). This allows us to define the actual object in a consistent way and not just format details.

Several tools exist to facilitate the generation of PREMIS data of which the library has chosen the excellent Archivists' Toolkit (http://www.archivist-stoolkit.org/). The output is a series of XML metadata documents included with the original objects that look something like this output file from JHOVE:

```xml
<?xml version="1.0" encoding="UTF-8"?>
<jhove xmlns:xsi="http://www.w3.org/2001/XMLSchema-instance"
xmlns="http://hul.harvard.edu/ois/xml/ns/jhove"
xsi:schemaLocation="http://hul.harvard.edu/ois/xml/ns/jhove
http://hul.harvard.edu/ois/xml/xsd/jhove/1.6/jhove.xsd"
  name="Jhove"
release="1.5" date="2009-12-19">
 <date>2010-02-24T16:13:13-05:00</date>
 <repInfo uri="C:\test\acpcc_35\bag-info.txt">
  <reportingModule release="1.3" date="2006-09-05">ASCII-
hul</reportingModule>
  <lastModified>2010-02-24T16:09:29-05:00</lastModified>
  <size>70</size>
  <format>ASCII</format>
  <status>Well-Formed and valid</status>
  <mimeType>text/plain; charset=US-ASCII</mimeType>
  <properties>
   <property>
    <name>ASCIIMetadata</name>
```

```
<values arity="List" type="Property">
<property>
 <name>LineEndings</name>
 <values arity="List" type="String">
  <value>CRLF</value>
 </values>
</property>
</values>
</property>
</properties>
<checksums>
 <checksum type="CRC32">19e7b527</checksum>
 <checksum type="MD5">02a7a1486a74dbb1cb9c68befeb13a5f
  </checksum>
 <checksum type="SHA-1">bd5707f0c74bb8b1c383930c41a9e7c27ed
  6f600</checksum>
</checksums>
```

A great deal of data can be gleaned from this file, including checksums for checking data integrity, format information, and dates modified. All of this helps ensure data integrity when depositing digital objects to the cloud. There are constant updates to these features as cloud-based storage vendors realize the need for greater precision in long-term data storage to protect against data degradation and errors in transmission.

After all of the metadata is applied and the object has been tracked it is placed on the Windows Home Server in a RAID array and then copied to the S3 cloud as part of a regularly scheduled job at 3:00 in the morning when the network has the least traffic. This schedule was worked out with our IT department for maximum efficiency. Strong communication with IT is vital. Although the storage is outsourced IT is still the network provider, and every effort should be made to make sure library operations do not affect the overall network adversely.

Assessment and Evaluation

Assessment is a vital part of any project, and so far it seems to have succeeded on several levels. The users, who include special collections librarians, catalogers, and archivists, seem pleased with the results. There was little additional training involved because the Electronic Resources & Information Systems Department (ERIS) took care of all the metadata creation.

The only real loss we have incurred while using this system was that one of our 1-TB removable drives that we use for transfer failed. This was a mechanical issue out of our control, but the lesson learned was to quickly move the data to a more secure medium. Fortunately, Amazon's S3 has proven very stable, with no downtime in the year the library has been using it.

Cost comparisons are another factor that continue to be considered. The library chose to model its backup scheme on OCLC's Archive product. We were

149

Table 13.1. Comparison of Costs for OCLC versus Amazon S3 for 5 TB

	OCLC	Amazon S3	NOTES
Set up	$3,000	$0*	*Does not include staff hours on design/setup
Ingest	$2,400	$0	
Annual storage*	$26,850	$8,610	*Assuming 5 TB
Monthly fee	$0	$716	
Interface	Provided by vendor	We would design	
Hardware costs	$0	$1,350	HP Windows Home Server: $600; five 2-TB drives: $750 ($150 x 5)
Internal staff requirements	None extra	$800	Use current staff, four days/year: $800 ($200/day)
Total costs	$32,250	$9,362	

150

able to duplicate most of the features at a fraction of the cost. The estimated cost for 5 TB of storage with OCLC was $32,250 at the time of this writing. With all library expenses included, such as staff time and hardware, the total cost for S3 was calculated at $9,362. The majority of that is the recurring annual cost for 5 TB of $8,610. If your library needs less space the cost would also be less. Table 13.1 shows a breakdown of the costs. The deciding factor for our library was the yearly storage fee of $26,850.

Conclusion and Future Direction

In the future, the Veteran's History Project may want us to take over their long-term storage. This is a much more complex task as there are many terabytes of data involved. Additionally, not all of their interviews have been digitized. Some exist as videotape in a variety of formats. Of the interviews that have been digitized the original high-resolution transcriptions were lost due to equipment failure. Furthermore, the digitized copies that we stream are highly compressed derivatives. In other words, we would have to start from scratch.

In terms of reliability and cost this solution has proven very acceptable to us. We are able to leverage our dollars more efficiently and just as importantly utilize the abilities of our staff. By developing a solution in house we are able to fix anything that breaks and are not tied to vendor contracts. Similarly the cloud computing solution from Amazon has worked marvelously and will likely continue to be used in the future. This is also a highly transferable solution, as the costs in terms of physical and human resources are remarkably low. As libraries struggle with budget shortfalls this kind of approach works well in an environment where the option to "buy it" is too expensive and the option to "build it" is limited by a lack of technical staff. With just one or two individuals and a modest commitment of resources, any library can save its precious objects in the cloud.

References

Caplan, Priscilla. 2010. "The Florida Digital Archive and DAITSS: A Model for Digital Preservation." *Library Hi Tech* 28, no. 2: 224–234.

Dougherty, William C. 2009. "MANAGING TECHNOLOGY Preservation of Digital Assets: One Approach." *Journal of Academic Librarianship* 35, no. 6: 599–602. *Library, Information Science & Technology Abstracts,* EBSCOhost.

Chapter 14

Keeping Your Data on the Ground When Putting Your (Lib)Guides in the Cloud

Karen A. Reiman-Sendi, Kenneth J. Varnum, and Albert A. Bertram

Introduction

The University of Michigan Library moved its research guides content into Springshare's LibGuides product in 2009. At the same time that the library was taking advantage of the benefits of the LibGuides software for authoring and managing the content of the library's research guides, there was a concern over losing the ability to access, index, and manipulate the information contained in the guides. Through Springshare's XML output process guide content was included in the library website's search and browse functions and made available to other parts of the site. Even though the library's research guides are hosted remotely, users have access to the content (through keyword searches, tags, and subject associations) in other parts of our library website. In this chapter, we discuss our decision to move to the cloud, what we gained and lost, and how we used existing tools to maintain a high degree of findability in our local website for the cloud content.

Background

The University of Michigan Library is one of the largest university library systems in the United States. The Ann Arbor campus library system holds more than 8.5 million volumes, employs over 500 talented staff, and serves 42,000 students in 19 schools and colleges.

From the mid-1990s through the late 2000s, websites for the University of Michigan Library's constituent libraries, services, and departments were locally managed. Each unit's site evolved independently from the main library site. To resolve the resulting confusion of interfaces, library administration launched a website redesign project in 2008, the goal of which was to remove location-based content or organizational silos and to present library information as well as web interactions into a single unified library identity while providing commonality to the website user experience. During this website redesign project, the librarians identified a unique category of content that would benefit from a single, user-friendly presentation: research guides.

Two questions about this content immediately surfaced:

1. Given the large, distributed staff, what tool or set of tools could we use to manage our subject and research guides (which included research guides to academic disciplines, guides developed to assist students enrolled in specific courses, and tutorials on specific software tools and library databases)? We use the terms "subject," "course," and "technology" guides to describe these three content types in this case study.

2. If hosted on an external vendor server, how could we connect the valuable guide content created by experts to our now centralized library website for users to discover?

This case study explores the decision process that led to our cloud-based solution.

Selection Process

Prior to the library website redesign project, we presented guide-like information across many library webpages in many different ways, including a custom-built PHP application. ResearchGuide, a tool developed at the University of Michigan Library in the mid-1990s and released as open source software (http://researchguide.sourceforge.net/) for later adoption by other libraries, accounted for some of the library's research guide content. Many library websites reflected the use of stand-alone HTML pages created by librarians; however, some guide content was stored on personal web space and not on the library web server.

Our main objective in this project was to select a tool that would simplify the authoring and user interfaces while at the same time preserving findability to the guide content throughout the library website. Any guide tool selected would need to integrate into our Solr-powered search function as well as into our academically focused and locally developed browse taxonomy, for the purpose of allowing this unique content discoverable through the website search and browse functions.

As we explored the landscape of options available, we quickly discounted the homegrown PHP application because it was not sufficiently powerful or flexible to meet the evolving needs of our content and could not handle Web 2.0-like features, such as integrating RSS feeds or embedding video clips. Its administrative and authoring interface was cumbersome for library staff to use, and the user display was simplistic and inflexible. We investigated existing modules in Drupal but did not find one that provided the necessary flexibility. Wishing to avoid a custom-built Drupal module, or spending the time and resources revamping existing applications, we looked for third-party solutions.

In 2008, there was only one viable commercial product on the market. Springshare's LibGuides product (http://www.springshare.com/libguides) offered a simple authoring environment, enabled sharing of individual content elements among guides within the LibGuides system, allowed some customization of the interface, and had an XML output format. This XML output feature was initially offered as the safety net for libraries, that is, a way for a library to get its data back at some future date if the library migrated away from Springshare's product or Springshare stopped offering it. We saw this as an opportunity to take advantage of the cloud to manage the guide content while still having access to our data for local integration and manipulation. In response to a request to enable frequent XML output (a feature that was not in the company's short-term plan), Springshare modified and developed a mechanism to allow for XML output of a library's guides on a weekly basis. When needed, the output can be manually refreshed on demand through a web interface. Here, as in other areas, Springshare's technical support group has proven responsive to our needs, confirming the experience other Springshare customers shared with us when we were exploring commercial options for our research guide content.

Implementation

At the time of our site redesign, we also dramatically expanded our locally developed subject taxonomy, used in many library-related tools. This expansion meant that few guides' content was directly relevant; most of the guides needed revision, and many subject guides had to be created to fit the new subject taxonomy. Thus, there was no automatic migration path from the existing tools and webpages into LibGuides; content migration was almost entirely manual and necessitated library staff moving or re-creating content in the new tool.

As we developed our Drupal website, we identified areas in which we wanted research guide content to appear. In particular, we wanted guide content to be featured in search and browse results and on guide authors' profile pages. Through the XML output described earlier, this was now easily achievable.

The metadata associated with Springshare's LibGuides is sparse; there is author information, a list of tags, and then the full text of the research guide. The LibGuides XML output itself is generally unremarkable: The XML is structured as a representation of the underlying relational database tables. Every week, Springshare generates the XML as a compressed text file that we download locally and ingest into our Solr index.

The interesting part is what we do with the XML output. In addition to normal tagging use, some special tags carry metadata managed within LibGuides but not expressed in the native LibGuides interface. For example, extra topic categories associated with a guide (only one is displayed in LibGuides),and our guide classi-fication (research guide, technology guide, or course guide) are available through the XML file but not through the web interface. We index the guide content along with information regarding special tags in our website's Solr index (see Figure 14.1 for a schematic of the data flows between LibGuides and our website).

Once the data is in our Solr index we can query and manipulate it to integrate within our Drupal website. The first and most prominent place we integrated con-tent stored in LibGuides is our search interface. When users search the library website through the search box in the site's standard navigation, the results are divided into categories based on what kind of resource was returned. Thus data-bases are shown separately from electronic journals or guides, and all of our resources can be searched from a single starting point.

The second way we integrate guide content from LibGuides is through the library website's browse function. Using our locally developed subject taxon-omy, the browse function allows a user to select a topic from a list to view all of our resources organized by broad category. Our guide content is findable through the website browse function thanks to the special tags we included on the guides.

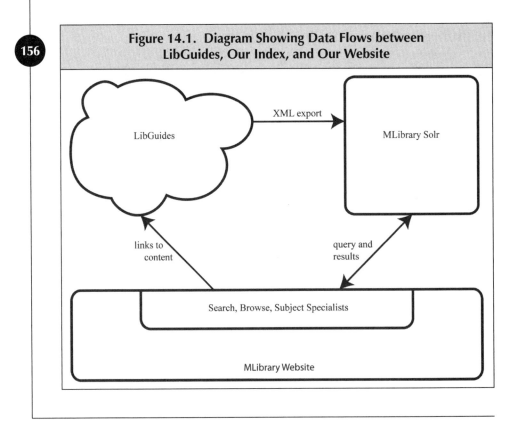

Figure 14.1. Diagram Showing Data Flows between LibGuides, Our Index, and Our Website

The final way we integrate guide content into the library website is in the subject specialist profiles. Each profile displays a dynamically generated list of each guide authored by that subject specialist.

Although we feel we made significant gains in the user interface by moving our guide content to the cloud, there were some minor losses along the way. As with any remotely hosted tool, the data owners lose some control over user interface and functionality of the application itself. This is not a criticism of this specific tool or vendor; it is part of the basic tradeoff of moving content and functionality off-site.

Of course, there are problems with the data ingestion from time to time. As mentioned previously, the XML output is a weekly process, which means that when a librarian edits, adds, or deletes a guide, the changed content is not reflected in the library website's search and browse results until the following week. We can manually download and process a fresh XML file whenever we wish, but the automated process is available to us, according to our current agreement, only on a weekly basis.

Assessment and Evaluation

As outlined in the previous section, our use of LibGuides to host and manage our subject-, course-, and technology-related guides while continuing to provide access through the library website has been successful. Library staff find the tool easy to use and have created almost 400 publicly available guides to library research in specific academic subjects, to library resources of particular use to students in specific courses, and to specific software packages or library databases. Through use of LibGuides tags—author-assigned keywords that conform to our local taxonomy—and the XML output, we have been able to provide links to guides in strategic places on the library site (in browse results, for example). Through the XML data we receive, links to relevant guides appear in search results.

From the user perspective, the tool has been similarly successful. The library's usability group conducted research on the guides in the summer and fall of 2009. (The full reports are online at http://www.lib.umich.edu/usability-library/usability-library-libguides-reports.) Changes based on our investigations have already been put into place.

For example, users were not at all disturbed by the change in interface between the library's website and Springshare's LibGuides sites. They appreciated discovering guides through both search and browse. However, in the original design of the site, guides were presented in search results as a list of titles with no descriptive or sample text. Users found this confusing, as they did not know what to expect. Because each guide's summary text is included in the XML output from LibGuides, we were able to incorporate the first 115 characters of each, in keeping with our standard "snippet" view of other items in site results lists. Guide authors have had to reword their descriptions, as a large number of the summaries began with phrases like "This guide lists the most important starting points for research in the area of Economics." This type of phrasing left the searcher with little context in which to understand the guide's presumed content.

Similarly, we also incorporated controlled vocabulary tags into the LibGuides tags, asking guide authors to use one of several set phrases to describe the kind of guide ("Course Guide," "Subject Guide," or "Technology Guide") so that we could label the results accordingly. By setting up rules and standards for guide authors, we have been able to enhance the findability of LibGuides content in our site through the search and browse results.

Conclusion

In terms of overall satisfaction with our hybrid of remote hosting of content and local discovery, we are very pleased with the result. We met our goal to integrate research guide content into our Drupal website without having to make a substantial investment of time or resources in developing or customizing a tool of our own. The user gets the advantage of LibGuides' ease of use and our website's focus on discoverability.

There are benefits of scale, as well. More customers using the same tool means that when a few customers request a feature that is subsequently developed, it immediately benefits all. A case in point is the ingestion of LibGuides content in Serials Solutions' Summon product announced in late October 2010. While our library had not requested this, we will be able to benefit from having our LibGuides content available through our Summon implementation. Going forward, we plan to expand the integration of the guides content into course-, department-, and discipline-specific pages, as well as to integrate LibGuides content into the University of Michigan's Sakai-powered course management system.

Chapter 15

Parting the Clouds: Use of Dropbox by Embedded Librarians

Caitlin A. Bagley

Introduction

This chapter highlights one file-sharing program in particular, Dropbox. The program has generated a great deal of buzz by users, and, while it certainly seems to be well liked by many single-source users, the question remains as to whether or not it is well poised to be used within the context of libraries. The following case study will show how the librarians and staff at Murray State University library used the service and will seek to offer input for libraries considering adopting the service. This chapter will give an overview of the service and how the embedded librarians within our library used it, as well as highlight other options we might have taken on in the cloud computing world.

Background

Murray State University is a midsize university with over 10,000 FTE students in Western Kentucky. The University Libraries see on average 3,500 students pass through the doors of the main library and use services every day. Because the library serves over a third of the entire student population daily, there is a tremendous strain on resources. We have two computer labs consisting of 74 computers total and a collection size of over 700,000 print materials. While it could easily be said that many of the students who use the library each day are using it as a central location to study, check e-mail, and grab a quick soda, this influx of students helps to determine how library materials are managed and allotted. The library Reference Department has watched as their traditional roles have changed, with focus shifting from providing in-depth research on a wide variety of topics to simply acting as the focal point of the library where they often become the go-to department for everything from research to help when a printer is faulty. Embedded librarians as part of the Reference Department have struggled to find the best ways

159

to balance their dual roles as frontline faces of the library and as teachers. Primarily, each department within our library system communicates to the others through the library listserv or shares files through the R-Drive, our local shared network drive. Although initially librarians were intrigued by the uses of Dropbox, few saw the benefits to using Dropbox over the R-Drive.

Selection Process

Overview of Dropbox

As of this writing, Dropbox can still be considered a relatively new program. Created in 2007 by Drew Houston, it has quickly grown to make a significant name for itself in the cloud computing market as a software as a service (SaaS) provider. SaaS is software that is typically provided on demand, within the cloud, and payment is typically open source or pay as you go. The way the program works is simple: users download a program onto any computer or device they want linked into the Dropbox system. For most people this link will be to their home and work computers, though others have chosen to link their smartphones to Dropbox as well. This program creates a Dropbox file folder on the computer that updates across all linked computers and devices. If a file is added to a Dropbox folder on a personal computer, the same file will then be added to the Dropbox folder on that employee's work computer as well. This creates local copies of each file in every location that we have specified to be synced with Dropbox. The concept of Dropbox holds up nicely with the LOCKSS (Lots of Copies Keep Stuff Safe) theory of library science because we end up with as many copies as computers that are regularly used to link to a particular Dropbox account or folder.

There are two different types of Dropbox accounts: users can create a free account giving them access to 2 GB of data, or they can pay for one of two tiered levels of data storage. For $9.99 a month, users can get up to 50 GB of data stored on a Dropbox node, and for $19.99 users can receive access to up to 100 GB of stored data. Although it is not an invite-only service, similar to many Google applications in their Beta stage, Dropbox does reward its users who bring new users to the site. Free users of the website have the potential to receive up to 8 GB of data storage if they refer enough friends to the service.

Dropbox's web interface is very clean and minimalist. Files and folders are listed out in easy formats similar to most Microsoft operating systems. There are a handful of tabs at the top row that help you navigate, but these are few and easy to understand. Users log in to the site with their e-mail and password, and then the first thing they are greeted by is their files. There is no need to make several clicks and wade through pages to get to the proper files.

Changes to the system can easily be tracked through the "Events" tab on the web interface of the site. Here is where the user can see what has been added and edited along with the day. There is a structural difference to this within the two versions of paid and unpaid accounts. Free accounts can only see changes made to the system within the past 30 days. Anything stored before 30 days cannot be accessed. However, paid subscribers at any tier level have access to all edits and changes in files through their system, Pack-Rat. This is viewable only through the web interface. If users upgrade to a paid account from a free account, they do not gain automatic access to their previous edits. Rather, users only get edits in the past 30 days and onward. It is not a retroactive program, and so it takes effect only from the moment you upgrade to a Pro account rather than from the beginning of your use of Dropbox. Having access to edits made to documents and the system is a great advantage, as it allows you to see older versions of documents as well as to (sometimes) see who made those edits.

Public versus Locked Dropbox Folders

Privacy is a major concern for libraries considering using the program. Librarians should consider the many potential outcomes with hosting internal documents on an external website not affiliated with their institution. Murray State's librarians wanted to ensure that they could limit who had access to certain documents. Every Dropbox account has a default Public Folder along with the private folders users create for themselves. When the user chooses to upload a file to this Public Folder, a permanent URL is created to that file so that the URL can be shared and seen by anyone in the world, not just Dropbox users. In this way a librarian can swiftly link to presentations and guides without having to pass out physical copies, and it give students a quick path to reference materials. However, unless the password to the Dropbox account is given out, then only the user has access to other locked files not kept within the Public Folder.

161

One thing that users should be aware of is that once something has been put into a public folder it can be difficult to unlink the file from the public view. Materials in this folder should only be things that the user wants available to the general public. Items can be deleted from the Public Folder, but they can also be easily restored through several means. If users try to follow a link to a former resource that has been deleted, they will be redirected to a standard 404 error page, but if the owner of the account tries to follow a link to a former resource he will be given the option to restore that link. Although we did not encounter any problems with deleted items, it seems that it could become a major security issue depending on how many people had access to the account.

Similar to the Public and Locked Folders are Shared Folders options. By far this option was used the most while working with the other librarians at Murray State, as well as with colleagues who were not associated with the institution. The librarians were able to specify for specific folders which ones they wanted to be shared and with whom. Some folders were shared with many people, and others were shared only by a few.

Other Options (drop.io)

Besides Dropbox there are several other cloud computing sources that libraries should take into consideration when deciding whether or not to take the leap. Murray State University has embraced many of the Google applications like Google Calendar, Documents, and Mail, among others. These are all options that many libraries are aware of, but another nascent technology that offers many of the same features of Dropbox that librarians may be unfamiliar with is drop.io. Created around roughly the same time as Dropbox in 2007, drop.io is an elegant and simple solution for file sharing and real-time collaboration. Users create "drops" or stable URLs where they can upload up to 100 MB of data for free. After that there are tiered levels of paid data storage. At $19 a month, subscribers can get the basic plan for 10 GB, and for $49 a month there is the professional plan for 30 GB. In terms of price to space available, it seems like Dropbox has the advantage on drop.io at the moment.

However, some of the advantages of drop.io are that it is more than simple data storage. It also offers a host of multimedia and Web 2.0 tools that have been deployed in an interesting manner. Every drop created is assigned an automatic e-mail address for the administrator to use as well as giving the administrator the potential to create voicemail and conference calling associated with the drop. There is a chat feature that is so carefully embedded that it is almost invisible to visitors on their first use, but, upon discovery, many users have enjoyed the capability to discuss topics right there on the site. Anyone can add files to the drop, but administrators still retain the right to delete any file they feel is inappropriate or not relevant. The sharing features associated with each drop have been quite well thought out. Whereas many websites and social networks will attempt to throw all possibilities at the user, drop.io gives a limited set of ten options for users to decide how they will disseminate the information. Of the ten options, there seems to be only a glancing nod toward the major players in social networking such as Facebook, Twitter, and Ping.fm. This seems to work exceedingly well without weighing down the interface with needless options the user will most likely not end up using.

Compared to Dropbox, drop.io has a multitude of customizable features under its settings. Some of these are excellent features to create standardized pages that would be consistent with the style and tone of your library or university. As there are many customizable options, it might seem as though it would be overwhelming for the new user to learn how to navigate the system. However, most options have been fairly streamlined so that users know what they are doing and can easily reverse changes. One pitfall is that there are multiple passwords for different components of the system.

Implementation

Embedded librarians seemed perfectly poised to use Dropbox. At Murray State University there are currently six embedded librarians, each frequently traveling to satellite campuses, and half of the embedded librarians maintain offices in their subject-specific department on campus. The embedded librarians travel a great deal, but they still need to access common files across all accounts, so Dropbox seemed like a natural fit. Although many of the librarians have the option to carry a laptop with them to their alternate offices and to the classrooms when they teach, Dropbox has provided another way to readily access their information when they are outside the typical library environment. The embedded librarians have used Dropbox most when they are off campus at conferences or preparing classes at home. It spares them the extra step of having to log in to the university VPN, as all they have to do with Dropbox is ensure that files have recently been updated in their Dropbox folder, and then they can access the same file that is stored on their work computer. Typically, when embedded librarians are teaching a class outside of the library, they will simply log on to the web interface of Dropbox and then download the lessons or presentations that they have already prepared and loaded onto the Dropbox server earlier. It quickly downloads, and their presentation is ready to teach in seconds.

At Murray State we opted for the free version of Dropbox, so the amount of stored data available to librarians and staff was comparable to that of a personal USB drive. One unexpected debate sprang from whether every librarian should have his or her own personal Dropbox account or whether there should just be a general Murray State account set up. If librarians were to create personal accounts they would have more space set up for just their work, but if a general account was set up for the entire department then everyone would have equal access to everyone's shared documents without the trouble of setting up unique sharing settings for every individual account. Eventually it was decided by the head of Reference that a general account would be set up with departmental folders. Then individual librarians created their own accounts that they used to get shared access to those folders.

Assessment and Evaluation

Ideally, before any library begins to use any form of cloud computing service it should consider the privacy concerns and protections that have been put in place by the system it is considering using, as well as any privacy policies it may already have in place. Dropbox has issued a privacy policy (https://www.dropbox.com/terms#privacy) that primarily addresses concerns about collecting personal information and how it is used. However, it gives only a very brief and cursory nod toward security of information without disclosing its methods. All data is password protected and encrypted, and supposedly only users with passwords can access their own data. Other concerns that libraries should be aware of are the reliability and availability of the data they have stored on Dropbox. Many coworkers at Murray State who were collaborating on shared projects found the Shared Folder option to be the most useful feature. Some pitfalls were that there were no notifications when edits or changes had been made to a document. Although those edits and changes would be noticed through the "Events" tab or by opening up the document itself, it was not something that was immediately apparent.

Overall the librarians were very pleased with the service and have continued to use it for several other small projects; however, the only major hurdle we seemed to encounter with Dropbox was that we already had an internal server that most librarians were used to using. The service became truly useful only when the embedded librarians were outside of the library teaching in other classrooms. Lesson plans and assignments were then easily accessed through the service. It is definitely a service that libraries should consider adopting into their own programs, as it adapts easily to the many needs of data storage that a library might have. The service would be recommended to anyone considering entering the cloud, as it offers a wide range of possibilities for temporary data storage that seem very well suited for the small or medium-sized library. As a personal service, it would be definitely recommended that individual librarians take advantage of this service if they have a need to access files in multiple locations. This is a highly accessible service that is ideal for the many different ways that libraries and librarians work.

Conclusion

Cloud computing seems to have many unique advantages over local servers and offers new methods of access to information for both students and librarians. As many people have already addressed, cloud computing has some very serious legal and security questions that may be off-putting to libraries before they attempt to store what can be massive amounts of data online. Although there are public options to Dropbox, it seemed that primarily when our librarians were using the service it became almost an internal application that many used to share files from coworker to coworker(s). Rarely were public documents kept on the service, and so we had very few privacy concerns to worry about.

If our library were to continue heavily using this service, we would probably opt for one of the paid versions of Dropbox, simply because 2 GB of space gets taken up quickly when you have multiple people using the service for varied projects. Probably the hardest part of using it was just in learning to break out of our old habits and remembering that we had the option to use it. There was a very minimal learning curve to using the site, and it continues to be used by many of the embedded librarians, who see it as an effective tool for organization across locations.

Chapter 16

From the Cloud, a Clear Solution: How One Academic Library Uses Google Calendar

Anne Leonard

Introduction

The instruction librarians of the Ursula C. Schwerin Library at New York City College of Technology were faced with an enviable problem: a vigorous and growing instruction program, a small core of instruction regulars, and one 30-seat e-classroom, the scheduling for which required great promptness and accuracy. A transparent way of creating a schedule for the library's electronic classroom, the room in which most library instruction occurs, was needed. At first librarians moved from a longhand, paper-based, and Excel-dependent schedule to the calendar feature of the college's e-mail system, GroupWise. When GroupWise mysteriously and spontaneously deleted dozens of scheduled classes from all library faculty members' calendars, and campus information technology services could neither recover the data nor help us learn how to prevent this problem from recurring, other online shared calendar tools were investigated. Some librarians were already using Google Docs and Gmail, so Google Calendar, a browser-based application available to any Google account holder or Gmail user, was easily within reach. Google Calendar proved to be a useful tool for e-classroom scheduling, and now the library's faculty and staff depend on ten different Google Calendars to communicate about classes, meetings, annual leave, and the reference desk schedule.

Background

The Ursula C. Schwerin Library serves the students, faculty, and staff of New York City College of Technology (City Tech), the largest public baccalaureate college of technology in the Northeast. Enrollment in fall 2009 surpassed 15,000 full-time and part-time students, according to the City University of New York's Office of Institutional Research and Assessment (CUNY OIRA, 2009). According to the *U.S. News & World Report's* 2011 college rankings, City Tech is the second most diverse regional college in the North (*U.S. News & World Report,* 2010). City Tech is a college in the CUNY system, which consists of 25 colleges throughout the five boroughs of New York City and enrolls nearly 260,000 degree-seeking undergraduate and graduate students. Since 2008, the library instruction regulars at City Tech have grown from a group of three instruction and reference librarians to a group of five librarians. Two new positions to support library instruction and information literacy were created and filled: a Coordinator of Information Literacy and an Instructional Design Librarian. As the instruction regulars, we take responsibility for planning, scheduling, and delivering the bulk of the library instruction program; our department chair determines how many classes each instruction regular should be assigned, with consideration given to tenure status and other responsibilities.

At City Tech, every student is required to pass English Composition I, and each section of that course visits the library for one library research lesson. In addition to teaching library research lessons for all sections of English Composition I, librarians coordinate other requests for library instruction, passing them along to librarian subject specialists as appropriate. All City Tech librarians are responsible for library information literacy instruction for the departments for which they are subject specialists. We also guide technology implementation in the electronic classroom and recommend software and hardware upgrades for purchase when we are fortunate enough to have a budget to do so.

The library's instruction program was growing quickly and demands on our teaching facility—one smart classroom equipped with 30 student computers, two projectors, and an instructor computer—were growing. Not only were there increasing numbers of English Composition I sections as college enrollment grew, there was increased interest in library instruction from departments all over campus, especially Speech, Nursing, Health Services Management, and Hospitality Management. Library faculty also formed a workshop group to plan and deliver workshops to students and faculty. The Information Literacy Librarian, supported by the department's curriculum committee, developed a credit-bearing course that can be taken to satisfy a core course requirement in the area of communications for two-year and four-year degree curricula. With multiple departments demanding library instruction, and the library itself expanding its instructional offerings, there was a great need for simple, quick, and transparent e-classroom scheduling that all librarians could easily access and update.

Selection Process

Before we switched to an online shared calendar tool, the instruction regulars (first three, then four, and now five librarians) had established a procedure for scheduling library instruction. Each semester, the most senior instruction librarian obtained the English department's schedule of classes and used a paper calendar template to write out a schedule in longhand. The handwritten calendar (Figure 16.1) was submitted to the department's Administration Office Assistant, who transcribed the

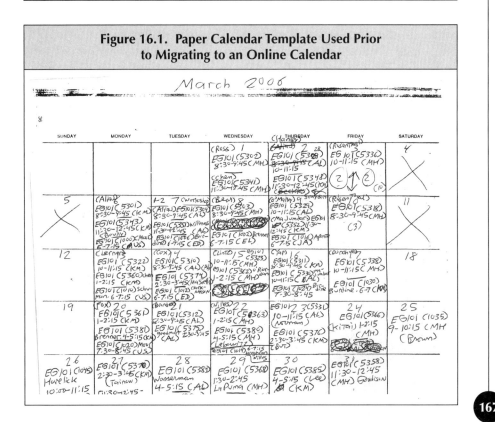

Figure 16.1. Paper Calendar Template Used Prior to Migrating to an Online Calendar

handwritten schedule into Excel. The Excel document was printed and distributed to all librarians with instruction duties, who would take a few days to check their teaching schedules against their existing calendars, reference desk schedules, and other department and college commitments. On approval of library faculty, the document was shared with the English department. Each time changes were made to the library instruction schedule, the Excel document had to be corrected and redistributed. All of the instruction regulars, however, needed to be able to update the e-classroom schedule and to communicate changes quickly to all librarians.

GroupWise

When librarians began to look to an online solution, they used the calendar event feature in GroupWise, the college-wide e-mail client. The ability to manage changes rather than working through one very busy staff member meant that schedule updates and changes were made quickly and with very little effort. With help from the college IT support, we created a new user account in GroupWise, LibraryClassroom, to which the instruction regulars had access. The Posted Appointments feature was used to create appointments on LibraryClassroom's calendar for library instruction sessions held in the e-classroom. If a GroupWise user edited or deleted an appointment that appeared on his or her own calendar and had originated from the LibraryClassroom account, it changed that appointment for everyone with permission to view the appointment. The college's limits on the amount of data stored in GroupWise means that about every six months, old calendar events and e-mails are deleted unless manually archived, one by one.

Google Calendar

Although troubled by the mysterious failure of GroupWise, we were reluctant to return to a print calendar. A few librarians already made use of other Google applications, including Gmail and Google Docs, for personal and professional communications and productivity. Because use of Google Calendar requires only a browser and an Internet connection, and does not require investment in software or storage media, moving the library instruction schedule to Google Calendar was an easily implemented solution to an urgent problem. The transition from GroupWise to Google Calendar went quickly; because we had kept careful records on paper, and had retained the class schedule from the English department, we were able to reconstruct all e-classroom events within a few days. We kept a GroupWise backup for a short time.

The introduction of Google Calendar bolstered a shift in attitudes about scheduling. As the transition from paper to Excel to web-based calendar tool has transformed the way we operate daily, how we conceptualize the task of scheduling has changed. Now the Google Calendar is the living document, and the spreadsheet generated at the end of each semester is the record, whereas before Google Calendar, the spreadsheet had to be both the living document and the record. Google applications, including the calendar, are imbued with "cloudiness"; they are meant to be transparent and accessible tools to facilitate sharing. GroupWise is more of a personal application with little to give a sense of a shared space for communication or documentation. When switching tools, we underwent a collective shift in attitude about ownership, privacy, and empowerment.

Implementation

When we first began to use Google Calendar, one librarian created a calendar using her own personal Google account and shared it with the other instruction regulars. It soon became clear that we would benefit from being able to view the reference desk schedule, colleagues' on- and off-campus meetings and appointments, and the annual leave calendar simultaneously. At that time, library administration created a Google account called "citytechlibrary." Only the department chair, the administrative services librarian, and the administrative assistant have access to edit calendars created by this account: Library Faculty Annual Leave, College Cultural Events, College Office Assistant Absences, and Public calendars (the Public calendar was developed to embed into our website or blog and promote library events).

All library faculty and the department's systems administrator have rights to create and edit all other calendars: College Meetings, Department Meetings, Professional Meetings, Reference Desk, Small Library Classroom, and E-Classroom.

The learning curve was steep at first. Librarians and library staff who did not already have Google accounts had to create them; there is no way to view a Google Calendar that is not made public without logging into Google accounts. Instruction regulars offered one-on-one training to all library staff and faculty on the creation and maintenance of calendar events. A protocol for entering data for library classes was quickly established; a consistent pattern greatly enhanced the search functionality. Now any librarian can view instruction responsibilities, reference desk shifts, or scheduled meetings from anywhere the Internet can be accessed.

The Information Literacy Coordinator early on recognized the importance of data backups and makes it a practice to regularly export the Google Calendar into a zipped file and save it on the college's Internet-based file storage system. Data is stored in iCal format. So far, we have not had to restore data from a backup zipped file; data seems secure in Google Calendar. As shown in Figure 16.2, Google Calendar allows multiple calendars to be viewed at the same time.

Figure 16.2. Google Calendar's One-Day Display of All Events in Ten Library Calendars

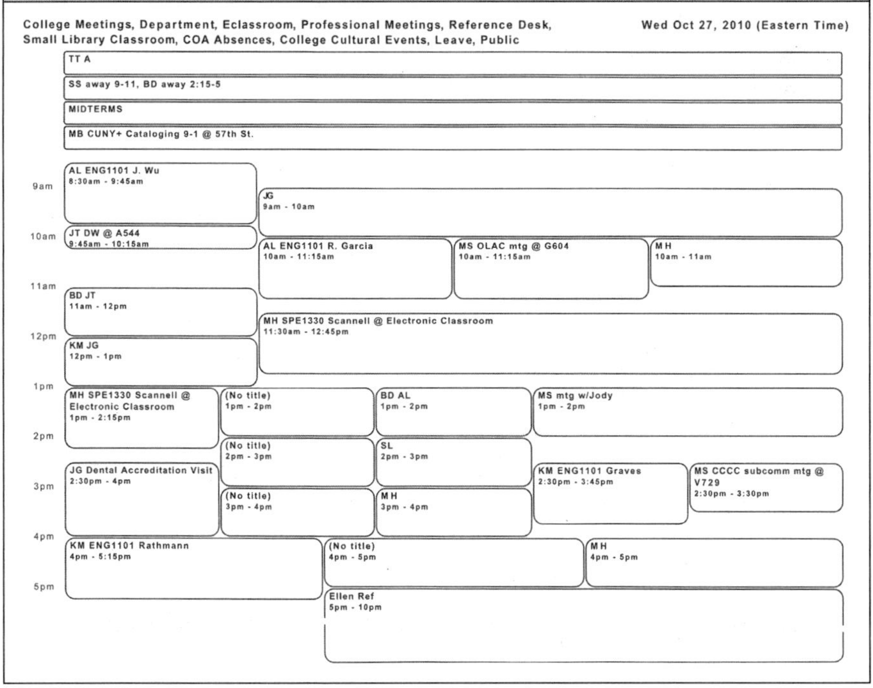

College Meetings, Department, Eclassroom, Professional Meetings, Reference Desk, Small Library Classroom, COA Absences, College Cultural Events, Leave, Public   Wed Oct 27, 2010 (Eastern Time)

TT A

SS away 9-11, BD away 2:15-5

MIDTERMS

MB CUNY+ Cataloging 9-1 @ 57th St.

9am — AL ENG1101 J. Wu 8:30am - 9:45am

JG 9am - 10am

10am — JT DW @ A544 9:45am - 10:15am

AL ENG1101 R. Garcia 10am - 11:15am

MS OLAC mtg @ G604 10am - 11:15am

M H 10am - 11am

11am — BD JT 11am - 12pm

MH SPE1330 Scannell @ Electronic Classroom 11:30am - 12:45pm

12pm — KM JG 12pm - 1pm

1pm — MH SPE1330 Scannell @ Electronic Classroom 1pm - 2:15pm

(No title) 1pm - 2pm

BD AL 1pm - 2pm

MS mtg w/Jody 1pm - 2pm

2pm — (No title) 2pm - 3pm

SL 2pm - 3pm

JG Dental Accreditation Visit 2:30pm - 4pm

3pm — (No title) 3pm - 4pm

M H 3pm - 4pm

KM ENG1101 Graves 2:30pm - 3:45pm

MS CCCC subcomm mtg @ V729 2:30pm - 3:30pm

4pm — KM ENG1101 Rathmann 4pm - 5:15pm

(No title) 4pm - 5pm

M H 4pm - 5pm

5pm — Ellen Ref 5pm - 10pm

Google Calendar offers some functionality that the college's version of Group-Wise does not: the ability to set e-mail or SMS reminders for calendar events for early morning classes, evening or weekend classes, or classes needing special preparation or setup. GroupWise offers pop-up reminders, but only in the desktop client, not in the web version.

Choices made about Google Calendar options included managing sharing and write rights. When the department adopted the instruction regulars' calendar techniques, editing rights were extended to all librarians for most calendars.

Assessment and Evaluation

As other units of the library have begun to use Google Calendar, it has eased our collective ability to schedule reference desk shift changes, schedule meetings, and reserve meeting or instructional spaces for occasional nonteaching use. With the exception of the annual leave calendar, we all have ownership over our own schedules and can make changes to reflect instruction or reference desk swaps; colleagues who teach less and may not consult the e-classroom calendar daily can easily see when the classroom is available. We are directed to the shared calendars by our department chair's daily e-mail summarizing meetings, absences, and college events. The use of several shared calendars began in spring 2009, and now the library uses ten calendars in total.

Now that we have relied on Google Calendar for several semesters, we have had the opportunity to reflect on its utility. Some members of the library faculty have expressed concern that we are too heavily invested in software that is not everlastingly guaranteed to be free of charge; if the fully functional Calendar evolved to a fee-based service, we would have to scale back our expectations of its functionality, migrate to another free calendar, or allocate funds to subscribe. Some are also concerned that our privacy is compromised; Google sets cookies to monitor user preferences and track user trends, and its server logs record user information such as IP address and software used. Communications, including e-mail, are also retained to "improve services" (Google, 2010).

While most of our colleagues are comfortable with most aspects of scheduling and editing calendar events, some errors are made from time to time. The most frequent and typical of these is the creation of a calendar event that is intended for all to see on a librarian's personal Google Calendar, which is not shared. In Google Calendar, the personal calendar of the account holder is the default, and those calendar events are visible only to the account holder. This is easily remedied, but only by the account holder. The application permits calendar events to be moved from one calendar to another and permits events to be copied from a shared calendar to the account holder's personal calendar. It also permits the setting of alerts by e-mail, text message, or pop-up browser window between one minute and several weeks before the event.

A few features would improve Google Calendar's robustness and utility. As of this writing, Google Calendar does not allow an easy way to output all events on a particular calendar as comma-separated values or another format easily imported into Excel or similar software (though it is possible to import .csv-formatted data into Google Calendar). The ability to easily export library instruction statistics into database or spreadsheet software would give us great power to analyze library instruction statistics and make meaningful comparisons among semesters. It is possible, but laborious, to copy and paste the Google Calendar into Excel; at the end of every semester the Information Literacy librarian manipulates our e-classroom Google Calendar into Excel, a very time-consuming task.

The ability to easily output the e-classroom calendar as a spreadsheet would also allow us to deliver the English department a schedule in a format that they had become accustomed to working with. A time stamp or history for each calendar event would be a great convenience. In the rare instance that multiple simultaneous reservations for the e-classroom are made, to be able to determine "who was first" would be very useful. We do not know how far back Google will permit us to store calendar data or whether the corporate policy will evolve to limit free browser-based storage, which is another compelling reason to back up and export data regularly.

On occasion a campus network problem seems to cause failure of Google applications, including the calendar, to load properly or completely. In May 2010, when the campus network regularly underwent periods of unexplained sluggishness, a colleague contacted campus IT services to find out more about the network's speed. We got an unsatisfying response: the Great Google Slowdown of May 2010 (as colleagues lightheartedly referred to it) was caused by an undiagnosed, unpublicized problem with Google, though many of us experienced uninterrupted Google Apps usage from off campus.

With Google Calendar meeting most of our scheduling needs, we have not yet seriously explored other scheduling software, either free or by purchase or subscription. Nor have we considered using the free version of Google Apps for Education. Most library staff and faculty who use the suite of Google Calendars are content with its transparency and immediacy, which were the primary goals of moving to a shared online solution. With our implementation, Google Calendar lacks the ability to empower classroom faculty to view available e-classroom times or instruction regulars' schedules or initiate the scheduling process. This could be done by making our classroom and instructional space calendars public, something not all of us are comfortable with. Giving editing privileges to individual classroom faculty members would be cumbersome, as each individual would need a Google account. There are risks as well: as the number of calendar users grows, so does the likelihood that someone will inadvertently delete or change the time or date of a calendar event or place it on a personal calendar that nobody else can see.

Conclusion

Migrating to shared online calendars for library instruction scheduling and for most other aspects of library work life has changed how some library faculty use Google Apps for productivity, including shared documents for collaborative writing projects and forms to survey classroom faculty about library instruction. A number of librarians now make use of Google Calendar and other applications for personal and other professional uses. At some point we may require more functionality and interactivity than Google Calendar can offer. We have learned that, when necessary, we can engineer what some might have regarded as a temporary fix into a long-term, hard-working solution.

References

CUNY Office of Institutional Research and Assessment. 2009. "Total Enrollment by Undergraduate and Graduate Level, Full-Time/Part-Time Attendance, and College." Updated March 26, 2010. http://owl.cuny.edu:7778/ENRL_0001_UGGR_FTPT.rpt.pdf.

Google. 2010. "Google Privacy Policy." Last modified October 3. http://www.google.com/privacypolicy.html.

U.S. News & World Report. 2010. "Best Colleges: Racial Diversity: Regional Colleges (North)." Best Colleges 2011. Accessed October 12. http://colleges.usnews.rankingsandreviews.com/best-colleges/bacc-north-campus-ethnic-diversity.

Chapter 17

Integrating Google Forms into Reference and Instruction

Robin Elizabeth Miller

Introduction

Google Forms offer librarians an array of opportunities to collect information from reference patrons and from students engaged in information literacy instruction. Part of the Google Docs suite of software as a service (SaaS) products, Google Forms have been recognized by librarians as an inexpensive and easy-to-use survey tool (Travis, 2010). Beyond surveys, libraries can use Google Forms to receive reference questions, and Google Forms offer a paperless alternative to the in-class worksheet often used in information literacy exercises. This chapter describes how Google Forms have been used in an academic library's reference and instruction services.

Background

The University of Wisconsin–Eau Claire is a public institution primarily serving undergraduates, with enrollment of more than 11,000 students. The McIntyre Library at UW–Eau Claire is a heavily used virtual and physical space. The library employs a variety of web-based instructional tools, including LibGuides, for general and course-integrated research assistance. Virtual reference—chat/IM, text message, and e-mail—is part of the McIntyre Library's standard reference service. "Chat with McIntyre Library" links are displayed in electronic resources, and chat/IM widgets are embedded in LibGuides. Virtual reference and web-based research guides are hardly unique among academic libraries; however, these tools are situated in the conceptual framework described by Lorcan Dempsey (2008: 111) as being "in the flow." As a library, we are working to adopt tools that enable us to connect with patrons within their research environment and at the point in their workflow where they need our assistance. Furthermore, because our reliance on web-based instructional tools and services is growing, we are actively searching for tools that will help us create "safety nets" at points where patrons become confused or frustrated by library resources (Veldof, 2008).

As the McIntyre Library's Reference and Instruction/Government Publications Librarian, I deliver information literacy instruction to a range of courses, including English 110 (a general education requirement) and upper-division research-intensive courses. Students from the classes I teach frequently contact me individually with complex reference questions. In the course of my teaching, I identified a need for flexible web-based forms with the functionality of a survey tool but with customization options that would make the forms appropriate for in-class exercises and for accepting reference questions. Instead of a worksheet printed on paper, I wanted to experiment with accepting in-class exercises through a web-based form. Using Springshare's LibGuides product, I generally develop a course-integrated research guide to which I direct students during a class session; I wanted to embed webforms into my LibGuides so that students could submit reference questions within the environment of the research guide designed to assist them. I was inspired to consider this by Dempsey's (2008: 111) exhortation that "we must build library services around their workflow (or learnflow, or researchflow, or . . .)." I hoped the forms would be a component of assessment, so automatically capturing each form's data in a spreadsheet was essential. Finally, I wanted a free tool that required little or no coding and that I could easily modify or customize, depending on the user group. In essence, I was looking for a webform that combined the function of a survey with qualities that would make the forms appropriate for in-class exercises and for accepting reference questions.

174

Selection Process

I first considered the tools already in use at my library and at UW–Eau Claire. Our library's website features webforms that enable users to request research consultations, schedule classroom instruction, or report a problem with an electronic resource. However, these forms collect information via e-mail, not in spreadsheets. In addition, I did not think our very busy systems department could accommodate a rotating array of requests for customized forms.

UW-Eau Claire faculty and staff have access to Qualtrics software, which can be used to create secure, web-based surveys. Any form created with Qualtrics can be distributed with a unique URL, and data collected can be downloaded in a variety of formats, including Excel. As a survey tool, Qualtrics is robust and more secure than Survey Monkey's freely available product; however, I was looking for a tool that functioned less like a poll and more like a web-based worksheet or question box.

Because my search for a form was focused partly on a tool that I could embed into LibGuides, I considered simply using one of LibGuides' comment boxes. However, I did not want to receive webform submissions via e-mail. Furthermore, I wanted the flexibility of a webform that I could install in LibGuides or another website, and I wanted to be able to e-mail a link to a webform or paste the link into another website or blog.

Other survey tools had the potential to meet the needs I had identified, but the free or "basic" products often lacked a single critical component. Marie and Weston (2009) succinctly review several online survey tools, including Survey-Gizmo, Survey Monkey, and Zoomerang. I considered the no-cost version of each of these tools, and I was especially impressed with SurveyGizmo, which offers Java script and HTML iframe tags for embedding the form. In a literature search about using webforms in higher education and libraries, Travis' (2010) description of a medical library's use of Google Forms for surveys convinced me that Google Forms is a sufficiently flexible product. Meanwhile, Gerhinger (2010) described integrating Google Forms into active learning exercises in computer science instruction at North Carolina State University. Based on these comprehensive assessments and my own experimentation, I concluded that Google Forms combined the qualities I sought, including a spreadsheet, into a single program that I could access anywhere.

Distinguishing Features of Google Forms

As a component of Google Docs, Google Forms is available to anyone with a free Google account. Following the software as a service (SaaS) product model, Google delivers Google Docs as a service to users, who can access word-processing documents, spreadsheets, presentations, a drawing program, and forms in a web-based interface hosted by Google. Google Docs runs inside conventional web browsers (Firefox 3.0, Internet Explorer 7 or 8, and Safari) installed on Windows, Mac OS X, or Linux operating systems (Google, 2010). A Google Form can be accessed and modified by logging into a Google Docs account. Like any Google Doc, Google Forms can have multiple collaborators, meaning that anyone with permission can modify a form.

Google Docs does not limit the number of forms one can create, and there is no cap on the number of responses per form. Google Forms offers a standard array of question types, and places no apparent restriction on form length. A Google Form can be revised and republished instantly without altering the form user's access to the form. Other attractive product features include:

- HTML iframe tags for embedding a form
- Automatic data collection in a Google Spreadsheet
- Customization of "thank you" or confirmation messages
- Section headers and page breaks for multipart forms
- Variety of background themes
- No advertising

Creating and Using a Google Form

No software installation was required before I could implement Google Forms, a distinct advantage to using SaaS products. A Google account is required to build a

Google Form (or to begin any other Google Doc). To implement Google Forms, I did not need to establish and keep track of another web-based product account, because my library already has a Google account for Google Voice and other services. Although a Google account is required to set up a Google Form and track the data collected, those who fill in the form do not have to log in or maintain a Google account.

To create a Google Form, a user must simply log into Google Docs (http://docs.google.com) with a Google account, select "Create New," and select "Form." A new Google Form is a blank canvas and each field of a new form is clearly labeled to indicate its purpose. Clicking on a specific field allows the form owner to edit that field. New questions can be added to each form by clicking "Add item." Selecting from the "Question Type" dropdown menu automatically alters the format of the question, depending on the question type selected.

A completed Google Form can be distributed in three ways. The form owner can e-mail it with the "Email this form" button that appears when the form is in edit mode. A unique URL appears at the bottom of the form when in edit mode next to the phrase, "You can view the published form here"; this URL can be copied and pasted for distribution via e-mail or as a link on a website. Finally, by clicking on "More Actions" within edit mode, the form owner can access an HTML iframe tag, which can be pasted into the source code of a website.

Implementation

When I set up Google Forms, I first built a form with a set of prototype questions. Colleagues and student employees at our reference desk "road tested" the forms, offering immediate usability insights and some suggestions for revision of formatting, question wording, order, and type. Following these revisions, I copied the HTML iframe tag from my form and pasted it into a LibGuides content box.

I first tested Google Forms in two upper-division history seminars in which students were beginning a significant year-long research project. In collaboration with McIntyre Library's Special Collections and Archives, I developed a LibGuide for the course and embedded a reference question webform into the LibGuide (Figure 17.1). I met with both seminars for 50 minutes each, highlighting the course LibGuide, and encouraging students to submit reference questions using the form embedded under the "Ask a Question" tab of the LibGuide.

After teaching both history seminars, I eagerly awaited receipt of a question submitted via Google Form. I did not expect that every student from the history seminar would choose to ask a question in the Google Form but hoped that the format was a desirable option for some patrons. In the two weeks that followed my presentation to both seminars, I received nine reference questions from seminar students. Four questions were submitted via Google Forms, three students asked questions in person in my office, one question was submitted via e-mail, and one patron used chat/IM to request assistance. The nature of the questions

Figure 17.1. Google Form Embedded in a Research Guide for Receiving Reference Questions

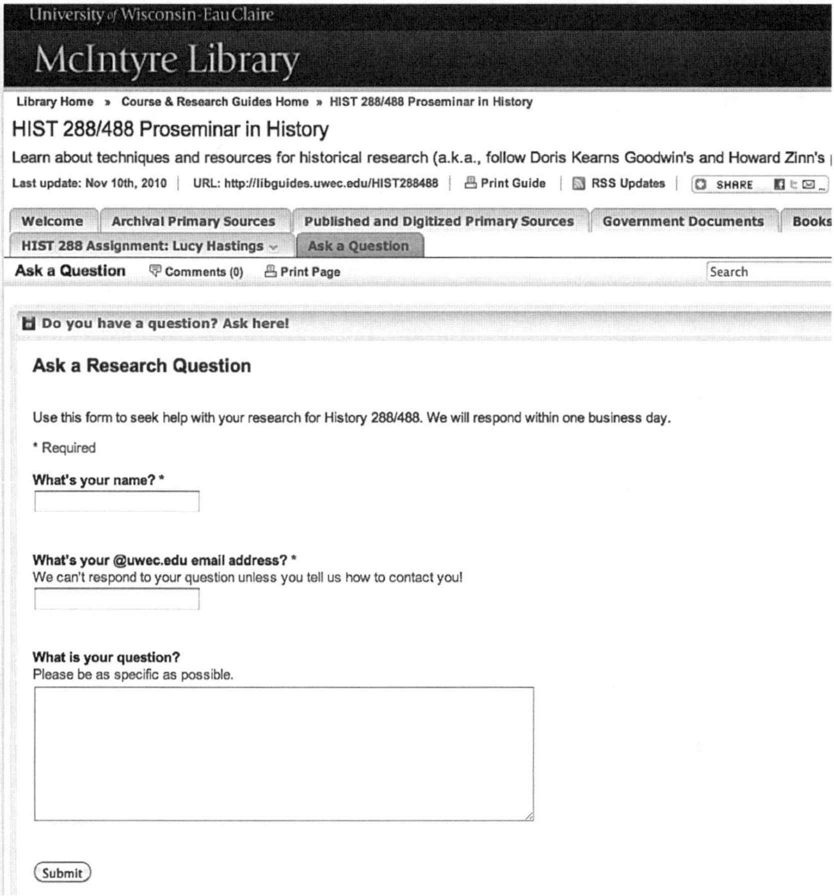

University of Wisconsin-Eau Claire

McIntyre Library

Library Home » Course & Research Guides Home » HIST 288/488 Proseminar in History

HIST 288/488 Proseminar in History

Learn about techniques and resources for historical research (a.k.a., follow Doris Kearns Goodwin's and Howard Zinn's |

Last update: Nov 10th, 2010 | URL: http://libguides.uwec.edu/HIST288488 | 🖨 Print Guide | 🔊 RSS Updates | ☐ SHARE 🗍 🖂

| Welcome | Archival Primary Sources | Published and Digitized Primary Sources | Government Documents | Books |

| HIST 288 Assignment: Lucy Hastings ⌄ | Ask a Question |

Ask a Question 💬 Comments (0) 🖨 Print Page   Search

🗒 Do you have a question? Ask here!

Ask a Research Question

Use this form to seek help with your research for History 288/488. We will respond within one business day.

* Required

What's your name? *

What's your @uwec.edu email address? *
We can't respond to your question unless you tell us how to contact you!

What is your question?
Please be as specific as possible.

(Submit)

submitted via Google Forms was similar to reference questions received in other modes. For example, one student asked how to locate historic census data, while another student sought help identifying appropriate search terms related to the eighteenth-century fur trade. Since piloting the form in these history seminars, I have embedded similar forms in research guides designed for other courses, occasionally changing the wording and format of the form fields to adjust to the particular research needs of the students in the course.

Data submitted through a Google Form is collected in a single Google Spreadsheet linked to the Google Form and accessible via Google Docs. Seamless data collection enables instant comparison of questions received from students who have attended a library instruction session or used a research guide. This data allows me to look for patterns that may indicate that the students are having difficulty with particular research concepts or library tools.

Google Forms also have applications for interactive classroom exercises. In information literacy instruction designed for an English composition class, I created a classroom activity to be completed in a Google Form embedded in the course LibGuide. During a 50-minute session, students are introduced to strategies for finding books and articles, and they compare their experiences with different library interfaces. When students apply their learning during each class activity, they fill out a brief form describing what they find.

After students submit the form I view the data they submit in a Google Spreadsheet. Although I believe assessment of student learning should extend beyond students' ability to find a book or an article, the data collected in these web-based worksheets enables quick assessment of whether students succeeded in executing the in-class activity. Asking students to fill out a web-based form is easy to integrate into the "flow" of a classroom activity that primarily utilizes computers and the Internet. Crucially, each student must have access to a computer in the classroom in order to access and fill out the form.

Based on successful implementation of Google Forms, future uses of webforms for reference questions will include linking the forms to course pages within D2L, the course management system used at UW–Eau Claire. Gerhinger (2010) provides a thorough overview of how Google Forms can be used in classroom instruction, both for engaging students in active learning exercises and for collecting opinions or answers to factual questions. McIntyre Library does not currently have access to clickers for instruction; however, one might imagine a Google Form that a librarian could use to conduct polls and collect other data from students who might otherwise use clickers. Clearly, Google Forms present many possibilities in instruction.

Assessment and Evaluation

In assessing my use of Google Forms in reference and instruction, I have considered whether and how the forms are being used; how the forms have functioned; and possible barriers to use. Library patrons are using the forms in two contexts. In the first context, history students have independently used the forms to ask questions, accessing the form within the LibGuide developed for their course. In the second context, students have used the forms at my direction in classroom settings instead of filling out paper-based worksheets.

To date, our Google Forms have functioned well, with no observed interruption in service or access. Submitting reference questions via a Google Form embedded in a LibGuide is optional; however, our initial experience with this option indicates that some patrons will use a Google Form to submit a question if the form is integrated into their research environment.

Students using the forms to submit classroom exercises have not revealed any frustration with the tool. However, one obvious barrier to using Google Forms as an instructional tool is that a webform may not fit into the "flow" of a classroom activity. For example, engaging students in small-group discussions about search results may not call for completion of a webform. Similarly, Google Draw (or another drawing product) may be a more appropriate tool for creating a Venn diagram to compare and contrast reference sources. However, Google Forms are a highly functional tool for eliminating paper-based worksheets in classroom settings, and McIntyre Library patrons have demonstrated that Google Forms are useful in the menu of options for asking a reference question.

Conclusion

When I began the hunt for a versatile webform, I wanted a product that was free and easy to build, customize, embed, and distribute. I was looking for a product with a variety of question types and with seamless data collection options. I looked to many online survey tools, but Google's SaaS product suite met each of these needs with Google Forms. The customization features of Google Forms have enabled me to create forms that do not inhibit patron questions with the character or word limits common to many online surveys. This has been particularly advantageous in instructional settings, because patrons are able to fill out a form just as they would an in-class worksheet. Implementing Google Forms in the McIntyre Library has shown that libraries may have uses for webforms beyond collecting survey data. Google Forms' ease of creation and customization, combined with low cost and no software installation or maintenance requirements, should be attractive features to librarians looking for paperless classroom assessment options and for new ways to connect with users.

179

References

Dempsey, Lorcan. 2008. "Reconfiguring the Library Systems Environment." *portal: Libraries and the Academy* 8, no. 2: 111–120.

Gerhinger, Edward. 2010. "Teaching Interactively with Google Docs." Paper presented at the Annual Conference and Exposition of the American Society for Engineering Education, Louisville, KY, June.

Google. 2010. "Getting to Know Google Docs: System Requirements." Google. Accessed November 1. https://docs.google.com/support.

Marie, Kirsten L., and Janine Weston. 2009. "Survey Says: Online Survey Tools for Library Assessment." *Library Media Connection* 28, no. 2: 50–52.

Travis, Lisa. 2010. "One of Many Free Survey Tools: Google Docs." *Journal of Electronic Resources in Medical Libraries* 7, no. 2: 105–114.

Veldof, Jerilyn R. 2008. "From Desk to Web: Creating Safety Nets in the Online Library." In *The Desk and Beyond*, edited by Sarah K. Steiner and M. Leslie Madden, 120–134. Chicago: Association of College and Research Libraries.

Chapter 18

Ning, Fostering Conversations in the Cloud

Leland R. Deeds, Cindy Kissel-Ito, and Ann Thomas Knox

Introduction

Custom social networking sites provide an environment that supports engagement with new ideas and resources. Cloud-based software as a service (SaaS) offerings like Ning and Wetpaint provide easily customized and implemented virtual space that fosters community and participant conversation. These services can also support collaborative, interactive teaching and learning. This chapter details how such SaaS social networking sites were used to meet the need for asynchronous training for staff in a theological library, resulting in the creation of a model that was later adapted for use by teaching faculty.

Background

Union Presbyterian Seminary is a small, stand-alone academic institution offering five masters degrees and two doctorates. Within the library there is one systems librarian, covering all internal information technology needs, and a campus Technology Services department, composed of four FTE responsible for all other communications infrastructure, support, and services. During the timing of both projects discussed, the campus was experiencing financial constraints. There was a need, from the projects' outset, not only to outsource the hardware and systems administration functions made available by "renting" virtual server space, but also to have these automatically bundled into a provided, supported, stable web-enabled environment. Planned goals for this environment included alleviating the need for local system administration, authentication, programming, storage, or server-based software installs. The environment also needed to provide remote file uploads, hosted web tools, a browser-based interface, stable service "up time," and support. The financial and staffing realities of the institution lead project leaders to pursue a cost-effective, cloud-based solution with these goals for both initiatives.

Training Series

In the spring of 2010 plans moved forward to offer a training series for staff in the library. The impact of requiring library staff to move among many individual web tools was discussed. The decision was made to search for a single cloud-based platform that would combine as much of the functionality desired for the project as possible in one place. The hope was that this decision would lower staff anxiety and resistance concerning technology training and encourage all communal comments or conversation to occur in a single location. A static Welcome page and the capability for all members to be able to give their responses to the instructional modules as blog posts were preferred. The training series also called for participants to be able to experience instant messaging, discussion forums and wikis, along with other Web 2.0 tools.

Summer Course

Simultaneously a member of the faculty was searching for a way to improve the at-home sessions of her course. The course, focused on teaching with technology, was part of the campus' Extended Campus Program (ECP). ECP provides a means for working adults to pursue part-time graduate study leading to a masters degree in Christian Education. Students engage in study at home and attend an intensive session on campus. Course materials are usually delivered through use of the institutional course management system. This system supports transmission of materials but does not provide a platform for an interactive, dynamic learning environment for the at-home portion of the course. The experience of the library's training series project leaders with cloud-based custom social networking platforms for asynchronous learning offered possibilities for a more collaborative model of teaching and learning in the ECP while also modeling the use of such tools for students' future professional work.

Selection Process

As the search began for a single, feature-rich, cloud-based platform to fit the institution's goals, as mentioned earlier, a list of desired features was established. Along with basic ease of use for participants, key capabilities were a static Menu or Welcome page, built-in instant messaging, discussion forums, timed release of content, individual participant blogs, built-in wiki, standard GUI editor, the ability to easily embed content/widgets from other sites, nominal cost, and privacy control. After some initial searching and conversations with associates at other institutions, the options were quickly narrowed to two custom social networking sites: Ning and Wetpaint. Each cloud-based platform offered unique advantages and disadvantages in the ways that they were structured.

The custom social networking site offered by Ning, for example, provides two places where almost all content is collected for sharing: the opening Welcome page and the individual member page, similar to other social networks' individual, member profile page. Outside of these two locations within the site all content is pooled by format type: blog post, discussion forum entry, uploaded picture, or uploaded video. The individual piece of content is clearly associated with the user profile that has created or uploaded it. The ability for participants to comment is available for all format types. This universal ability to comment on material was quite important for each project.

The custom social networking site provided by Wetpaint offers most of the same sought after functionality but delivers it differently. Wetpaint also offers a default Home menu. It shows subpages, new activity, and members, which are displayed as widgets along the page sides. Wetpaint lacked, most importantly, integrated blogging. Instead of blogs as an available format type, Wetpaint uses "pages," operating like moderated wikis that have multiple assigned writers. This structural design led to a very clunky interface and caused concerns about participants' potential confusion regarding how to author new content.

One of the goals for a cloud-based environment for both projects was either a free or low-cost set of services. When both custom social networking sites were initially reviewed as solutions, both were free but displayed advertisements in order to generate revenue. Wetpaint's design for displaying these advertisements was much more aggressive. The distinction in how each custom social network site managed new user content, along with Wetpaint's very heavy use of advertisements, drove the decision to select Ning.

It is worth noting here, however, that midway through the initial project, during the training series for library staff, Ning changed to a completely fee-based model. Shortly after, Wetpaint chose to focus their development on fan sites for TV or movies target markets. More will be said later about the impact of these changes, but they only reinforced the original choice. Ning's price for an annual subscription, as of May 2011, was $19.95 for Mini, $199.95 for Plus, and $499.95 for Pro. Wetpaint's Premium Services offering was $239.40 in November 2010.

Implementation

Training Series

In May 2010 the Web 2.0 introductory series for library staff was created using the selected Ning social networking platform. The custom social network that was designed used all the following components: blogs, forums, photos, and chat. One of the key features, wikis, was not available from Ning. Other resources outside of the custom social network had to be relied on for those needs.

Each learning unit was developed as a blog post by one of the project leaders and linked to the splash page's menu as an embedded hyperlink in the unit's title. These individual learning units were timed to release to participants on set dates, so the series could follow a planned schedule that also included "open lab" times in the library's media lab when project leaders would be available to answer questions and assist staff experiencing issues. Participants were then issued invitations to join the custom social network that was called "7 Signposts to Library 2.0." Their activity as they progressed through the series generated individual blog posts, threaded discussions in the forums, and exposure to instant messaging using the network's built-in chat feature. Other activity occurred outside of the site but was then discussed in reflection pieces created as blog posts.

Summer Course

The course's custom social network utilized the library training series' Ning site as a template. Registered students were invited to participate and were introduced to the work of the course through the main page of the social network. This page included information regarding course purposes, methods, and assignments, with a link to the syllabus. A sidebar depicted members and detailed course activity. Content material presented perspectives on the weekly topic, with minimal reliance on a printed course textbook. Exploration of online sources led to articles, websites and video/audio resources on educational practice, Internet usage, and teaching in religious education, which became embedded links in the course site. The Ning blog, associated with the support subsite, directed the project leaders to valuable information and examples of networks that specifically use Ning in education (http://education.ning.com; Classroom 2.0, http://www.classroom20.com/).

After engaging the materials, students were invited to experiment with web tools such as Flickr (http://www.flickr.com/) and VoiceThread (http://voicethread.com/). Assignments asked students to discuss the content and their experiences with technological tools through blog and forum posts, components of the Ning system.

Assessment and Evaluation

Training Series

The performance of the Ning social network was positive, though issues were experienced. It was stable. Only one service outage was experienced. Participants found the social network reasonably easy to use. The network's structure of pooling all member blog posts, while providing a means to allow browsing all available posts or filtering by author, met all project expectations. The ability of participants to share among one another while also feeling the network was a "safe" or "private" learning environment succeeded in fostering a willingness to comment on one another's work.

During the training series for staff (prior to the development of the course site for students), Ning ceased all free custom social networks. All network creators were faced with migration of content or submitting to a subscription fee. The decision was made to stay with the network that had already been created. It was felt that too much effort had been invested in the series to transition. This also avoided forcing participants to move to another learning platform.

The most significant disappointment was communication based. Participants expected to receive e-mail notifications when others added content to the training series' Ning network. In initial tests among the project leaders, this had been successful. Once the project launched, the participants did not receive such e-mail. It was initially thought that the issue may have arisen because network members had not been required to "friend" their colleagues. Testing proved this assumption to be false. The root of this particular issue was never found. Attempts to contact Ning's support staff, now that the institution was a paying customer, failed. This occurred during the period that only support tickets associated with billing and subscriptions were receiving prompt attention. This unexpected issue left project leaders with no choice but to rely on using "all member broadcast" messages as network administrators. This did not make up for individual participant notification when new content and comments had been added by other participants, a reminder that had been counted on to help drive conversation on the networks. Ning, therefore, met 11 of 12 of our goals for a cloud-based environment and provided nine of ten key features.

Summer Course

The course use of Ning as an educational platform was successful. Students gained both an academic knowledge of teaching with technology and technical knowledge of Web 2.0 tools. Ning had partnered with Pearson to offer a free "Ning Mini" specifically developed for educational purposes, which was requested for the course's social network. Despite immediate registration, notification was not received within the term.

The most important assessment focuses on the collaborative learning environment of the custom social network. The process of learning moved from transmission of information to collaborative engagement. The changing roles of the instructors serve as a metaphor for this educational shift. Initial consultation among project leaders involved a conference between two experts. The librarian colleague contributed knowledge and experience of social networking as an educational platform. He also contributed the necessary technical skills that supported the use of Ning. The faculty member had primary responsibility for the educational content, process, and student evaluation. These roles became more fluid, as instructors responded to students' reflections and experiences. Both colleagues began to contribute content, gave technical support, and engaged in discussion through blogs and discussion forums. Students also became "experts" who posted valuable resource materials on course topics. One student articulated this educational shift well in her final evaluation: "Previous coursework primarily involved transmission of information by the professor to students. Assignments were submitted to the instructor and evaluated. Other students in the class participated by reading peers' reflections and comments. Use of the network demanded engagement of all class members with each other and with the instructors."

Conclusion

Even with the specific issues experienced using Ning, the custom social networking service successfully met all but one of the initial criteria set for a cloud-based environment. Both projects involved multimedia files, requiring upload and storage. Multiple leaders were involved with both projects and were able to work jointly across locations successfully. Ning proved to be stable, without authentication error, and sufficiently low cost. The project leaders were freed to focus all effort on project development with a short schedule and limited learning curve. The service's interface proved easy to use for project participants. No internal campus resource had to be tapped or consulted. For all these reasons, there is a great deal of potential in cloud-based web services like Ning where not only content needs to be delivered, but the space and functionality to foster community and participant sharing are vital and where institutional resources for such efforts are minimal. With menu-driven customization and domain name mapping (for Plus and Pro level accounts), platforms such as Ning offer smaller educational or cultural institutions a low-cost, feature-rich, easily implemented springboard for service development.

Chapter 19

Not Every Cloud Has a Silver Lining: Using a Cloud Application May Not Always Be the Best Solution

Ann Whitney Gleason

Introduction

Libraries are increasingly looking to technology to solve issues of integrating instruction and reference services into academic courses, which may be offered partly or wholly online. Cloud-based web conferencing software offers features such as chat, screen sharing, and video to effectively present library instruction in an interactive, engaging way. Many students may be unfamiliar with web conferencing, especially older nontraditional students returning to the workforce or upgrading work skills. In our search for the perfect web conferencing software, we thought we had found the solution in a cloud application with all the features we were looking for in the free version, only to find out a year later that the software had been sold and the service was being discontinued for all users. Users with free accounts had three months' notice before their accounts were closed, while paying customers were able to keep their service until the end of their contract. As we reflect on our experiences, we find that although some cloud-based applications offer low-cost, easy-to-use, feature-rich software, they may not always be the best solution for critical library programs.

Background

The University of Washington (UW) is the largest university in Washington state, with three campuses enrolling over 45,000 students. We serve the educational needs of researchers, faculty, staff, students, and health professionals for the WWAMI region (Washington, Alaska, Idaho, Montana, and Wyoming). Students who use the Health Sciences Library are mainly upper-division students from all over the state. Many of these students are older nontraditional students juggling career, family, and education.

187

The UW Health Sciences Library has the largest and most comprehensive collection of health sciences materials in the Pacific Northwest. Our online web portal offers off-campus access to a large number of health-related resources. We also provide video and HTML tutorials on a variety of popular resources on our website. In spite of the popularity of online, self-paced tutorials, there is often a need for one-on-one training, especially for nontraditional students who may be returning to the workforce or upgrading skills and who may not have the computer skills of the younger generation. Many students, young and old, may also prefer to get help from a librarian face-to-face, especially when working on a large research project that requires accessing several different resources, all with different interfaces and search methodologies. Finding the resources needed for research can be daunting, involving hours of sifting through huge databases of information to find a few key articles.

In our work in an academic medical library, librarians are called on more and more to integrate library instruction with nontraditional courses such as evening, online, or hybrid offerings. Communicating with students who we may see face-to-face only once, if at all, is a huge challenge. When our nursing liaisons were asked late in December to teach the research component in a large (50 students) project-oriented winter course that would be largely offered online, we needed to think creatively in order to come up with a distance education solution that would offer the traditional benefit of in-person library instruction and consultation to off-campus students. Web conferencing software offers the advantages of face-to-face instruction, but at a distance. The solution we were looking for needed to be easy to use and not be dependent on the fast network resources we are used to on campus. We were looking for a solution that would allow us to do electronic chat and video and screen sharing so that we could discuss the students' research needs and guide them through search strategies and resource discovery. All of this needed to be done in an environment of diminishing budgets with limited technical support. The timeline also made it imperative that there be minimal training of librarians needed. The software we were looking for also needed to be easy to access for students of all ages and abilities with technology. We preferred applications with no software to be loaded on the student's computer and limited setup before use. The solution we came up with was to use the free version of a web application called DimDim. This solution proved to be very successful, although we encountered several challenges during and after implementation.

Selection Process

We originally chose a free cloud service because we had no budget for the project and it needed to be implemented on very short notice. We had originally looked at several web conferencing applications, including free cloud offerings, for-pay cloud services, and commercial software. We chose DimDim because of the ease of use for host and client, extensive features, and of course the free price tag. It also seemed to be well established and was built on open source software. DimDim was advertised as "real-time collaboration made real easy." DimDim allowed us to e-mail a meeting invitation, which contained a clickable link that took the participant directly to the meeting. Screen sharing, document sharing, and a built-in whiteboard were included. Participants could even share their computer screen with the librarian, which is helpful when troubleshooting problems with accessing resources. Meetings could be hosted and accessed online from anywhere at anytime the librarian was available and were not dependent on specific hardware or a particular browser.

After spending considerable time and effort choosing and implementing a cloud application for online web conferencing for the nursing distance education program, we were notified the software had been sold and we were given three months to save our files before our login account would be closed on March 15, 2011. Those who paid for the added features of subscription service are supported only until their subscription runs out, and no new accounts are being accepted. All users, free or paid subscription holders, were advised to download files and conference transcripts from DimDim before the expiration period. Under the license agreement we approved when signing up for a free DimDim account, it was clear that they had the right to discontinue services at any time. We just had not counted on that happening so soon.

Although it was built on open source software, the DimDim developers decided to sell the code to a for-profit company after being offered several million dollars. The code will be integrated into existing commercial software, expanding an existing social platform for business communications to include web conferencing. The new owners of the software, Salesforce.com, have announced that besides shutting down the cloud version of the software, they will also not be supporting the further development of the open source version, which has not been well maintained recently. Although a fork of the code called MidMid was announced (http://code.google.com/p/midmid), we are not aware of another service using either the original DimDim or forked code. We do not have the staff to further develop this software on our own. Salesforce.com has announced that with the purchase of DimDim they plan to integrate the software into their existing social collaboration platform, Chatter. This integration will allow them to offer an integrated collaboration and communication platform in the future, but it is not yet available.

After learning that DimDim was discontinuing their cloud services, we needed to again form a committee to re-review web conferencing software. Fortunately, due to a campuswide licensing program, we were able to purchase an Adobe Connect account for a discounted rate. This software offers all of the features we were looking for when we chose DimDim but is not as easy for librarians or students to use. Unfortunately, we have to pay phone line charges to get a good audio connection, and sometimes students have trouble accessing the conference due to limita-

189

tions of their computer software or network connection. We will continue our search for the perfect web conferencing software, but we have concerns that inexpensive solutions will not last and our budget will not support the more expensive solutions.

Conclusion

The most important lesson we learned was that the best software for a particular application is sometimes not free. We will probably not use a free cloud application for a critical project again. We continue to use both free and inexpensive cloud applications for online polling, sharing documents, IM, and surveys. Paying the extra fee for a "pro" account with established cloud applications seems more secure than relying on a completely free service. As we have seen with DimDim, however, that is not always true. Another option would be to pay for cloud applications offered by established software companies, although again there is no guarantee that the specific product will be any more likely to be continued if it is not deemed successful by the company.

While cloud applications can save a lot of money on computer hardware and infrastructure as well as programming staff, there are some dangers to be aware of when using it for critical library programs. Non-business critical programs are fine with these risks, but for critical programs and websites, it may still be better to host your own data or website and/or develop your own product using open source software that is well established and has an active supporting community. For more information about these types of issues, see the chapters by Rosalyn Metz, H. Frank Cervone, and Carl Grant in Part I of this book.

Although we have purchased Adobe Connect web conferencing software and are able to continue our program offering online reference assistance and screen sharing, we still have problems with ease of use, audio lag time, and other quality-of-sound issues. We have formed a committee to explore new web conferencing options as they emerge. The field is very dynamic right now, and we have high hopes that new technology will emerge to integrate online web conferencing into the library workflow in a more seamless way and at an affordable price.

Chapter 20

Speak Up! Using VoiceThread to Encourage Participation and Collaboration in Library Instruction

Jennifer Ditkoff and Kara Young

Introduction

Imagine for a moment a group of people gathered around a piece of artwork in a gallery. The group may be collectively or individually discussing the piece, offering opinions, background information, or interpretations of the exhibit. Each person may have something of value to contribute, but louder opinions sometimes drown out the more soft-spoken voices. Similarly, the experience of soliciting feedback from students during instruction sessions can be disappointing when the same three students (or worse, none at all) answer all the questions. What if there was a forum that could offer equal time to everyone? The cloud technology tool VoiceThread offers just that, and, as a bonus, it is easy to set up and fun to use. Offered as software as a service (SaaS), VoiceThread allows users to upload still images, documents, or videos to a custom display and invite others to view and comment on the materials. These presentation modules, appropriately titled "VoiceThreads," allow individuals to share and exchange ideas around a common object. It is easy to integrate this cloud technology into library instruction in a variety of ways.

191

Background

Keene State College in Keene, NH, is a public liberal arts college with an approximate enrollment of 5,000 students and an active and growing information literacy instruction program. At Mason Library, eight librarians teach more than 250 sessions over the course of an academic year. This instruction takes place across all majors and course levels. Because all incoming freshman are required to take the interdisciplinary course Thinking and Writing, innovative approaches to reducing "IAKT" (I Already Know That) syndrome are always of keen interest.

At Keene State College, the exploration and utilization of low-cost or free tools in the classroom is a way to develop cutting-edge library instruction without being financially burdened or committed. The online tool VoiceThread allows collaborative conversations around multimedia presentations, encouraging participation from students in nontraditional ways. The discussions take place in the cloud without the need for downloading or hosting software, something to consider when the library does not have access to a server. Despite the relative simplicity of the program application, VoiceThread can be used in a variety of ways depending on the desired learning outcomes of the instructor using it. The flexibility and adaptability of the program allows for easy customization and application beyond the four walls of the traditional classroom. Promoting an ongoing collaborative educational experience rather than a static resource page, VoiceThread can be embedded in course management software, accessed through the web, or linked from subject guides. This functionality provides the opportunity to enhance content and build dialogue around course materials and subjects extending beyond the class session and even the campus itself.

Incorporating cloud technologies, like VoiceThread, into instruction helps engage beginning students and focus more advanced library users on the session content. It also gives librarians and professors the ability to assess student learning outcomes and teaching effectiveness.

Selection Process

192

Although there are other programs similar in focus to VoiceThread, and while VoiceThread itself is a mashup of several Web 2.0 concepts (online communities/forums, Facebook, Slideshare, YouTube, etc.), it is still unique in how it builds upon these existing frameworks. We chose VoiceThread because of the low cost and the way modules can be created using technologies we are already familiar with, including PowerPoint, Jing, and LibGuides. VoiceThread has been available since 2007, winning awards for its innovative application of collaborative software. It has also been featured periodically on educational blogs (http://www .webware.com/html/ww/100/2008/winners.html and http://sloanconsortium.org/ effective_practices/voicethread-enhanced-community-increased-social-presence-and-improved-visual-lea).

We see students for a relatively limited time during the semester, and VoiceThread provides a way to encourage participation in the class community. This tool is valuable because of the distinct way it engages students during class and continues the conversation after the class session and beyond the physical space of the library in the computing cloud. However, before using this, or any other technology, it is important to consider the learning outcomes for which the tool would be useful. VoiceThread isn't used for every class, only those in which the features of the tool enhance or help to achieve student learning outcomes.

We chose to use the free account of VoiceThread, which allows each registered account up to three VoiceThreads. This means that a classroom can only have three "sessions" in play at any time. This may be a problem if librarians anticipate using this tool in multiple classes. Like many cloud programs, VoiceThread requires payment to unlock greater functionality or storage space.

As much as we like using VoiceThread, we have not yet chosen to upgrade to a paid account due to the cost of doing so. For Higher Education users, a single license for a Pro account (including the ability to manage up to 50 Basic accounts) is $99 for one year, while a departmental account (up to 10 Pro accounts and 250 Basic accounts) currently costs $699 per year. Site-wide licenses are available upon request and vary on the size of the institution. With the increase in costs come greater functionality, storage space, and user account management features not available at the lower tiers. Additionally, there are account options available for users not affiliated with Higher Education.

After creating a VoiceThread account, it is easy to create modules. Materials are uploaded to VoiceThread from one's computer, media sources (Facebook, Flickr, the New York Public Library, or another VoiceThread), a URL, or an attached webcam. Once items are uploaded, VoiceThread can be shared with others via a custom URL, or it can be embedded in a variety of social media platforms using the code automatically generated. Publishing options allow a user to choose privacy settings. Playback options are somewhat adjustable for the free account, with greater functionality available to the paid account users. For a fee, archival quality versions of the VoiceThread can be exported.

193

Implementation

Jennifer's Implementation: VoiceThread to Encourage Community Growth as Part of an Instruction Toolkit

After providing one-shot library instruction sessions in connection with programmatic and student learning outcomes specific to that course, students still have questions and need more help. I use VoiceThread to build course support modules for students to revisit the materials presented in class. These modules reinforce information literacy skills to help students gain mastery of the material. They also give help specific to library technology tools such as databases and the catalog. The modules include topics such as how to search the catalog, how to authenticate access to databases from off campus, and how to search databases efficiently and effectively. I uploaded a screenshot tutorial on these topics into VoiceThread and offered the embedded VoiceThread for posting in the course management system for that class. Students were encouraged via e-mail to discuss and ask questions about the concepts using the VoiceThread module with voice, text, or video. Contributing students developed a community beyond the physical face-to-face interactions of the classroom and extended learning to the virtual world, sharing their own perspectives.

Students gained further understanding of the material as they asked and answered each others' questions. I monitored the VoiceThread and contributed as well. The VoiceThread module prompted students to actively participate in their own learning experience by revisiting the course materials throughout the semester. The presentation was left up for the entire semester so the students could continue to add content, ask questions, and receive feedback. The VoiceThread allowed me to continue to contribute to student learning after the research session by providing the space to give students tips on search strategies and help with procedural glitches, such as, "How do I activate my bar code?" VoiceThread has provided opportunities for me to see what learning outcomes students are struggling with, thus helping me design future information literacy sessions.

Kara's Implementation: VoiceThread for Peer-to-Peer Evaluation and Topic Focus

One common challenge in undergraduate research classes is a lack of topic focus. As part of the required interdisciplinary general education class Thinking and Writing, students are assigned a 15–20 page research paper. Students frequently arrive for library research sessions with very broad and unrefined topics. Even if provided the opportunity to read general reference sources and search databases for further information, they are often still unsure of how to narrow their focus even several weeks into the research process. Based on my observations, this can occur because students have not read about the general topic from several different angles and thus have not developed more appropriate keywords.

Cognizant of maximizing my time during my face-to-face sessions with the students, I am always trying new ways to give assistance to the entire class individually while still covering all the subject material. Recognizing that most students need one-on-one assistance in how to better approach their individual topics, I sought a way to (1) offer personal help to as many students as possible given the size of the class of 20 students and the 90-minute time frame, (2) offer students an engaging and different experience than they may have had before in library instruction, and (3) provide them with a resource they can use after the instruction session.

To achieve these goals, I adapted the following exercise:

1. Each student receives a blank piece of paper and writes on it the following: topic statement/question in its current form and why he or she is interested in the topic.
2. The papers are redistributed equally around the room.
3. Students and the instructor take time to read the topics and make suggestions about each. "Suggestions" could take the form of a comment or question about the topic, an alternate keyword to use, a recent event related to the subject area, etc.

This exercise works well to engage students and encourage peer-to-peer evaluation of the class topics, but I wondered if participation could be further enhanced through the use of cloud technology. The added bonus of using such a tool would be the enduring record of the collective work of the class (at least for the short term).

Having worked with VoiceThread previously, I thought it offered the perfect opportunity to boost the traditional tried-and-true approach to the virtual level. This program could move the discussion to the online environment, which might encourage more students to participate and encourage higher quality participation. I imagined that each student would be able to get feedback from others in the class through VoiceThread's text commenting capabilities. With this in mind, I adapted the previous exercise as follows:

1. Either ahead of time or during the first part of class (though beforehand saves time), each student e-mails the librarian a PowerPoint slide with two pieces of information: the topic statement/question and why this topic is of individual interest.
2. The librarian combines the slides into one PowerPoint file and uploads it to VoiceThread.
3. A brief tutorial is provided to the class on how to use VoiceThread, with the librarian offering a live example of how to add a text comment to a slide.
4. Students are encouraged to supply at least one comment/item for consideration/question on each person's slide, with the librarian also participating.
5. After a set amount of time, students find their own slides and view what others have suggested. The suggestions are condensed into keywords that are employed in new search strategies in the library's online databases.

Preparation before the session included creating a generic VoiceThread account using a free e-mail account I set up for this purpose. Every student was able to successfully log in to the software using the same account. However, the unfortunate drawback to this approach was that each comment came from "the same" user; it is visually more appealing while using VoiceThread to see the individual icon of each user around the periphery of the image in the center. At the conclusion of the session, I was able to quickly export the code for the VoiceThread community we had created together and embed it into the class LibGuide, showing the students where to find it before the end of the session.

Assessment and Evaluation

It is always an experiment to try new technologies in library instruction sessions. Situational factors, including some outside the instructor's control, can contribute to success. VoiceThread successfully achieved the goal of using a low-cost, easy setup cloud technology to encourage participation and collaboration in library instruction.

Jennifer's implementation of VoiceThread supports library instruction sessions by encouraging nontraditional participation. Students less likely to speak up in class or ask questions were given the opportunity to do so in a low-risk environment. Creating and embedding presentation modules is straightforward, allowing quick setup and ease of use. Although higher participation rates were hoped for, there are some reasons for low usage. The necessity to create an account to make comments and ask questions may have discouraged students. Although the class professor was interested and supportive, VoiceThread might not have been promoted well during the class. In the future, students will be given time in class to create an account so they can try out the system and see how easy it is. This will also allow the professor a hands-on chance to become involved during class. Professors will also be asked what types of VoiceThread presentation modules are needed for the class. This will give the professor buy-in from the start, increasing the marketing of the materials for use.

Kara was pleasantly surprised in doing the analysis of her implementation to see that each student had commented on an average of about 11 slides per class and that the feedback provided was meaningful. Thought-provoking concepts for further study and excellent critical questions were the norm in peer-to-peer comments. This showed that VoiceThread did increase student participation and collaboration in library instruction.

Students were completely engaged in the activity and the instruction classroom was abuzz with the flutter of keyboard activity. Informal feedback indicated that the exercise did help students think about aspects of their topics they had not previously considered. In observing search behavior after the VoiceThread exercise, some students were expanding their keyword usage beyond the few they had been using before the session. To maximize the session and take advantage of the community feel of VoiceThread, it will be beneficial in the future to set up a VoiceThread account for each individual student. Additionally, it would save time to gather student topics and questions about topics before the day instruction is to take place. This gives the librarian time to build the class PowerPoint ahead of time, including a final slide soliciting feedback on the exercise.

Conclusion

Using the cloud technology tool VoiceThread has been easy and fun. We look forward to developing other projects using this tool to enhance and support library instruction in the future. Here are some recommendations we have developed for the use of VoiceThread:

- **Discussing and recommending resources:** Take a screenshot of a book cover or take a picture of someone holding an item. Record a brief review of why the source is a good choice for a given research topic. Students then find a resource of their own to recommend to the group and record a message describing their choice.

- **Class discussion:** Post slides from library instruction sessions with added questions. Have students record their answers. This keeps a discussion going beyond class, allowing nonverbal processors to participate.
- **Library orientation:** Upload pictures of the library. Have students view this virtual tour and ask questions or make comments.
- **Tutorials:** Capture screen images to provide a step-by-step tutorial incorporating the visual with the auditory on how to find and use library resources.
- **Blended learning:** Use this platform to engage a group of people who have never met before. The pictures and voice recordings allow unique discussion opportunities for virtual and blended classrooms.
- **Student learning outcome assessment:** Upload a two-picture slideshow asking students these questions, "What did you learn today?" and "What questions do you still have?" to create ongoing or end-of-session evaluations.

Overall, integrating VoiceThread into our instruction sessions has been a success. It facilitates collaborative teaching and learning among the students, professors, and librarians by supporting conversations in multiple modes around a common object. It encourages participation within the classroom and allows learning to take place beyond the physical classroom. VoiceThread also gives students control over their learning experience as they revisit presentation modules. We would use free or low-cost cloud technologies such as VoiceThread again because they give libraries the chance to experiment with new technologies without being financially invested. Cloud technologies are more convenient to use than traditional software packages because they can be learned and utilized in a short period of time. The time-consuming work of setting up or configuring a server, or learning a fully featured program is not an issue with the proliferation of such low-cost and low-barrier programs hosted on the web. We have used VoiceThread to enhance instruction sessions and look forward to using it in the future for teaching information literacy skills and addressing student learning outcomes.

About the Editors and Contributors

Edward M. Corrado (http://ecorrado.us/) is Director of Library Technology at Binghamton University, Binghamton, New York. Corrado has written articles presented at multiple conferences on various library technology topics. His research interests include cloud computing, open source software in libraries, social software in libraries, and the role of libraries in Democracy 2.0. Corrado earned his Master of Library Service from Rutgers University, New Brunswick, New Jersey, and his Bachelor of Arts in Mathematics from Caldwell College, Caldwell, New Jersey.

Heather Lea Moulaison (http://www.moulaison.net) is Assistant Professor in the School of Information Science & Learning Technologies at the University of Missouri. Dr. Moulaison studies web technologies as they pertain to organization of information and has presented at numerous international, national, and local conferences. Dr. Moulaison earned a Master of Arts in French and a Master of Science in Library and Information Science at the University of Illinois, Urbana–Champaign and a PhD in Library and Information Science from Rutgers University, New Brunswick, New Jersey.

✍

Susan W. Alman directs distance education in the School of Information Sciences at the University of Pittsburgh. She holds degrees from Washington and Jefferson College and the University of Pittsburgh. Dr. Alman's areas of interest include asynchronous learning, marketing libraries, and interpersonal communication.

Caitlin A. Bagley is an Assistant Professor and Reference Librarian at Murray State University in Murray, Kentucky. Her research interests are web technology in libraries and information literacy. Bagley earned her Master of Library Science from Indiana University in Bloomington, Indiana, and a Bachelor of Arts in Classics and English from the University of Kentucky in Lexington.

Albert A. Bertram (bertrama@umich.edu) is the Lead Web Developer in the University of Michigan Library's Web Systems group. Bertram earned a Master of Arts in Computational Linguistics at the University of Washington, Seattle, and a Bachelor of Science in Computer Science and Cognitive Psychology from the University of Michigan, Ann Arbor. Bertram has been working with web technologies for 9 years and specializes in information retrieval and data mining.

Marshall Breeding is the Director for Innovative Technology and Research at Vanderbilt University. He is the creator of Library Technology Guides (http://www.librarytechnology.org). In 2010 he authored *Next-Gen Library Catalogs* for Neal-Schuman and has written or edited five other books. Breeding writes a monthly column for *Computers in Libraries,* is a Contributing Editor for *Smart Libraries Newsletter,* has authored *Library Journal's* "Automation System Marketplace" since 2002, and has written many other articles and book chapters.

H. Frank Cervone is the Vice Chancellor for Information Services at Purdue University Calumet, Hammond, Indiana (http://www.cervone.com). The author of four books and a frequent speaker at library and information technology conferences, he writes a recurring column in *OCLC Systems and Services.* He is the LITA Representative to the International Federation of Library Associations and Agencies. Cervone holds a Master of Science in Education with a specialization in Online Teaching and Learning from California State University as well as a PhD in Management and Information Systems from Northcentral University.

Karen A. Coombs (http://www.librarywebchic.net) is the Product Manager for the OCLC Developer Network. Coombs has presented at many conferences on topics related to web services, mashups, and open source software in libraries. She is the author of two books— *Library Blogging* with Jason Griffey and *Open Source Web Applications in Libraries* with Amanda Hollister. Coombs earned her Master of Library Science and Master of Science in Information Management from Syracuse University, Syracuse, New York.

John Davison is Assistant Director for Digital Resource Management at the Ohio Library & Information Network (http://www.ohiolink.edu/). Davison's research interests include cloud-based distributed computing, open source software development, and digital object preservation. Davison earned a Master of Library and Information Science from the Kent State School of Library and Information Science and a Bachelor of Arts from the Ohio State University.

Leland R. Deeds is Librarian for Academic Computing Support at Union Presbyterian Seminary, Richmond, Virginia. Deeds has presented on topics related to web technologies, assessment, and training. Deeds earned a Bachelor of Arts in Religion from Bard College, a Master of Theological Studies from Emory University, and a Master of Science in Information Systems from the University of Tennessee, Knoxville.

Jennifer Diffin (jdiffin@umuc.edu) is the Assistant Director for Systems and Access Services at the University of Maryland University College in Largo, Maryland. Diffin has written articles and presented at national and regional conferences on several topics, including the effective use of Microsoft SharePoint in libraries. Diffin earned a Master of Library Science from Simmons College, Boston, and a Bachelor of Science in computer science and math also at Simmons College.

Jennifer Ditkoff is the Collection Development Librarian at Keene State College in Keene, New Hampshire. She has presented at several conferences on using low-cost, low-barrier technologies in the classroom. She earned her Master of Science in Library and Information Science from Syracuse University in Syracuse, New York.

Heidi M. Nickisch Duggan is the Associate Director at the Galter Health Sciences Library at Northwestern University's Feinberg School of Medicine. Nickisch Duggan holds a Bachelor of Arts from the University of Nebraska–Lincoln, a Master of Arts in Library Science from the University of Missouri–Columbia, and a Master of Science in Communication from Northwestern University. Her research interests include library leadership, organizational change management, and scholarly communication.

Nicole C. Engard (nengard@gmail.com) is the Director of Open Source Education at ByWater Solutions. In addition to her daily responsibilities, Engard keeps the library community up-to-date on web technologies via her website "What I Learned Today. . . ." (http://www.web2learning.net). In 2009 Engard was the editor of *Library Mashups,* a book published by Information Today, and in 2010 she authored *Practical Open Source Software for Libraries,* a book published by Chandos.

Michelle Frisque is Head of Information Systems, Galter Health Sciences Library, Northwestern University's Feinberg School of Medicine. Frisque is a former President of the Library & Information Technology Association (LITA), a division of the American Library Association. Frisque graduated with a Master of Library and Information Science from the University of Pittsburgh and is currently pursuing a Master of Learning and Organization Change at Northwestern University. Frisque has written articles and presented at conferences on library IT management issues.

Ann Whitney Gleason is the Head, Systems at the University of Washington Health Sciences Library. Her research interests currently center on the use of educational technology in libraries. Gleason worked as an educational technology specialist for several years before receiving her Master of Library and Information Science from the University of Rhode Island. She received a Bachelor of Arts in Education from The Evergreen State College.

Carl Grant is Chief Librarian at Ex Libris. Grant's commitment to libraries and librarianship is known from his participation in ALA; ACRL, LITA, Exhibits Round Table; and on the board of the NISO, where he has served as board member, treasurer, and chair. *Library Journal* has also named Grant an industry notable. Grant holds a Master's degree in information and library science from the University of Missouri at Columbia.

Edward Iglesias is the Systems Librarian at Central Connecticut State University and part of the ERIS (Electronic Resources and Information Systems) group in a variety of capacities, ranging from ILS Systems Administration and Coordination to overseeing digital initiatives and encouraging technical curiosity. He just authored a book, *An Overview of the Changing Role of the Systems Librarian: Systemic Shifts,* published by Chandos. Iglesias earned a Master of Library and Information Science at the University of Texas and a Master of Arts in English from Texas A&M International University.

Cindy Kissel-Ito is Director of the Extended Campus Program and Affiliate Assistant Professor of Christian Education at Union Presbyterian Seminary, Richmond, Virginia. Kissel-Ito's academic interests focus on supporting student investigation of the curriculum and developmental theory that shape religious education theory and practice. Kissel-Ito received a PhD from Union Theological Seminary–Presbyterian School of Christian

201

Education, a Master of Divinity from Wesley Theological Seminary, and a Bachelor of Arts in Anthropology from Albany State University.

Ann Thomas Knox is Director of the Instructional Resource Center at Union Presbyterian Seminary, Richmond, Virginia. Knox has a particular interest in ways that web technologies can be used in teaching. Knox earned a Bachelor of Arts in History from Austin College, Sherman, Texas, and a Master of Arts in Christian Education from the Presbyterian School of Christian Education, Richmond.

Anne Leonard is an Instruction & Reference Librarian and the Coordinator of Resource Sharing at New York City College of Technology of the City University of New York. Her varied professional interests include the faculty and professional status of academic librarians and academic integrity among undergraduates. She earned a Master of Library Science from the University of Texas at Austin and a Master of Science in Urban Affairs from Hunter College.

Rosalyn Metz (http://www.rosalynmetz.com) is a project manager for Viget, a web consulting firm located near Washington, DC. She has written about cloud computing on her blog (http://www.rosalynmetz.com/ideas) and for *EDUCAUSE Quarterly*. Additionally, Metz has presented at multiple conferences on the cloud, including ALA Annual. She has a Master of Library Science from the University of North Carolina at Chapel Hill and a Bachelor in Political Science from George Washington University.

Robin Elizabeth Miller (millerob@uwec.edu) is Reference and Instruction/Government Publications Librarian at the University of Wisconsin–Eau Claire. Miller earned a Master of Science in Library and Information Science from the University of Illinois at Urbana–Champaign and a Bachelor of Arts in Political Science from the University of Oregon.

Erik Mitchell (http://erikmitchell.info) is the Assistant Director for Technology Services at the Z. Smith Reynolds Library at Wake Forest University. He holds a Master of Library and Information Science from the University of South Carolina and a PhD in Information and Library Science from the University of North Carolina at Chapel Hill. His research focus includes metadata and cloud computing and the role that these technologies play in information experiences. His most recent work focused on exploring the role of cloud computing in library IT. He currently writes a recurring column for the *Journal of Web Librarianship*.

Dennis Nangle (dnangle@umuc.edu) is a Document Management Technician at University of Maryland University College in Largo, Maryland. Nangle has written multiple articles and presented at local and national conferences on the topic of establishing effective library workspaces using Microsoft SharePoint. Nangle also worked on a project through ALA's Emerging Leaders program, which provided best practices for LITA members working in ALA Connect. Nangle earned his Master of Library Science at the University of Maryland, College Park.

Christopher R. Nighswonger is Network and Systems Director at Foundations Bible College and Theological Seminary, Dunn, North Carolina (http://www.foundations.edu/). Nighswonger has been involved in a variety of segments of the IT field for 25 years and in active development for the Koha open source ILS project since November 2007. In February 2010, he was elected Release Maintainer for Koha 3.2. Nighswonger earned his Master of Theology from Foundations Bible College and Theological Seminary, Dunn.

Karen A. Reiman-Sendi (karsendi@umich.edu) is the Digital Information Services Librarian at the University of Michigan Library. Reiman-Sendi has presented and published on topics such as Library 2.0 applications, web projects, information literacy, virtual reference services, collection assessment, and integrating desktop applications for public services desks. Reiman-Sendi earned a Master of Information and Library Science from the University of Michigan and a Bachelor of Arts in German Languages and Literature from the University of Toledo.

Christinger R. Tomer, University of Pittsburgh Associate Professor, teaches asynchronous and blended classes. He holds degrees from the College of Wooster and Case Western Reserve University. Dr. Tomer's areas of specialization include open source computing and scientometrics.

Kenneth J. Varnum (varnum@umich.edu) is Web Systems Manager at the University of Michigan Library. Varnum has presented at national conferences on topics including Drupal, user-generated content, personalized search, and website redesign. Varnum earned Masters of Information and Library Science and Russian Studies from the University of Michigan and his Bachelor of Arts from Grinnell College.

Kara Young is the Systems Librarian at Keene State College in Keene, New Hampshire. Young enjoys working with technology every day and sharing her experiences with low-cost, low-barrier web applications by presenting at workshops and conferences. She earned her Master of Science in Information Systems and Master of Public Administration degrees from the State University of New York at Albany.

Index

Page numbers followed by "f" indicate figures; those followed by "t" indicate tables.

205